Rebirth in the Life
and Works of Beatrix Potter

ALSO BY RICHARD TUERK

*Oz in Perspective: Magic and Myth
in the L. Frank Baum Books* (McFarland, 2007)

Rebirth in the Life and Works of Beatrix Potter

RICHARD TUERK

McFarland & Company, Inc., Publishers
Jefferson, North Carolina

LIBRARY OF CONGRESS CATALOGUING-IN-PUBLICATION DATA

Names: Tuerk, Richard Carl, 1941– author.
Title: Rebirth in the life and works of Beatrix Potter / Richard Tuerk.
Description: Jefferson, North Carolina : McFarland & Company, Inc., Publishers, 2020 | Includes bibliographical references and index.
Identifiers: LCCN 2020000802 | ISBN 9781476680620 (paperback: acid free paper) ♾
ISBN 9781476639307 (ebook)
Subjects: LCSH: Potter, Beatrix, 1866–1943—Criticism and interpretation. | Potter, Beatrix, 1866–1943—Correspondence. | Potter, Beatrix, 1866–1943—Diaries. | Children's stories, English—History and criticism. | Regeneration in literature. | Authors, English—20th century—Biography.
Classification: LCC PR6031.O72 Z88 2020 | DDC 823/.912 [B]—dc23
LC record available at https://lccn.loc.gov/2020000802

BRITISH LIBRARY CATALOGUING DATA ARE AVAILABLE

ISBN (print) 978-1-4766-8062-0
ISBN (ebook) 978-1-4766-3930-7

© 2020 Richard Tuerk. All rights reserved

No part of this book may be reproduced or transmitted in any form or by any means, electronic or mechanical, including photocopying or recording, or by any information storage and retrieval system, without permission in writing from the publisher.

On the cover: *Beatrix Potter* by Delmar Banner, 1938, oil on canvas © National Portrait Gallery, London; background © 2020 Ellerslie/Shutterstock

Printed in the United States of America

McFarland & Company, Inc., Publishers
Box 611, Jefferson, North Carolina 28640
www.mcfarlandpub.com

To Becky, Michael, and Roz

Table of Contents

Acknowledgments	ix
A Very Personal Preface	1
What to Call Beatrix Potter	5
An Introduction to the World of Beatrix Potter	7
Potter's Realism	33
Fairies, Fairytales and Beatrix Potter	43
Potter's Vocabulary and Readership Awareness	49
The Tale of Peter Rabbit	55
The Tailor of Gloucester	66
The Tale of Squirrel Nutkin	69
The Tale of Benjamin Bunny	76
The Tale of Two Bad Mice and *The Tale of Mrs. Tiggy-Winkle*	82
The Tale of the Pie and the Patty-Pan	88
The Tale of Mr. Jeremy Fisher	94
The Story of a Fierce Bad Rabbit, *The Story of Miss Moppet*, and "The Sly Old Cat"	101
The Tale of Tom Kitten	105
The Tale of Jemima Puddle-Duck	109
The Tale of Samuel Whiskers or The Roly-Poly Pudding	114
The Tale of the Flopsy Bunnies	122
The Tale of Ginger and Pickles	126

The Tale of Mrs. Tittlemouse	128
The Tale of Timmy Tiptoes	130
The Tale of Mr. Tod	134
The Tale of Pigling Bland	143
The Tale of Johnny Town-Mouse	147
The Fairy Caravan: Beatrix Potter's Book for an American Audience	152
The Tale of Little Pig Robinson	159
Sister Anne	170
Three Posthumous Works: *Wag-by-Wall*, *The Tale of the Faithful Dove*, and *The Tale of Kitty-in-Boots*	177
A Very Personal Conclusion	182
Notes	189
Works Cited	199
Index	205

Acknowledgments

I am grateful to Judy Taylor Hough for getting me a copy of George Middleton's *Echoes of Ambleside and Beyond*. I could not get one for myself since the publisher wanted payment in pounds, and I could find no way to get a check to him in pounds. I am also very grateful to her for all the work she has done making Beatrix Potter's previously unpublished work available to a large reading public. In works like *Beatrix Potter's Letters* and her separate collection entitled *Letters to Children from Beatrix Potter*, Taylor has provided both general readers and scholars with many insights into Potter's life and thoughts that readers would have great difficulty getting in any other way. Taylor's study of Potter's life, *Beatrix Potter: Artist, Storyteller and Countrywoman*, and her introductions and notes to her collections of Potter's letters as well as Potter's letters to children and her edition of Potter's *Holiday Diary* have also provided great insights for readers.

I am also grateful to the late Leslie Linder, who has contributed immeasurably to readers' understanding of Potter through works like his translations of her code writing in her journals and his *History of the Writings of Beatrix Potter*. Linder's pioneering studies of Potter have created the bedrock on which all studies of Potter must stand.

In fact, readers of Potter have been provided with incredible riches in the form of the work critics and scholars have done writing about her, beginning with some of her contemporaries and going into the twenty-first century. Also, a number of books about things like Potter's gardens, houses, and artwork are aimed at a general audience but are still of value to scholars.

I am also grateful to the many undergraduate and graduate students who have endured the classes I taught that involved Potter's works and who have interacted with me and with others in the class concerning Potter's writing and ideas. They have added greatly to my understanding of Potter and her works. Also, audiences at conferences I have attended have reacted favorably to my presentations on Potter and have shared ideas about her and her works with me. I am grateful to them.

My good friend C. Jason Smith read and commented extensively on the

Acknowledgments

manuscript of this book. For his careful work, I am very grateful. I also am grateful to my colleague, Dorys Grover, for encouraging me in my work and for being a good friend. Jacob Pichnarcik, the library associate in charge of interlibrary loans at Gee Library at Texas A&M University-Commerce, was an immense help in locating and getting for my use books and articles that otherwise would have been unavailable in Commerce, Texas. Joe Shipman of Luminous Productions did wonders handling the illustrations for this book, just as he did for my book on L. Frank Baum. I am also grateful to my editor, David Alff of McFarland, for his help and encouragement.

A Very Personal Preface

For me, exploring Beatrix Potter's works involves an entrance into a strange new world. I find it difficult to conceive of the kind of life she led. The Victorian and Edwardian England in which she was born in 1866 and grew up and the pre- and post–World War I and pre–World War II England in which she spent most of her adult years are themselves foreign to me, as is England from the entry of that nation into World War II until her death in 1943. I have vague memories of Baltimore, Maryland, during World War II. I was born four months before Pearl Harbor, but my experiences in Baltimore during the war hardly involve the kinds of experiences Beatrix Potter had during this period.

Potter's writing for children slowed down markedly after she married in 1913, at age 47. Many of the works she published after this date were reworkings of older material, but some of the revisions were substantial and significant, and refreshed the storyline, similar to the finetuning executed on several of her best works from before she was married, including *The Tale of Peter Rabbit*, *The Tailor of Gloucester*, and *The Tale of Squirrel Nutkin*.

It is difficult for me to believe that she had trouble finding a publisher for *The Tale of Peter Rabbit*, but she did. She sent it out without finding a publisher to around a half-dozen publishing companies. She even published at her own expense two editions of the book and then revised it again for publication when it was finally accepted by Frederick Warne and Company.

Helen Beatrix Potter was born on 28 July 1866. She died on 22 December 1943. That makes her my contemporary, since I was born in 1941. I remember how astonished I was when I discovered that her life and mine overlapped, but this contemporaneity did not make it any easier for me to comprehend the kind of life she lived. She lived through all of World War I and a great part of World War II. I lived through the entire time the United States was involved in World War II, but I was too young to know what was happening. So this overlapping did not help me much in my attempts to comprehend the kind of life she led. Even though my father was on active duty in the United States Army from 1941 until 1946, and in Europe for 18 months, serving under

General Patton in the Battle of the Bulge and being one of the liberators of Buchenwald, I was isolated from what was happening because of my young age and distance from the war itself.

The isolation of her childhood combined with the great wealth of her family and, later in life, her own great wealth, add to the challenge of my understanding the world in which she and her works grew. I have difficulty conceiving of a life involving the kind of wealth the Potters had. Living in the large house they occupied during Potter's childhood in London and the large houses in which they vacationed also is difficult for me to conceive of, although from the time I was eight until I was nineteen, my family lived in the Superintendent's House at Spring Grove State Hospital, later called The Mansion, a large house that was part of the hospital. It had a finished basement, two floors, and an attic; it also had servants' quarters that my brother and I used for various hobbies; and it had what were to me strange things like a butler's pantry and powder room as well as four full bathrooms. However, we did not own the house—the State of Maryland did—and large as the Superintendent's house was, the houses the Potters lived in and rented dwarf it. Even reading Susan Denyer's lavishly illustrated *At Home with Beatrix Potter* did not make me feel comfortable with the house her parents owned and the houses they rented or the kinds of houses Beatrix Potter owned after she married. The one exception is Hill Top Cottage, which she bought, as part of Hill Top Farm, in 1905. But she lived in Hill Top Cottage only for short periods during which she visited Near Sawrey before her marriage to William Heelis in 1913. I too lived in a cottage for a while, the Paradise Avenue Gate House at Spring Grove. It, however, was a fairly small cottage with a living room, kitchen, rumpus room, and dining room on the first floor; two bedrooms and one bathroom on the second floor; and a decidedly unfinished basement. It was heated by a coal furnace into which my mother shoveled coal; the coal dust got over everything in the poorly lit basement. I was often terrified when I went into the basement, especially when I had to accompany my mother into it when she shoveled the coal; when I was much older, she told me she took me with her because she was afraid of the rats there. After a while, we got a cat, and the rat problem apparently ended. I was eight when we left the gatehouse and moved into the Superintendent's House.

After Beatrix Potter's marriage, she kept Hill Top Cottage to use as a kind of studio and retreat as well as a place to store things connected with her books and artwork and pieces of oak furniture that she collected, additional things that make her life foreign to me. She also let friends and relatives stay in it from time to time. Having the wealth to keep a "cottage" of this sort for a study, retreat, and storage is difficult for me to conceive of. After she married, she also bought large tracts of land and several houses in the English Lake District, not exclusively for her own use but with the object of giving them to the British National Trust either during her lifetime or after her death.

The geographical landscapes of her life, which became source material for the landscapes in her works, are also foreign to me. I went to England once, in 1959, right after I graduated from high school, during the summer I turned eighteen. At that time, I knew next to nothing about the English Romantic poets, and I do not remember having any knowledge of the Lake District or of Beatrix Potter, who vacationed in the Lake District when she was still living with her parents and lived there after she married. Only during my undergraduate and graduate years did I find out anything about the Lake District when I studied the Romantic poets in one of the British literature survey courses I took at Columbia College in New York City and the Romantic literature course I audited in graduate school at Johns Hopkins University in Baltimore, Maryland. Then, my main concern was with the ways landscape appeared in works by writers like Wordsworth and Coleridge, both closely associated with the Lake District.

None of my university education involved the study of children's literature, unless it also was considered adult literature. In an undergraduate humanities course I took at Columbia, we studied Swift's *Gulliver's Travels*, but we certainly did not study it as children's literature, and we read the whole book, not just the section on the Lilliputians, which is the part most people think of when they think of the work as children's literature. In an English survey course, we read Defoe's *Robinson Crusoe*, but, again, not as children's literature. Yet some of my happiest moments as a child involved being read to and later reading children's books for myself. And as an adult, some of my happiest moments involved reading to my children and teaching children's literature to undergraduates and graduates.

Travel is now difficult for me. I still dream of going to England and walking some of the paths Beatrix Potter walked and touring some of her houses. But walking is a problem for me. Many of the names of places where she lived are, in my mind, not connected with anything tangible other than things I have read and pictures I have seen in books and magazines. I need to keep reminding myself that the robins that appear in *The Tale of Peter Rabbit* are not the same as the robins I see hunting for worms in my front yard, and the pictures of the robins in her books are accurate. I have the same kind of problems with the squirrels in her works, and I am glad that in *The Tale of Squirrel Nutkin*, she uses American red squirrels that were becoming common in the England of her day. She even uses an American chipmunk in one of her works, *The Tale of Timmy Tiptoes*, published in 1911. So I am able to find some kind of grounding in her world. Moreover, her works, I am delighted to say, have a kind of universality that makes it possible for me to participate in them without having visited the places where they are set and without seeing daily all the kinds of creatures that inhabit them.

Until relatively recently, the works of Beatrix Potter were unknown to me. I do not remember my mother's reading any to me when I was young. When I went to college and graduate school, I never heard of a course involving children's literature being taught in an English department. Only after I began teaching at East Texas State University in Commerce, Texas, in 1972, did I find myself in an English department that taught children's literature. In the meantime, I started reading stories to my own children, including those by Beatrix Potter.

At East Texas State University, when in about 1982, an undergraduate course in children's literature needed a teacher, I immediately volunteered to fill the position. Preparing for that course—and continuing to prepare for it during the years that followed—was a joy for me, as was teaching that course and a number of other ones my colleagues and I developed, especially several graduate courses that led to master's and doctoral degrees in English. My discovering that children's literature was a valid area of exploration for English graduate students and professors was a revelation. I am sure that had I suggested when I was in graduate school doing a dissertation exploring the works of writers like L. Frank Baum and Beatrix Potter, I would have been greeted with derision and probably told to pursue my doctorate elsewhere.

After more than twenty years of teaching children's literature and especially writing about it, I began to consider myself somewhat of an authority in the field. I have a number of publications and presentations in the field, including some on Beatrix Potter. This book represents the culmination of my work on children's literature in general and on Beatrix Potter in particular.

What to Call Beatrix Potter

What to call Beatrix Potter has been a real problem for me. My first impulse is to call her simply Potter throughout, the same way that we call Chaucer, Shakespeare, and Faulkner by their last names. However, when I write about her in the context of her family, calling her simply Potter can, at times, be confusing. Adding to the problem is her own desire to no longer be called Beatrix Potter or Miss Potter after she married. In fact, she sometimes got very upset with people who called her either of those names after her marriage to William Heelis. She then insisted on being called Mrs. Heelis.

Still, to call her Mrs. Heelis when dealing with most of her published works seems strange to me since she wrote at least part of most of them before she got married, and she continued to publish works as Beatrix Potter after she married. One that she apparently wrote almost entirely after her marriage—*The Fairy Caravan*—she chose to publish under the name of Beatrix Potter. Yet in it, when the animals refer to her, they call her Mistress Heelis. She also chose to publish it with Alexander McKay in Philadelphia instead of the Warnes in London.

Another late work in terms of publication is *The Tale of Little Pig Robinson*, also published in America by McKay. It contains some work she did much earlier, and it too was published under the name of Beatrix Potter.

I finally decided to call her Potter whenever I think no confusion would arise. When I think confusion might arise, I use Beatrix Potter. I use Mrs. Heelis only when quoting from someone or discussing her in direct connection with her marriage or her own preference for Mrs. Heelis.

An Introduction to the World of Beatrix Potter

In work after work by Beatrix Potter, the protagonists go through a series of events that roughly correspond to processes of initiation in which a kind of rebirth occurs. In the course of their adventures, many escape from what looks like certain death. Some protagonists grow from their experiences; others remain the same; some deteriorate. For example, in *The Tale of Peter Rabbit* (1902), Peter grows as a result of his experiences. In *The Tale of Jemima Puddle-Duck* (1908), Jemima grows in no discernable way. In *The Tale of Samuel Whiskers or, The Roly-Poly Pudding* (1908), Tom Kitten's adventures change him, but not entirely for the better.

Anthropologically, rebirth involves a "threshold passage," an initiation into some sort of "mystery," perhaps involving moving from childhood to adulthood or transitioning from the realm of life to that of death. Ritualistically, it is represented through "imagery of re-entry into" and emergence from the womb (Campbell, *Masks* 62). Imagery associated with rebirth is, in fact, a central concern of many of Potter's most successful works. At the time of an episode that seems to be leading to imminent death of one of her characters, the character is almost always within some kind of enclosing, womb-like structure. The pattern can be found in work after work by Potter, including, in addition to ones named earlier, *The Tale of Mr. Jeremy Fisher* (1906), *The Tale of Squirrel Nutkin* (1903), *The Story of Miss Moppet* (1906), *The Tale of the Flopsy Bunnies* (1909), and *The Tale of Pigling Bland* (1913). A psychological biography would probably explain the centrality of this kind of imagery in Potter's works in terms of her own life, in particular her desire to create for herself a world of her own, to free herself from her domineering parents.

Helen Beatrix Potter was born on 28 July 1866, daughter of Rupert and Helen Leech Potter. Her parents kept her isolated from most other children except her brother, Bertram, who was born on 14 March 1872, when Beatrix was five years old. She was so secluded during her childhood that by modern standards, she seems to have been abused, spending most of her time in the third-floor nursery of her parents' house on 2 Bolton Gardens in London. In later life, she showed no love for the house and the city where she was born. In a letter dated 20 November 1942, she writes to Bertha Mahony Miller, founder of *Horn Book*, a magazine devoted to children's literature, that she and her brother "hated" the city in which they were born (*Beatrix Potter's Americans* 191). When Bertha Mahony Miller asked Potter during the 1940s for some biographical information for *Horn* Book, Potter responded by writing of what she calls her "unloved birthplace," that it was "hit by shrapnel" and she is glad that it is "no more!" (*Beatrix Potter's Americans* 213).

Her brother left for his first boarding school on 19 April 1883, when he was eleven, leaving Beatrix alone at age sixteen. That same year, her parents hired a new governess for her, Annie Carter, who was employed primarily to teach German to Beatrix. Annie Carter, later Annie Carter Moore, was three years older than Beatrix. Although Beatrix considered her mother's hiring of Annie Moore a betrayal of trust, she and Beatrix eventually became good friends. Beatrix's parents continued to rule her life even after Beatrix reached her thirties and continued to try to control her after that. According to Linda Lear, even when Beatrix Potter entered into negotiations with Frederick Warne & Company about publishing her books, her father had to be included in some way since, though she was thirty-five, she was unmarried and thus needed her father's consent to enter into a legal or financial agreement (148). Norman Warne handled negotiations with Potter for Warne and later proposed marriage to Potter; unfortunately, he died before the marriage could occur. In a letter to Norman Warne, dated 22 May 1902, she discusses legal arrangements for *The Tale of Peter Rabbit*, saying, if her father accompanies her to discuss those arrangements, Norman should recognize that her father is extremely "fidgetty [sic],"[1] so Norman should not be upset, and adds that even though what she is writing about her father is not "respectful," she wants Norman to know that her father is at times "a little difficult." She concludes that since she is thirty-six years old, she can do what she likes about the book (*Letters* 62).

Beatrix Potter's parents retained control over her as long as she had to rely on them for money.[2] In her journal for 14 December 1895, she mentions that for several days, she was "very much down" and explains that she consoled herself by reading Matthew Arnold's letters. She also writes that she consoled herself reading the Old Testament and Wordsworth (*Journal*, complete ed. 411). She probably also needed consolation after, on 11 December 1895, she told her father's doctor, Charles Aiken, that it would be difficult for her father to go abroad for several months for his health, and she admits in her journal, that she wants to help her father, but she cannot "face" accompanying him "abroad." She also recognizes that having money gives her some comfort. Now that she has some money for books, she can hope to be independent but "forlorn" (*Journal*, complete ed. 411), an idea that combines her knowledge of her need for a source of money independent of her wealthy parents with her knowledge of the problems she had finding happiness.

When she finally married at age forty-seven, her parents still tried to exert incredible control over her. Beatrix Potter had problems with her father, who died on 8 May 1914; nonetheless, he seems to have been easier to get along with than her mother was. Alexander Grinstein, a psychiatrist and psychoanalyst who wrote a book about Potter, points out that although Potter's journal shows "a depth of feeling about both of her parents," he calls her "thinly veiled hostility" toward Mrs. Potter "especially evident" (21–22). Nonetheless, Potter's relationship with her father as revealed in her journal seems far from ideal. In her journal for 3 November 1895, she writes about her consternation at not being recognized by Sir William Flower, the director of the Natural History Museum, when he saw her in and outside of the museum. During the 1890s, she spent many hours in the museum studying fungi, one of her passions. She was present when her father engaged Flower in conversation. She was especially upset when Flower did not recognize her when she went for some kind of social event at the home of Mr. and Mrs. John Paget. John Paget was a barrister whose family the Potters knew since Beatrix's mother and Mrs. Paget and her daughters used the same milliner (Lane 39). According to Lear, Beatrix hoped to speak with Flower about lithographs of insects she was commissioned to make for the Morley Memorial College for Working Men and Women.[3] Then, she writes that she cried when she got home because her father was "as usual deplorable [...]" (*Journal*, complete ed., 408). It seems impossible to tell which upset her more: Flower's not knowing who she was or her father's actions. Beatrix was twenty-six at the time!

It is probably a good thing her father rather than her mother was the one involved in Potter's legal and financial affairs. Her mother would probably have forbidden her from entering into any contract with the Warnes, and her father certainly did not like her to deal with what he and his wife called people in trade. Beatrix encountered problems at home about dealing with the Warnes about her books. In 1903, she sent a list of possible topics for additional books to Harold Warne, who invited her to visit their offices before she left with her parents to spend the summer at Fawe Park in Keswick. She wrote back to Harold that she could not visit before leaving and thought she could deal with the publishers through the mail. She also told him she wishes she had not brought up the idea of another book, since she has had "unpleasantness [...] about the work."[4]

Buying Hill Top Farm in Near Sawrey in the English Lake District was Beatrix's first giant step in eventually freeing herself from her parents'—especially her mother's—despotism. As her biographers indicate, when she bought it, she told her parents she was doing so as an investment, but probably had in mind living there from the first.

She understandably had little love for the house where she was born and grew up. In a letter to Marian Frazer Harris Perry, one of her American correspondents, dated 13 July 1936, she writes that she is cleaning out the house in London where she grew up and comments that she was not sentimentally attached to the London house since she was "discontented and never strong" when she lived there (*Beatrix Potter's Americans* 73).

Marriage to Norman Warne presented a possible escape long before her mother's death. Norman, a member of the family that published her books, handled more and more of the interaction between Potter and the firm. On 25 July 1905, Norman sent her a letter proposing marriage. Apparently, she was in London at the time she received this letter.[5] Potter's parents, of course, objected to the marriage. As Margaret Lane points out, her parents were "affronted" by the idea that their daughter should marry someone in publishing, and they strongly opposed it (*Tale of Beatrix Potter* 83). Still, Beatrix intended to marry Norman. Lear possibly understates when she writes that opposing her parents' wishes was for Beatrix "a near-revolutionary act" (200). In deference to Beatrix's parents, Norman and Beatrix decided to keep their engagement quiet. However, the marriage was not to be. On 25 August, one month after Potter received the letter of proposal, when the Potters were vacationing in Wales, Norman died of lymphatic leukemia. According to Lear, just that morning, Potter received a telegram from the Warnes telling her that Norman was dying and that she should come to London (203). On 27 August, the Potters left Wales. Beatrix apparently got to London in time to view Norman's body shortly before he was buried. Lear comments, being at home with her own disapproving parents and "Bereft of her own story's happy ending [...] Beatrix fled London for Wales" (204).

Not long after Norman's death, on 23 December 1905, in a letter to Norman's sister Millie (her birth-name was Amelia), Beatrix comes close to expressing an explicit desire for a kind of rebirth. She sent the letter to Millie from her home in London with a sketch of a barley field in Llanbedr in Wales; apparently, she made the sketch from a watercolor she made of the scene on 24 August 1905, the day before Norman died. In the letter accompanying the sketch, apparently commenting on the scene in the sketch and referring to Norman, she writes that she tries "to think of the golden sheaves, and harvest," adds that Norman had a short but "useful happy life," and asserts that during the next year, she needs to "try to make a fresh beginning" (qtd. in Taylor, "Postscript" 58).

Lane points out that Potter produced most of her small books for children over thirteen years from her middle thirties to shortly after her marriage to William Heelis. Lane adds, then the "secretly self-reliant Miss Potter" became "another person" (*Magic Years* 9). Lane, of course, writes metaphorically here about Potter's becoming "another person," but the metaphor is not far removed from the reality. Later, in the same book, Lane writes that when what she calls Potter's "magic years" of creativity ended (*Magic Years* 198), a real "personality-transformation" occurred, a transformation, Lane feels, caused by Potter's work and a legacy an aunt left her that brought her some "independence," and the independence led to her being able to fulfill her "interest in farming and to a happy marriage" (*Magic Years* 9). That marriage should transform Potter in so many ways should not be surprising, since in her journal for June 1894, she calls "a happy marriage [...] the crown of a woman's life [...]" (*Journal*, complete ed. 321). Apparently, she really believed these words when she put them in her journal shortly before she turned twenty-eight and, in light of her own happy marriage, continued to believe them for the rest of her life.

On 15 October 1913, she married William Heelis; she was forty-seven years old. Heelis was a country solicitor in the Lake District. Her parents greatly objected to the marriage, so much so that, Linda Lear says, after Beatrix told her parents she was going to get married, a "contest of wills" occurred, and Beatrix's "health broke down" (248). After her marriage, she was, in effect, reborn as Mrs. Heelis. She entered what her friends and biographers call the happiest period of her life. On 4 July 1913, Beatrix wrote to Norman Warne's sister Millie, calling Norman "a saint" and adding that she did not think Norman "would object" to her marriage to William Heelis, since Beatrix's sickness and what she called her "miserable feeling of loneliness" finally made her decide to marry William (qtd. in Taylor, "Postscript" 60).[6]

At any rate, on 21 October 1913, six days after her wedding, Beatrix again wrote to Millie, this time saying that she was "very happy, & [...] satisfied with" her husband, and adding that she felt it was "best now not to look back," and assuring Millie of her continued friendship (qtd. in Taylor, "Postscript" 60).[7] She wore the engagement ring Norman gave her until her death, at one point writing to Millie (on 8 November 1918) how upset she was about losing Norman's ring in a cornfield and how glad she was when she found it again (Taylor, "Postscript" 61). Judy Taylor points out that in her will, Potter left her "shares and debentures" in Warne to Frederick Warne Stephens, and comments that bequeathing this material to one of the Warnes shows that until her death, "Norman had remained in her heart [...]" (Taylor, "Postscript" 62), words that are most likely true.

A distant cousin of Beatrix by marriage, Ulla Hyde Parker, who became quite close to Beatrix, recalls that Beatrix and William Heelis, "were certainly a happy or, perhaps better, a contented couple" living "harmoniously" (23). After her marriage, she no longer replied to mail addressed to Beatrix Potter. Lane comments that Potter's "creative period" ended when she married ("Secret World" 30). Before her marriage, Potter was, Lane asserts, "imprisoned, as it were, in an extended childhood" ("Secret World" 26). Lane further explains, when Potter married William Heelis, she grew up: she exchanged "the secret world of her childhood" for a world "totally practical and as different as possible" ("Secret World" 30). Lane explains that after her marriage, Potter grew "testy about her celebrity, and hated being addressed as 'Miss Potter.'" She no longer wanted to be "reminded of the stifling past," Lane continues a little melodramatically, during which she was "a captive in the dark Victorian house which she called 'my unloved birthplace'" ("Secret World" 31). Still, she did not manage to escape entirely from her "stifling past." As Andrew Norman points out, thirteen days after she got married, she was summoned back to London because her mother was having servant problems. Amazingly, Potter left her husband to answer her mother's summons. Andrew Norman argues, Beatrix's parents "were still determined to keep Beatrix at their beck and call, and she [...] was equally determined not to let them down" (134).

According to her biographers, once she married, although she tried to remain in some ways a "dutiful daughter,"[8] she entered the happiest period of her life. In her introduction to *Beatrix Potter's Americans*, a collection of letters Potter sent to American friends, Jane Crowell Morse writes about Potter after she married, that Potter no longer wanted "to be known as Beatrix Potter," and she no longer wanted "to be bothered by visitors." Nonetheless, she welcomed what Morse calls "many admiring American visitors" (xi). Lane goes so far as to comment, Potter "deliberately buried Miss Potter of Bolton Gardens, and became another person" (*Tale of Beatrix Potter* 112–18). However, her mother still apparently continued to haunt and even to a certain extent control her while Helen Potter was alive and perhaps even after Helen Potter's death.

Making friends seems to have been a problem for Beatrix throughout her life, probably because of the isolation she experienced in childhood, largely as a result of her mother's desire to shield her from the world. Ulla Hyde Parker writes about Beatrix, "she did not invite friendships." Even with people "she had known for years," she did not have "real friendships," but, Hyde Parker adds, "She was always kind [...]" (19). Whether some of the children—and adults—she intimidated would say she was always kind is another matter.[9]

When Beatrix was 28, while still living with her parents, she voices in her journal displeasure with her mother: on 13 September 1894, she writes in her journal, which she kept in code, about "defying the enemy," meaning her mother, by going for "a delightful drive" (*Journal*, complete ed. 346), apparently in her mother's carriage. Linda Lear comments about Helen Potter that although she was very wealthy, she was "stingy" with her daughter (348). One of the things Helen Potter was stingy about was letting Beatrix borrow her carriage.

An Introduction to the World of Beatrix Potter

Beatrix and her family vacationed at Lennel during the summer of 1894. Lennel was a large house in Coldstream on the border between England and Scotland. She enjoyed herself but realized there was much work with natural history and fossils left for her to do, since she had not "half worked through the district," she writes in her journal for 10 October 1894, but she could console herself knowing she had "done a good summer's work," and adds that she hopes to return when she becomes "an old woman" unless she "becomes a fossil" herself, "which would save trouble" (*Journal*, complete ed. 363). Such a comment again is on one level simply a joke, but on another level, when the words, "which would save trouble," are added to the comment, they point to her feelings of lack of self-worth and depression. She also comments about the difficulties of staying at Lennel for "a season of enjoyment" accompanied by people who "constantly" look "for matters of complaint," probably referring to both her parents, especially her mother. Still, she was pleased with the stay since it gave her a chance to examine lots of fungi; she and Elizabeth the maid, she thought, were the only ones there "who were thoroughly pleased," leading her to believe that the two of them should someday go back to Lennel (*Journal, complete ed.* 364). Thus, in spite of her mother, Beatrix was able to enjoy herself and still get work done.

In 1930, Beatrix Potter was trying to raise money so she could buy Monk Coniston, a huge estate, and eventually give it to the British National Trust (Lear 359). Her mother, however, refused to give a penny toward the purchase. She refused even to lend some money to her daughter to make the purchase. In a letter to her cousin, Caroline Clark, Beatrix voices her frustration with her mother's attitude. After saying her mother is ninety-one years old and in excellent health—better health than Beatrix is in—she calls her mother "a regular miser" and writes that "death duties" will waste the money her mother "has hoarded [...] up" (*Letters* 336). Adding to her frustration with her mother are the facts that her father was interested in and supported the Trust and some of the land Beatrix hoped to buy belonged to Beatrix's great grandfather, Abraham Crompton. As Linda Lear points out, Rupert Potter was an early Life Member of the National Trust, but Beatrix's mother refused to give any money to the National Trust and to loan her own daughter money to use to buy land for the Trust, things that added to Beatrix's consternation. Lear then quotes from one of Potter's letters dated 21 October 1929, to Samuel Hamer, secretary of the National Trust, in which Beatrix writes that because people know Beatrix's mother is very wealthy, they do not subscribe to help Beatrix, and concludes the letter, writing about her mother, "She is hopeless" (359).

When her mother was dying, Potter wrote a letter, dated 18 December 1932, to Alexander McKay, the American publisher of *The Fairy Caravan*, saying she hopes McKay and the McKay family are having "a Merry Christmas," and adds, "I am *not*. My old mother is refusing to die," and explaining that her mother is in much pain and "cannot recover, [...] so we hope it will soon be over [...]" (*Beatrix Potter's Americans* 51). Lear comments that Potter's words "seem harsh," but "they betray only her customary realism and the desire to move on." Lear adds that Potter's relationship with her mother was always "awkward, often adversarial"; the "charity and understanding" they had for each other "is less calculable" (368). Actually, there seems to have been just about no "charity and understanding" of the mother for the daughter and, towards the end, less and less of the daughter for the mother. Potter's mother died on 20 December 1932, two days after Potter wrote those words to Alexander McKay. However, even with her death, the daughter probably was not entirely free from the yoke of her mother since she still carried parts of her mother inside her.

Nonetheless, in a letter to Caroline Clark, dated 15 February 1937, when Potter was 70, Potter writes that she began "to assert" herself "at 70" (*Letters* 384). Since her mother died when Beatrix Potter was sixty-six, that would place her as beginning to assert herself four years after her mother's death! Actually, Potter is using hyperbole here, as her letter to Fruing Warne of 29 May 1919 shows. In this letter, she objects strongly to Fruing's criticism of a story she sent him (*Letters* 257).[10] Clearly, she began to assert herself earlier than her seventieth year, as some of her statements about her mother before her mother's death and some of the accounts of interactions between Potter and others also indicate. Nonetheless, her statement about asserting herself indicates that she too placed after her mother died the time when she began asserting herself.

In the letter of 15 February 1937 to Caroline Clark, Potter answers a question Clark asked about how Potter liked growing old, writing that she minded "it little (with one or two reservations)." Then, she quotes someone she calls "a friend," to describe her own feelings: she is grateful that she has "the seeing eye," and explains that she can "lie in bed" and "walk [...] on the fells and rough lands seeing every" detail of the landscape over which she will never walk again; and she asks Clark whether Clark does "not feel it is rather pleasing to be so much *wiser* than quantities of young idiots?" (*Letters* 384). This ability to use "the seeing eye" seems central to her work as a writer and artist who was able to reimagine the natural world so vividly in her works and to fuse animal and human so well.

Helen Potter's real concern may not have been so much with her daughter's health as with her own, an idea Helen herself reinforced by having Beatrix care for her when she was ill. It seems incorrect to say that in Helen Potter's case, mother-love turned to smother-love since usual mother-love seems to have been missing from their relationship. Shortly after Beatrix's death, Caroline Clark wrote to William Heelis, saying she thought she knew "more" of Beatrix "than almost anyone," and adding, "She was delicate & her Mother tried to keep her as a semi-invalid far too much." In another letter, Caroline Clark wrote that Beatrix's mother was not "much help to her." According to Clark, when Beatrix was a child, Beatrix placed her brother first and then her father, but adds that although her father was proud of her and the books she wrote, he did not feel "she had the right to her own life" (qtd. in Lear 442–43).

Margaret Lane calls Helen and Rupert Potter "a terrible pair for a child to have as parents, particularly one like Beatrix" who, Lane feels, "was little more than an only child for much of her childhood [...]." Lane calls Beatrix, "the dutiful daughter," who could not even get away to go to school as her brother Bertram did. As a result, Lane argues, Beatrix became "pathologically shy" and almost "a chronic invalid." According to Lane, Beatrix Potter's upbringing "was enough to turn any child into a neurotic." Yet Lane feels that Potter's journal along with her "secret world of childhood fantasy" led to her "serious and happy middle and old age" ("The Secret World" 25). Even Andrew Norman recognizes that Potter's journal enabled her to retreat into a "secret world" in which she expressed "herself freely, set to rights the wrongs, real or imagined, of the world" and was able to "create something [...] for her eyes only" (36). Yet for the most part, the journal shows how conventional she was, how she adopted the conventions of her parents' world as her own. Still, it contains small glimmerings of the subversive element that a critic like Humphrey Carpenter finds so important in her books for children that he uses the term "subversive element" as part of his subtitle for his 1989 essay on Potter.[11]

Once, while working on the book that was to become *The Tale of Two Bad Mice*, Beatrix wanted to go to Surbiton to visit Norman Warne's house and draw a dollhouse he built for his niece, so Norman invited her. Beatrix's mother objected, for, according to Judy Taylor, she was starting to feel she needed to end Beatrix's "friendship with the Warne family" because it "had gone far enough," so she told Beatrix she could not go (*Beatrix Potter: Artist* 94). Beatrix, the "dutiful daughter," sent regrets to Norman. Not understanding the situation, Norman then responded by inviting her to bring her mother with her. In a letter to Norman, dated 18 February 1904, Beatrix says that her mother is not "likely to want to go to Surbiton" and adds that people seeing her mother "casually do not know how disagreeable" her mother "can be when she takes dislikes." She does add, however, that she "should have been glad enough to go" (*Letters* 86). Beatrix then was thirty-seven years old!

Andrew Norman also argues that Beatrix "was by nature an introvert" and as a result, led an isolated life because she chose to live that kind of life (182). Scholars will never know whether Beatrix was an introvert by nature or by nurture. It really does not matter. Even if shyness and a desire for isolation and privacy were somehow parts of her DNA, her parents' way of bringing her up exacerbated those traits. To expect her in later life suddenly to enjoy spending her time dancing and partying once freed from her parents seems very strange. When the term "rebirth" is used in this study, it is important to remember that it is a metaphor, both in regard to Beatrix Potter's life and to her works. As Potter no doubt knew, a caterpillar becomes a butterfly or moth and a tadpole becomes a frog or newt, but they still remain in many ways essentially the same as they were before the metamorphosis occurs. There is also much continuity between Potter's characters after their initiatory experiences occur. There is also much continuity between Beatrix Potter and Mrs. William Heelis. In "Beatrix Potter: The Missing Years," Lane writes of carefully examining the published version of Potter's journal, trying to find out about Potter's early years, years during which the people Lane spoke with after Potter's death claimed "Nothing Happened" (291). After reading the journal, Lane felt that most of it is "so very impersonal" (296), but not all of it. Instead, Lane finds in the journal the later Mrs. Heelis "in the larval stage [...], half-buried [...] under drifts of detail and alluvial deposits of words, but" nonetheless "still there" (299).

The rebirths in Potter's works are limited in many ways, and so was that in her life. As a married adult, she did not go out of her way to go to parties and dances. Her husband often went to dances without her. Sometimes she went—to watch and sketch but never to dance. She did go to Heelis family gatherings and participate in them. She did not avoid crowds and interacting with many people, especially when that interaction involved buying oak furniture at auction or what became her true passion, Herdwick sheep. That marriage changed her and she became happier is undeniable. That some people would say it did not change her enough is a valid point. For example, even after her marriage, when her mother called her to come to London to help her straighten out problems involving servants and her parents' health, Beatrix, the "dutiful daughter," left her husband in the Lake District and went. After her father died, she moved her mother to the Lake District so Beatrix could be near her without having to travel to London, a place she claimed never to have liked.

There are many indications she suffered from depression, something that could have been hereditary or acquired or both. Actually, that she should suffer from depression is certainly not surprising. In a journal entry for 27 April 1885, she mentions some people who died recently (*Journal*, complete ed. 146). In her very next journal entry, she alludes to an explicit desire to commit suicide, exclaiming, "Oh the beautiful spring!" and adding, "If one's spirit was assured to haunt Birds' Place, suicide in the duck pond might be worthy of consideration," and concluding with the following sentence: "Wild ducks nest" (*Journal*, complete ed. 146). Birds' Place is in Camfield. Potter recollects this place in *The Fairy Caravan*: in Chapter 7, entitled "Springtime in Birds' Place," Potter drew upon the garden she saw at Birds' Place.[12] This journal entry combines the idea of suicide with that of new life in several ways: mention of spring and ducks' nesting and even one's spirit's haunting a place.

In a letter Potter sent to Norman Warne on 21 July 1905, two days before she received Norman's proposal of marriage, Potter gives one of her most explicit indications that she was depressed: she tells about her pet mouse, Hunca Munca, falling off a chandelier and breaking her neck and writes that she cannot forgive herself for letting the mouse fall, adding, "I do so miss her," and she thinks that had she "broken" her "own neck it would have saved [...] trouble" (*Letters* 122). Though hyperbole is probably involved in Potter's choice of words about her pet mouse, any statement that breaking her own neck would save trouble seems important. These words might be dismissed as some kind of joke, but even a joke that involves wishing for death is, so psychologists say, important.

In *Beatrix Potter: Her Inner World*, Andrew Norman observes that in "her late teens and early twenties, Beatrix suffered a prolonged period of intense depression" caused, he asserts, from "having contracted" an undiagnosed "infectious disease" (11). Another illness followed. Andrew Norman diagnoses the disease as infectious mononucleosis followed by "post viral fatigue syndrome" (35–36). However, she wrote the letter to Norman Warne about breaking her own neck one week before her thirty-ninth birthday, long after the period Andrew Norman discusses. Incidentally, causes of depression seem much more complex than attributing it to illness alone would indicate.[13] Alexander Grinstein feels that her depression "was aggravated by episodes of illness" and adds that for many people, "the more serious the illness, the more they are inclined to withdraw into themselves and feel depressed and discouraged" (29); he does not say the episodes of illness caused the depression. He theorizes that her illness was rheumatic fever and she "developed rheumatic heart disease" (32). Grinstein notes that during the period from 1883 to 1888, "the most central theme" in Potter's journals is "her depression and the various ways in which it was manifest" (27). Margaret Lane simply recognizes that Potter suffered from "recurring depression" and was "increasingly lonely, suffered from faintness and rheumatic pains, was always tired" (Lane, *Tale of Beatrix Potter* 52). It seems possible that the depression even caused some of the physical symptoms; it undoubtedly exacerbated them. Even if infectious mononucleosis and post-viral fatigue syndrome along with rheumatic fever caused some of the symptoms, the physical disease and the emotional distress probably worked together to enhance her suffering. Her cousin by marriage, Ulla Hyde Parker, who became quite friendly with Potter, theorizes that Potter had a "stern exterior and firm, almost forbidding manner" that "hid many fears which she carried within her since" she was a child (36).

Beatrix Potter probably did not know that depression was what she suffered from, but she seems to have come up with a time-worn method of countering it: keeping busy.¹⁴ According to Lear, Potter discovered that memorizing Shakespeare plays involved a concentration that was "diverting and provided mental exercise" (95).¹⁵ In her journal for 6 November 1895 is a chart showing her progress in memorizing plays (*Journal*, complete ed. 408). It indicates that she mostly concentrated on history plays.¹⁶

Several entries in her journal indicate problems with depression. Most of them come during the period Andrew Norman focuses on. Fortunately, in the first edition of Potter's journal, Leslie Linder makes most of these entries easily accessible by bunching them under the entry in his index entitled, "Potter, Beatrix, personal views."¹⁷ Surprisingly few page numbers appear in this section of the index, and many of those numbers point to journal entries that indicate depression. As several critics and biographers note, there are very few personal reflections in her journal. Most entries involve straightforward descriptions and narrations of events. Margaret Lane, who wrote two ground-breaking biographies of Potter, notes that in the journal, there are "no dangerous secrets, nothing revolutionary, nothing much that (at a pinch) could not have been shown to her parents [...]." Potter was, Lane writes, not "a rebel" and calls her "one of nature's conservatives, a born traditionalist," something that led to her remaining "a genuinely dutiful daughter to the end" ("The Secret World" 24).¹⁸

Thus, the personal items stand out from the rest of the journal. For example, in 1883, on the day before Bertram was to leave for boarding school, Mrs. Potter told her sixteen-year-old daughter that she had engaged a new governess for her. The governess was three years older than Beatrix. Linda Lear writes of this event that Beatrix "was understandably furious" that her mother hired the governess and adds that Beatrix "felt betrayed" (55). In her journal for 25 April 1883, Potter contemplates her mother's announcement of the coming of the new governess, writing that she was "up one day and down another," and adding that she had that day "been a long way down." Then, she asks whether things would "never settle" and wonders, "Is this being grown-up?" If her parents say she must have the governess, she will, only her temper will be "very nasty." She was, she writes, not happy about having to study anything other than painting. Then, she writes, "Only a year, but if it is like the last it will be a lifetime [...]," and adds, "There is nothing to be done, I must watch things pass—Oh *Faith—Faith*" (*Journal*, complete ed. 39–40). As mentioned earlier in this study, the governess was Annie Carter, later to become Annie Carter Moore, with whom Beatrix became good friends and to whose children she wrote some of her most important story letters, including the one that eventually became *The Tale of Peter Rabbit*.

The deaths of some of Beatrix's pet animals added to her depression, as her reaction to the death of Hunca Munca clearly illustrates. Among the animals Potter mourned, Lear lists a green lizard named Judy, a family of garden snails, and a green frog named Punch (59). Other kinds of losses also depressed her; Lear lists the loss of Dalguise as a summer residence, the loss of her brother's companionship and of her old governess and her grandparents, and "her enforced companionship with two hypercritical parents" and adds that Beatrix's depression was "compounded by unspoken disappointment at having her own needs unacknowledged and worse, ignored" (60).

On Christmas Day 1884, Beatrix comments in her journal that Bertram has a bad cold and she caught the cold "from him," and adds, "General depression. I wonder how they all feel underground" (*Journal*, complete ed. 123). Here, she refers explicitly to depression, probably not meaning clinical depression but simply a feeling of despondency. But the reference to death—"I wonder how they all feel underground"—certainly ties the journal passage to clinical depression. For the Potters, Christmas was a pretty drab affair, especially when compared to the celebrations of their neighbors. Since her parents were strict Unitarians in Victorian England, they did not condone much in the way of celebrations at Christmas. This particular Christmas obviously impressed her as being particularly unpleasant, so much so that it made her wonder how the dead feel. Only after her marriage did she celebrate Christmas joyfully.

Several of her darker periods involved her birthdays. For example, on 28 July 1883, she writes that she has just turned seventeen. She has "heard it called 'sweet seventeen,' no indeed, what a time we are, have been having, and shall have—." She then goes on to narrate an episode involving catching a small perch (*Journal*, complete ed. 49). And on 28 July 1884, after narrating an episode in which John Millais, a particular friend of her father and of Beatrix herself, was painting a portrait of W.E. Gladstone and asked Gladstone to be still and telling what they talked about, she writes that she is eighteen that day and comments that she used to have "funny notions of life" when she was "a child!" concluding that turning eighteen is "a queer business—" (*Journal*, complete ed. 104). These comments seem all the more poignant because of the unemotional material that surrounds them.

On 29 April 1884, she writes in her journal that someone sent her father two tickets for a private viewing of a Millais painting and comments that she feels as though she would "almost [...] like to see it, but if he takes a lass," he will probably take someone else since she feels "like a cow in a drawing room"; her "head is uncertain now" (*Journal*, complete ed. 83), alluding not only to physical discomfort but, through the simile, to her feeling of awkwardness, of being out of place, even of being grotesque, feelings that surely stemmed from her depression and added to her depression.

On 8 May 1884, she comments about her desire not to go back to Dalguise where she was so happy, for she does not want to see it changed. "I feel an extraordinary dislike to this idea, a childish dislike," she writes, but thinks of her memories of Dalguise as "the only bit of childhood" left to her. She concludes the thought by writing, "the future is dark and uncertain, let me keep the past" (*Journal*, complete ed. 84–85). However, as her journal makes clear, there are large parts of her "past" that were, for her, anything but happy.

A particularly telling entry appears on 12 October 1884, when she writes, "This day last year, how time moves and what it brings! So cold and stormy," but having "gleams of peace and light" that make "the darkness stranger and more dreary," and then asks, "How will it end for me?" (*Journal*, complete ed. 109). On 13 December 1884, she writes that she is feeling better than she has since the preceding summer. Recognizing she has "many things" for which "to be thankful," she nonetheless concludes, "these odious fits of low spirits would spoil any life" (*Journal*, complete ed. 122).

On 29 May 1885, Potter writes in her journal that she "always thought" she "was born to be a discredit to my parents." However, on that day "it was exhibited in a marked manner [...]." She then goes on to narrate an episode in which, because her hair was cut short as a result of illness, probably the one Andrew Norman diagnoses as infectious mononucleosis, her hat blew off her head into a fountain at the International Inventions Exhibition at South Kensington and "drifted off," she writes, "to the consternation of my father, and the immense amusement of the spectators." (*Journal*, complete ed. 149). Earlier, on 28 March 1885, she writes of "A lamentable falling off." Commenting that most of her hair came off because of her illness, on that day she had had the rest of her hair cut short: "Now that the sheep is shorn, I may say without pride that I have seldom seen a more beautiful head of hair than mine" (*Journal*, complete ed. 143–44). The jocular tone here hardly covers the consternation she must have felt at having her hair cut off. Perhaps the "beautiful head of hair" refers sarcastically to the hair that had been cut off.

She continues the narrative of the episode at the International Inventions Exposition, writing that she and her father had to wait for someone to come and get the hat out of the fountain, and when it was retrieved, it was too wet to put on. Still, she writes that she "did not care" since "one of the peculiarities of my nature" is "that when there *is* anything to be shy about, I don't care in the least, and I caused a good deal of harmless amusement" (*Journal*, complete ed. 149). If these words about not caring were true, why does she write about the incident at all? Had she ended the narration here and had she not introduced it by saying she thought she was born to discredit her parents, readers could dismiss the whole incident as a typical adolescent reaction to a slightly embarrassing situation that the adolescent herself dismisses. But she adds that she wishes her father had not been there since he takes her out infrequently, and she doubts "he will do it again for a time" (*Journal*, complete ed. 149). Linda Lear understates when she calls this episode "enormously embarrassing" (66). Immediately after treating this episode, Potter, as is usual with her, writes about an everyday matter, in this case, the weather *(Journal,* complete ed. 149).

It is difficult to understand how her losing her hat could show her that she really was born to be and had become a "discredit" to her parents, especially since she could not control losing her hair and probably had no choice about cutting short what was left. She also had no control over losing her hat. Even worse is her reasoning that because of this episode, her father will not take her out again for a long time, although the reasoning may be correct. His not showing concern for her feelings is itself an indication of how little Rupert Potter cared about his daughter and how little attuned he was to his own daughter's feelings—or at least how little his daughter felt he cared about her and was attuned to her feelings.

On 7 September 1885, she refers to the engagement of her cousin Kate Potter, who she thinks is entering into a marriage that will give her little in the way of "position or wealth" and will be unpleasant. About her father and herself, she writes that if he had a "beautiful daughter," he certainly "could marry her very well" and comments that she is "content to have a red nose and a shorn head." Being lonely, she writes, is better than having "an unhappy marriage" *(Journal,* complete ed. 156), words that again indicate her low self-image exacerbated by her illness and, incidentally, her own snobbishness.

On 31 December 1885, at age 19, she writes, "I am terribly afraid of the future" and adds, "Some fears will inevitably be fulfilled, and the rest is dark" *(Journal,* complete ed. 168).

On 11 October 1895, she writes about her mother's being ill and comments that although people suppose there is "some angelic sentiment" about taking care of people who are sick, she does not "associate angels with castor oil and emptying slops," apparently commenting on her having to serve as a nursemaid for her mother. She acknowledges she caught a "violent" head cold, and her father was troubled by kidney stones, events that she felt predicted "every prospect of a hard winter." So she became, she writes, "lower than is the habit with me, a cheerful person" *(Journal,* complete ed. 407). Still, if her journal is at all reliable, she certainly did not seem to be very cheerful for a large portion of 1885 to 1895 and certainly not on 11 October 1895.

Depression in many people seems to go in cycles. For Potter, it seems the same. At any rate, on 28 July 1896, she comments, "I am thirty this day," mentioning letters from her Hutton cousins congratulating her on her birthday, and adds, "I feel much younger at thirty than I did at twenty; firmer and stronger both in mind and body" *(Journal,* complete ed. 427). So, if readers can trust her words, she apparently had come out of her depression.

Nonetheless, it seems that she never got entirely free of depression. According to Lane, Beatrix contracted in 1909 an illness following her parents' opposition to her wanting to marry William Heelis, and "Depression settled on her" which was "difficult to shake off." In fact, Lane writes of "two spectres which gloomily haunted her in Bolton Gardens—loneliness and depression" (*Tale of Beatrix Potter* 109). Judy Taylor points out that when in 1927 Potter told Fruing Warne about an offer she had to write a column for the *Daily Graphic*, an upset Fruing visited her. She agreed not to write the column, but the "visit," Taylor writes, "had depressed Beatrix deeply." His visit, Potter wrote Fruing, "brought back such a nightmare of painful realities" (*Beatrix Potter: Artist* 160). Fruing's visit occurred about four months before she turned fifty-eight.

Anne Stevenson Hobbs detects "an underlying melancholy" throughout Potter's work. Hobbs feels, "Anxiety, vulnerability and pathos are implicit in the attitudes of her animals, belied by the outward serenity of her sunlit paintings," and Hobbs adds, "In the nocturnes of her late books one senses unease, loneliness and fear" (23). E. James Anthony, a psychiatrist and psychoanalyst, detects in her work, an "undercurrent of deeper anxieties that," he claims, "propelled" her "stories willy-nilly into the hearts and minds of the younger set" (xv). Certainly, her animals have reason to feel "anxiety" and "vulnerability" since they are typically small creatures living in a world of predators. So it seems that a good case can be made for seeing a sense of depression and anxiety throughout her work, not just in the journal entries of her late teens and early twenties, a sense of depression that goes hand-in-hand with the realism that pervades her books both on and under their surfaces.

Maurice Sendak is justly praised as masterfully combining anxiety and security in his books for children. In an essay on Potter, he focuses on the scene in *The Tale of Peter Rabbit* in which Peter is slumped against a locked door and an old mouse cannot answer his question about escape because her mouth is too full. Sendak says that in this scene, one finds "the exact quality of nightmare: the sense of being trapped and frightened and finding the rest of the world (in this case, an old mouse) too busy keeping itself alive to help save you" ("Beatrix Potter/2" 75).[19] When one lives in a world of predator and prey in which predator can become prey and prey become predator, it seems sensible to be aware of the darker aspects of life, and when one describes such a world, the quality of nightmare is appropriate. Also, when one is brought up the way Beatrix Potter was with parents as undemonstrative as hers were—especially undemonstrative of love for their daughter—for her to have escaped depression and anxiety would seem miraculous. The combination of anxiety and security at work in her books is similar to that in many of the fairytales that she loved and drew on heavily in her writing. One of the attractions of these tales for children is hearing them in a situation in which the children are safe. An ideal situation is while sitting in the lap of a loving parent or other adult or at least very near that adult. Even for many adults, feeling anxiety in a setting of safety is pleasurable: hence, the popularity of horror movies.

Most scholars that deal with Potter's life indicate that, as a child, her lack of interaction with other children her age was somehow involved in what appears to be her difficulty as an adult dealing with children. There is much debate about her attitude toward children.[20] As Andrew Norman points out, when Potter was a child, she "existed in a world almost totally devoid of children," so she did not learn "to relate with them on a personal level" (85). Her first extensive experience with young children other than her brother seems to have been her interaction with the children of Annie Carter Moore, an interaction that occurred after Moore stopped being her governess and married Edwin Moore. On Christmas Eve, 1887, the Moores' first child was born; the child later received the story letter that later metamorphosed into *The Tale of Peter Rabbit*.

Potter's great-nephew by marriage, John Heelis, asserts that Potter "did not always understand the ways of children," but he is "sure she did not dislike them," but he also asserts, "she liked them to be well behaved" (56). John Heelis recalls that some children were frightened of her (54). Yet John Heelis points out that Tom Storey, her shepherd for many years, said, "I don't think she liked children" (50).

Willow Taylor knew Beatrix Potter when Willow Taylor was a young child, but by that time Potter was a grown woman who was married to William Heelis. Willow Taylor writes that she believes that Potter "truly did not understand children," and adds, "I doubt whether she had ever played a child's game in her life, because she had no friends" (W. Taylor, *Through the Pages* 25). In the "Introduction" to *Letters to Children from Beatrix Potter*, Judy Taylor quotes Willow Taylor as saying that Potter "was not the sweet old grandmotherly type," and Willow Taylor added that she sometimes wonders whether Potter "resented the fact that we were enjoying the kind of childhood she had longed for" and concluded, "It isn't that Mrs [sic] Heelis disliked children," but she "didn't understand their ways" (10). Willow Taylor exaggerates: Potter's biographers show that as a child, Potter did have some friends. Her younger brother, five years her junior, was for many years her only close friend. She spent some time with several cousins, but mostly after she reached adolescence. Potter's mother, who had tremendous fear of disease and especially of her daughter's catching diseases from other children, shielded—or perhaps blocked—her from close contact with young children. Andrew Norman argues that, since Beatrix Potter suffered from several maladies and as a child seems not to have been very robust, Mrs. Potter's fears for her daughter may not have been purely pathological. Still Potter's cousin, Ulla Hyde Parker, speculates that Potter's mother's fear of germs (what Hyde Parker calls, "her mother's great fear" [36]), added to other fears from childhood that kept

Potter from being able to be friendly or even relaxed with many people. Of course, Willow Taylor's and Ulla Hyde Parker's speculations about Potter's childhood are just that: speculations, since neither knew Potter when Potter was a child. Readers need to go to Potter's journal, letters, and biographers to find support for those speculations. And there one finds plenty of support.

Willow Taylor is on much firmer ground when she writes about Potter's attitude toward children when Taylor knew her. Taylor recalls being intimidated by Potter and writes that she and the other children never thought of Potter as an author or artist: "She was simply Mrs. Heelis, a farmer and villager, and someone to be wary of" (25). Moreover, Willow Taylor recounts the wonderful times she and the other children had playing in the farmers' fields during haying time, "all the farmers except Beatrix Potter that is. Most of us were never allowed into her fields" (24). She further recalls that Potter was a generous woman, but was unwilling to have anything she grew given away. Whatever she grew, she wanted sold. Willow Taylor says that people who did give away some of the things Potter grew had to do it without Potter's knowledge. Instead, Potter's "generosity was centered on the National Trust and [...] on the preservation of the Lake District" (24). It is easy to understand that young children really were not concerned with the National Trust and preservation of the Lake District, so Potter's generosity would be of little interest to them.

In 1929, Beatrix Potter proposed to write a book derived from Aesop's fables that Potter titled *The Folly of Vanity*.[21] In a letter written on 29 May 1919 to Fruing Warne, she reacts negatively to his desire to have her not write that book but to write one involving pigeons, referring to what eventually became *The Tale of the Faithful Dove* (published posthumously in 1955), asserting that the only "lever" Fruing has with Potter is her "sympathy with you and the old firm" and that "nothing else would induce me to go on at all." She has plenty of money and she does not care "for popularity or for the modern child; they are pampered and spoilt with too many toys and books." (*Letters* 257). She may have meant her words about "the modern child" here, or they may have been written just to gain leverage with her publisher. At any rate, she does seem to have liked some "modern" children.

Nonetheless, Potter could show a surprising callousness toward children. Judy Taylor tells of Potter's giving chocolate to five-year-old Alison Hart to feed to her two dogs, Chulah and Tzusee. According to Judy Taylor, Alison's mother was amazed that it never occurred to Potter that the child might herself like some chocolate (*Beatrix Potter: Artist* 199–201). The year was 1942, when chocolate was difficult to get in England. Was Potter entirely ignorant of the implications of what she was doing, or was she just unaware of what was going on in the lives of children? Could she not see the disappointment of the child and the amazement of the mother, or was she completely blind or even indifferent to both?

One scholar, Judy Taylor, who has edited many of Potter's works and written extensively about her, concludes in *Letters to Children from Beatrix Potter*, "We shall never know [...] whether or not Beatrix Potter liked children," but Potter "had a strong *rapport* with them through her writing." To Judy Taylor, the letters Potter wrote to children furnish "incontrovertible evidence" that Potter liked "children very much" (11). The letters and books also show that she had a keen understanding of children's needs, perhaps from tapping her own unfulfilled needs when she was a child. One undated series of letters that she wrote to John Hough is particularly telling concerning Potter's understanding of children and their needs. Each letter is signed by a different one of the Flopsy Bunnies. In the first, Mrs. Flopsy Bunny tells John, "We think Miss Potter is lazy" (*Letters to Children* 168). The rest of the letters are from the Flopsy Bunny children wishing John Hough a merry Christmas. The final one, from "4th (Miss) F. Bunny," reads in its entirety, "I have not learned to rite prop perly" (*Letters to Children* 169). It is easy to understand why such a series of letters would be especially pleasing to a young child.

In the final analysis, Potter seems to have liked some individual children and disliked many others. But she does seem to have had a difficult time getting along with most children, probably because she had so little contact with them when she was a child. It seems fair to conclude that for the most part, she liked children from a distance, separated from them at least by her books or long distances, not from close up, unless they were "well behaved."

One could not expect the child of Rupert and especially Helen Potter to have been entirely uninfluenced by their meanness. In fact, she does seem to have had a mean streak that became especially noticeable when she was herself an older person. Willow Taylor seems to hear echoes of the influence of "old Mrs. Potter" in some of the things Beatrix Potter said. Willow Taylor even feels that Beatrix Potter "frequently made herself unpopular with the villagers by interfering in their lives" (27).

One of the first persons to write literary criticism of Potter's books was the novelist Graham Greene. His essay, "Beatrix Potter: A Critical Estimate," appeared in the January 1933 issue of *The London Mercury*, when Greene was a young novelist starting on his career. His essay about Potter has often been reprinted. Ever since it appeared, other critics have had trouble figuring out Greene's point of view. Janet Adam Smith calls it "an admiring and affectionate joke" (39). Others recognize the essay's importance as a genuine piece of criticism. For example, Paula Weiderger, writing in *The Independent*, an English newspaper published in London, for 6 October 1993, says, "[...] Greene was adulatory, his subject was her genius." In *Smithsonian* for January 1989, Timothy Foote calls it a "celebrated essay," noting Potter's "evolution from simpler to more complex stories." Foote claims that Greene writes "(with tongue barely in cheek). that" before Potter wrote *Mr. Tod*, "she had experienced a gloomy epiphany" so that her later books "were marked by smiling villainy and a much darker view of human (or is it animal?) nature" (82). Peter Hollindale recognizes that Potter uses "concealment through irony" in her works and that "in turn her critics must be something of an ironist," and adds, "probably the best achievement of ironist criticism of Potter's work is Graham Greene's essay" ("These Piglets" 142–43).

Greene's essay contains what many critics agree is some of the most penetrating criticism of Potter's stories. Nonetheless, Potter reacted extremely negatively to it. In *Collected Essays*, published in 1969, Greene appends to the essay a note saying that Potter sent him what he calls a "somewhat acid letter" in which, Greene says, she corrected "certain details" of the essay, denied she went through "any emotional disturbance" when she was writing *The Tale of Mr. Tod*, but said she did suffer from "the after-effects of flu." Moreover, Greene writes, "she deprecated sharply 'the Freudian school of criticism'" (240). Potter seems to have objected most particularly to Greene's assertion that "between 1907 and 1909 Miss Potter must have passed through an emotional ordeal which changed the character of her genius" (236).[22] Unfortunately, Potter's letter to Greene seems to be lost. When Greene first published the essay on Potter, he was twenty-eight years old.[23] When she sent him the letter is unknown, but presumably it was not sent much later than his essay appeared in *The London Mercury*.

Margaret Lane, Potter's first biographer, writes of sending a letter to Potter in 1939 telling her what she was writing and asking to visit Potter to check some facts by submitting to her what Lane had written, "for her approval." Lane received in response what Lane calls "the rudest letter" she ever received. Lane says Potter wrote back saying, in effect, "nothing would induce her to see me." She also wrote, and Lane quotes her, "My books have always sold without advertisement, and I do not propose to go in for that sort of thing now." Lane then comments that Potter's reply "could hardly have been more offensively worded if I had asked her to sponsor a deodorant advertisement" and further comments that Lane tore up the letter, not knowing that she was one of many people who "had had the breath knocked out of them by her acerbity" ("Ghost of Beatrix Potter" 283). One of the ironies of the exchange between Lane and Potter is Potter's having in effect extensively advertised her own books, especially in the form of spin-offs from which she collected a great deal of money. In an article in *Smithsonian Magazine* for January 2017, Joy Lanzendorfer argues that Potter's "sweet stories [...] helped hide a savvy business mind—and an author who was among the first to realize that her readers could help build a business empire." Potter showed an interest throughout her writing career in creating income from her stories, including not only song and painting books but also, according to a partial list Lanzendorfer gives, "wallpaper, slippers, china, silverware, handkerchiefs, bookcases, stationary, almanacs." Lanzendorfer calls Potter's "approach unique," because of "the amount of merchandise she sold and the patents she was able to secure." Potter encouraged her publisher to help with the merchandising of these things and designed many of them herself, even stitching some of the dolls and advising Warne where to have them manufactured. It is easy to conclude that, rather than rejecting the idea of advertising her books, Potter really wanted a monopoly on the advertisements for her books and wanted most of the income derived from those advertisements!

Potter was, Lane writes, remembered in the Lake District as an eccentric person who wore "the odd bundle of country clothing" but was "full of good humour, of authority, of sudden acerbities which could flash out quite brutally and inflict hurts where she probably never intended them." Her neighbors in the Lake District, Lane learned, respected "her as a person it was dangerous to oppose, but very safe to love" ("Ghost of Beatrix Potter" 287).[24] Whether Potter "intended" to inflict hurts is impossible to judge, but in some cases, including that involving Lane, she certainly *seems* to have intended to do so.

One of those "people who had had the breath knocked out of them" was Janet Adam Smith (Mrs. Roberts) who sent Potter a copy of an article she published in *The Listener* on 21 January 1943 entitled, "The World of Beatrix Potter." In an article that includes *The Listener* article as well as information about the exchange with Potter, Smith writes that *The Listener* article "was written with enthusiasm and love" and she "hoped it would please Beatrix Potter" (39). On 2 February 1943, Potter wrote back to Smith that she already received a copy of the article and read it with "gratitude and stupefaction—the writer seems to know a deal more about the inception of the Peter Rabbit books than I do!" Smith, Potter wrote, says Potter's works "are founded on the work of the Immortals—all names which" Potter reveres, but, Potter claimed that "the only one" she "tried to copy was Randolph Caldecott, and you say there is no resemblance." She ends with a PS, saying she did not like being addressed as Miss (Smith 36). Smith says she was "appalled" by Potter's reply in which Potter very obviously acted insulted by Smith's article; Smith asks, "How could she have so misunderstood me" (39). On 7 February 1943, Potter wrote to Arthur Stephens, one of her editors at Warne, who sent her the article from *The Listener*: she called the article "great rubbish? Absolute bosh" (*Letters* 455).

Smith then sent a letter to Potter trying to clarify the meaning of what she had written, indicating to Potter that Smith meant to compliment her, not criticize her. Smith explains, "I never meant her work was 'founded' on anybody else's; only in the atmosphere conveyed by her pictures she was 'of the company' of Blake, Calvert, and Samuel Palmer," and Smith added that in the letter to Potter, Smith wrote, "her pictures had that quality of 'dewy freshness' a critic found in Constable. Now she thought I was comparing her to Constable!" (39).

On 8 February 1943, Potter replied, "We seem so much at 'cross purposes' that its [*sic*] not much use pursuing the subject," objecting especially to what she perceived as Smith's suggesting that her painting-manner "is founded on that of Constable." She added that Smith writes, "nicely," but Smith did not have "enough knowledge" to write the article, and then tells Smith "the secret of good writing": "Try and write […] about country wayside objects—if you are a beginner—and write them for your own children" and adds that Smith should "have something to say," and concluding, "for goodness sake don't write any more rubbish about me" (Smith 38).[25] Smith concludes, "It was hopeless to explain further" and adds, "I was sad that words written in admiration should have caused such offence" (39). Smith goes on, trying to defend Potter by saying, after Smith read Taylor's edition of Potter's letters, she understood that Potter saw Smith's article and letters "breaking into" Potter's "privacy" (39). Yet it is difficult to understand how Potter determined that the article was attacking her and even more difficult to see what she found insulting about Smith's second letter to her. At any rate, Potter's role in this exchange and the one with Lane and probably the letter she wrote to Greene was mean-spirited. She seems to have derived some pleasure from bullying people who were in a position of powerlessness to her. Is it not possible that she was unwittingly imitating the way her parents treated her?

One person Potter surely meant to hurt was Bruce Logan Thompson, who served the National Trust in various capacities, including, beginning in 1936, as land agent for the Trust's northern district, thus becoming the first land agent the Trust had anywhere in England. Before Thompson's appointment, Potter informed the trust that she and William would stop managing Monk Coniston when 1936 ended (Lear 394). However, Thompson's appointment seems to have upset Potter in some way that is difficult to understand. Perhaps she thought the Trust would beg her to stay on or at least make clear to her that anyone appointed to the position would be decidedly subservient to her. At any rate, she seems to have taken an instant disliking to Thompson, finding fault with everything he did and insulting him outrageously. Even a biographer as sympathetic to Potter as Linda Lear could not excuse Potter's attacks on Thompson, commenting that Potter's "scornful personal remarks about Bruce Thompson […] reflect poorly on Beatrix," and adding, "The privileges of age, wealth and patronage had made her careless and inconsiderate of others in the preservation community with whom she needed to cooperate" (401). Lear adds that Potter "allowed petty jealousies, mere bagatelles of turf, to get the better of her basic generosity and her profound concern for the future of the Lake District," and she praises Thompson for not allowing Potter's actions to have "disastrous results" (402). In a letter to D.M. Matheson, dated 9 May 1938, Potter writes that Thompson "seems to have no understanding about anything; and he is not learning either" (*Letters* 389). Matheson was

National Trust secretary and thus one of Thompson's superiors. In a letter to Matheson dated 17 October 1939, she says she thinks Thompson "seems to have no sense at all" and adds that Thompson is incapable "of learning." Upset because Thompson apparently wanted to cut down some trees that Potter thought necessary for the beauty of the landscape, she further writes that Thompson has no "pictorial sense of trees arranged in landscape" and his "imagination is blank," so "He wastes time & wages in the woods." Much of the hardwood in Monk Coniston, one of the estates Potter bought for the National Trust, Potter thought could be cut, but, Potter writes of Thompson that he "is too deficient in experience and taste […] to choose" which trees should be cut. She closes the body of the letter, writing that Thompson should not be allowed "to sell anything extensive without reference to the committee" and adds that she wants Matheson to "show the Estates Committee" what she has written. However, apparently not able to stop there, she adds after her signature that Thompson "has had no discretion in the past; and no experience (except disastrous) in timber & wood selling" (*Letters* 410). In the course of the letter, she comments, apparently about Thompson, "some folks would sell their soul for 6d" (409). To direct letters of this sort to Thompson's supervisor with directions that they also be passed on to the committee overseeing Thompson shows an extremely mean streak. Were it an isolated example, it would be fairly easy to excuse Potter on grounds of "age, wealth and patronage," as Lear does. Surely wealth and patronage were involved. But just plain meanness also seems to have been at work here.

In "Notes from the Hill" in the *Beatrix Potter Society Journal and Newsletter* for April 2016, Judy Taylor tells of what she calls "the first really anti (and extraordinary) Potter story I have ever read." She then tells of George Middleton's recounting his meeting with Potter in his book entitled, *Echoes of Ambleside and Beyond: Reminiscences and Recollections of an Ambleside Octogenarian*. In the chapter in his book entitled, "Social Event in Hawkeshead," Middleton tells of going with a friend to an event in Hawkeshead, where Potter told him he "was not welcome." According to Middleton, Potter's "last words were: 'Be gone if you do not want a taste of this,' and showed me the whip that I knew she invariably carried inside her cape" (55).

It was, Middleton feels, because of Potter's association with Middleton's grandfather's printing business that she recognized Middleton and turned him away, apparently thinking that since he was not from Hawkeshead, he should not be there.[26] As he started to walk home, he met a friend of his from Hawkeshead, Jack Pooley and his family. Pooley asked him where he was going, and he told Pooley what had happened. Pooley invited Middleton to join him and his family. Thus, Middleton returned to the "entertainment," as Middleton calls it. Pooley told Potter he invited Middleton, so Middleton "was not turned away again" (55). Middleton was about fourteen when Beatrix Potter died; he was probably about thirteen when the event he tells about occurred. Since he wrote his memoir in 2012, when he was about eighty-one, he may have forgotten or exaggerated some of the details of the encounter.[27]

In a series of three books, W.R. Mitchell writes of his "quest for Beatrix" in the Lakeland country she loved so well. In the last one in the series, his quest, he says, "revealed many facets about her life among us. Not all of them praiseworthy," and he adds, "No one is perfect" (129). Thus, like most of Potter's biographers, he recognizes her basic humanity, that is, her mixture of admirable and not-so-admirable traits. It is important to remember that although many heroes in Classical mythology are indeed not wholly human, heroes in more modern literature usually are. Potter was indeed human. Given some of the depths of Potter's early despair and the happiness she achieved in later life, she can easily be regarded as a kind of hero who herself went through an initiatory process that would have destroyed many people. For her, it led to the kind of happiness she found in her marriage and later life. Even as early as 1894, she wrote in her journal that she considered "happy marriage" to be "the crown of a woman's life" (*Journal*, complete ed. 321). A happy marriage certainly seems in many ways to have been the "crown" of her own life.

That Potter also retained some of her mother's snobbishness becomes clear in a letter she sent to two of her neighbors, Daisy Hammond and Cecily Mills, on 30 March 1939, shortly before she was to have a hysterectomy. In it, she writes that if she dies, she thinks it would be best for her husband to remarry, "provided he did not make a fool of himself by marrying, or not marrying, a servant" (*Beatrix Potter's Letters* 398). She here seems to have forgotten her brother's secret but happy marriage—albeit his first and only one—to Mary Welsh Scott, a woman who was not a servant but the daughter of a wine merchant and who once worked in textile mills.

However, clearly, her process of initiation did not involve a literal rebirth or a making-over of her entire personality. Many of the aspects of her later happiness can be found in her earlier life in which she managed to find the strength to free herself from her parents and achieve an independence of mind and body. Her struggle—in spite of her parents' objections—to find a means of supporting herself in the kind of affluence to which she was accustomed, her ability to escape from the criticizing of her parents and to overcome her sorrow and disappointment over the death of Norman Warne, who provided her with a real glimpse of possible happiness, and her ability to endure her parents' objections to William Heelis, who was, they were sure, too far beneath them and their daughter socially, all show the kind of tenaciousness that leads to heroic action. It should not be too surprising that Potter was able to work this kind of heroism into her books for very young children.

The patterns of rebirth Potter uses in her books correspond to initiation rites in which the initiate goes through what Mircea Eliade calls "the initiatory ritual of the ordeal (= fight with the monster), of symbolic death and resurrection (= birth of the new man)" (136). "Initiation," Eliade writes, "included a ritual death and resurrection" (144). There are many kinds of initiatory ordeals, not just the one literary critics seem to focus on most that inevitably ends with one becoming a hero. As Potter's work recognizes, one may fail one's initiatory ordeal. In some societies, failing the initiatory ordeal results in genuine rather than symbolic death. In Potter's work, however, the failed initiate lives. Jemima Puddle-duck, Jeremy Fisher, and Tom Kitten are just three examples. Peter in *The Tale of Peter Rabbit* comes close to having a successful initiation. In a later work, *The Tale of Mr. Tod*, Peter seems to be a genuine hero. In that work, his initiation is certainly successful, as is that of Pigling Bland in *The Tale of Pigling Bland*.

Fortunately for Potter, she survived her own initiation and became a stronger person as a result. Unfortunately for her readers, as she grew older, her literary creative period came mostly to an end as she immersed herself in married life and in another kind of creativity: farming; raising, buying, and selling sheep; and buying land for the National Trust. Yet Beatrix Potter, like so many of her characters, survived her own initiation, and in the course of that initiation, she contributed immensely to the world.

Potter's Realism

One of the most amazing things about Beatrix Potter's books for very young children is the way they combine stark realism with fantasy. In a letter written on 17 September 1921, Sylvester May Heelis, Beatrix's husband's niece, asked Beatrix for advice about writing for children. Beatrix wrote, among other things, "We were matter of fact little people," but immediately added that they "believed in fairies and the sweeps," alluding to both figures of fancy—fairies—and chimney sweeps, children involved in some of the most disturbing aspects of Victorian life in England. Beatrix also writes that she believes her books "succeeded by being absolutely matter of fact, & *thorough*" (*Letters* 272), words that seem very strange when applied to her fantasies. However, like traditional fairytales, her works treat many of the more unpleasant aspects of life—both natural and domestic, including awareness that rabbits, under certain circumstances, become rabbit pie and even articles of fur clothing for people; pigs become food for people; foxes and badgers eat other animals; owls eat small animals; frogs swallow fish; fish swallow frogs; people kill mice and rats; rats even kill small animals, including kittens. She usually depicts nature as being "red in tooth and claw,"[1] and the people in her works often add to the potential or actual carnage. However, cooperation is not unknown in her works: as one of Potter's illustrations in *The Tale of Peter Rabbit* shows: Peter Rabbit's sisters cooperate as they harvest blackberries (17). In *The Tale of Samuel Whiskers*, even the despicable Samuel Whiskers and Anna Maria cooperate in getting the ingredients for a roly-poly pudding. And Potter usually characterizes families as being cemented not by enmity but by love, as she does in *The Tale of Peter Rabbit* and *The Tale of Mr. Tod*. But sometimes, cooperation among animals proves very difficult, as it does in *The Tale of Ginger and Pickles*.

In a letter to eleven-year-old Tom Harding, written 21 December 1917, Potter clearly describes for an individual child the violence of life on Hill Top Farm. She speaks of some of the animals whose names appear in her works, including Jemima Puddleduck and Mr. Puddleduck, but she also writes about eating one of her own ducks named Sago and eating rabbit pies made "of the young ones" (180). In a letter to an unidentified child named Dulcie, written on 18 October 1918, she again mentions eating Sago because he was a male (*Letters to Children* 180–81). In another letter to Dulcie, dated 29 July 1924, she writes matter-of-factly about slaughtering animals and writes of a cat that catches rabbits and gives them to a cat named "Tabbitha," who skins and then eats the rabbits (*Letters to Children* 185–86). Thus, she clearly shows violence in domestic life since the episodes she narrates in the letter to Dulcie occur on a farm and involve farm animals. In fact, many of the letters to children that Judy Taylor collects in *Letters to Children from Beatrix Potter* show not only her recognition of the kinds of violence that occur on farms but also her willingness to communicate to children about that violence.

Her drawings and paintings in her books show her ability to create animals that have the realistic characteristics of animals even when they dress in human clothing and speak a human language, and the pictures and words show her not avoiding depictions of the aspects of their lives that include horror as well as joy. Thus, the literary fairytales she creates resemble traditional fairytales with their combination of fantasy and stark realism and their happy endings.

As a child, she collected live animals, often took them back to her nursery, and even took some with her on trains when the Potters went on vacations to the north of England and into Scotland. She and her brother dissected some animal carcasses they found and boiled some down to skeletons and put the skeletons together. Critics and biographers try to describe what is often called her "curious double vision" that allowed her to see and draw animals that are so accurate yet so much a part of her works of fantasy in which they are both animals and people simultaneously. In her journal for 13 August 1896, Potter discusses the death of John Millais, the painter, one of her father's friends, whom Beatrix admired and of whom Beatrix had become quite fond, writing that he complimented her by saying, although many "people can *draw*," Potter and Millais' "son [...] have observation'" (*Journal*, complete ed. 429). So she recognized that Millais understood that she had a special kind of vision that later became vital to her artwork. Her cousin by marriage, Ulla Hyde Parker, tries to describe this vision and her ability to embody it in her artwork. Hyde Parker's difficulty describing it becomes obvious in the course of her attempt. Potter, she writes, "loved animals. They were her real friends [...]." Potter studied animals, played with animals, and took them with her on trips. "She sketched them, making beautiful drawings or watercolours and revealing their individual beauty and character, even personality." For Potter, Hyde Parker writes, "animals did become people, real people." Hyde Parker even calls them "people animals" (8).

Lear recognizes that in the 1890s, searching for ways "to market her fanciful drawings," Potter used "human costume and activity" to anthropomorphize the creatures in them and set them in real places and "in real, rather than imagined, nature" (*Beatrix Potter* 130). According to Lear, Potter ultimately produced a new kind of "animal fable" with "anthropomorphized animals" that "behave always as real animals with true animal instincts" that "are accurately drawn by a scientific illustrator." In Potter's stories, Lear writes, "The gap between animals and humans is so narrow [...] that we scarcely notice the transition between the two" (*Beatrix Potter* 153). This realistic depiction continues throughout her work. At the same time, in her books, Potter creates realistic threats of death for them to face. However, when Lear asserts that Potter's animals "behave always as real animals," she exaggerates. No real rabbit could hand one of her daughters a basket, as Peter's mother does when Peter's sisters are about to leave to gather berries in *The Tale of Peter Rabbit* (9), nor could she button her son's jacket before he goes out on his adventures, as Peter's mother does to him (13).

Margaret Lane wrote two books and several essays about Potter and then revised one of the books. Lane contacted Potter when she was alive, but Potter refused to help Lane. In fact, Potter rebuffed Lane in what Lane describes as a very unpleasant manner. After Potter's death, however, William Heelis, Potter's widower, gave Lane access to some of Potter's manuscripts and unpublished paintings. In her writing, Lane also wrestles with trying to elucidate Potter's vision involving animals. *The Magic Years of Beatrix Potter* was the second of Lane's books on Potter, written after Leslie Linder published the first edition of his translation of Beatrix Potter's coded journal. In it, Lane writes about Potter's pet hedgehog, a creature that became a large part of the inspiration for *The Tale of Mrs. Tiggy-Winkle*. After treating Potter's taking her hedgehog on train journeys, Lane writes about what she calls Potter's "curious 'double vision'" that in Potter's work, one finds "the absorbed naturalist, observing, recording, perhaps even discovering minutiae of animal behavior," and "the poetic vision" that translates "the fastidiously clean habits of a species into the diligent laundry business of Mrs [*sic*] Tiggy-Winkle" (53).

In a later essay, Lane writes that Potter combines "a child's vision of the natural world and a child's fantasies about animals" with the ability of a "serious" naturalist to observe and the "integrity of approach" of an artist (Lane, "Secret World" 26). She then quotes from Potter's journal of 17 November 1896 in which Potter writes, "What heaven can be more real than to retain the spirit-world of childhood, tempered and balanced by knowledge and common-sense; to fear no longer the terror that flieth by night, yet to feel truly and understand [...] a very little, of the story of life."[2] Lane then concludes that these words are a "clear, brief statement of the vision and the common-sense balance" Potter "achieved" (Lane, "Secret World" 26). Lane does not quote the passage just before the words she quotes in which Potter writes that when she was a child, she "half" believed and "wholly" played "with fairies" (*Journal*, complete ed. 435).

In an essay on one of Potter's late, atypical stories, *Sister Anne* (1932), a long retelling of the Bluebeard story, Rose Lovell Smith focuses on one picture from an early Potter work, *The Tailor of Gloucester* (1902), in an attempt to understand this double vision.[3] It shows a very ornately dressed female mouse holding a hand mirror but apparently looking ahead at the reader rather than into the mirror. According to Lovell-Smith, the "main effect" of the picture "is to slide the animal and the human on top of each other into a single image." In doing so, Potter situates "human nature and animal nature as uncomfortably close to each other, as looking uncomfortably like, yet unlike, each other, and as unstable, even interchangeable in their differences." This "effect," Lovell-Smith writes, is found "in much of Potter's works" (6). Lovell-Smith's words, of course, tell the effect on some adult readers. Most child readers probably do not feel uncomfortable at all. In fact, many of them may consider it a matter of course that human nature and animal nature are extremely close to each other, just as many of them believe that their toys, especially those that resemble people or animals, are alive.

In *Aesop in the Shadows*, Peter Hollindale writes of "the double perspective" readers find in Potter's books for children. "The anthropomorphic human comedy," Hollindale writes, "is the conspicuous thing, but encoded into it there is precise, uncompromising natural history" (*Aesop* 13). The natural history and the human comedy, however, seem to some readers to interpenetrate one another; neither seems more conspicuous than the other: both seem, to use Hollindale's term, encoded into one another.[4]

Closely observing animals undoubtedly contributed to Potter's ability to depict them and their activities realistically. She and her brother Bertram kept many pets. In addition to the usual dogs, cats, and birds, she kept many animals usually considered wild, including rabbits, mice, hedgehogs, snails, frogs, birds, newts, lizards, even bats, rats, and snakes. Among their birds were an owl and a falcon, both of which belonged to Bertram. They observed them carefully in the wild and in captivity. Beatrix also raised and observed domesticated animals carefully, including ducks. When she was an adult living in the Lake Country and managing several farms that she owned, she raised her favorite kind of sheep—Herdwicks, as well as cattle, pigs, even keeping a pet pig in her house.

In a letter to the printing firm of Edmund Evans, dated 28 February 1910, she writes, in parentheses, that she is "a one horse farmer" (*Letters* 176). Always practical, Potter writes in the letter that if published, it should be signed, "N. Lancs [sic], as a female farmer is silly on paper [...]" (*Letters* 176). She wrote the letter to the printing firm in connection with a pamphlet she published in leaflet form signed, "Yours truly, North Country Farmer," that argued that the government should not take farmers' horses for war work since the farmers need the horses to produce food. In *Beatrix Potter's Letters*, Taylor publishes two letters to the Evans firm that discuss the pamphlet, one for 28 February 1910 and one for 8 March 1910. She adds to the second letter that that letter must not indicate it was "written by a *female*" (177–78). The published pamphlet is entitled "The Shortage of Horses."[5]

Potter was able to embed her love for animals into her books for very small children, though she simultaneously recognized how perilous their lives are. She also had the ability simultaneously to love animals and devour some of the ones she kept; that is, she did not have what she considered a simple sentimental attachment to animals raised for food. In fact, she was quite forthright in acknowledging her willingness to slaughter animals for food and other purposes. Lear quotes a letter Potter sent to Millie Warne on 30 August 1907, in which Potter writes about photographing lambs before sending them off to slaughter, stating forthrightly, "it does not do to be sentimental on a farm" and adding that she will have "lambskin hearthrugs" (220). Eleanor Louisa (Louie) Choyce worked on Potter's farm during World War I when male workers were largely unavailable because of the war. The friendship that developed between Choyce and Potter lasted long after Choyce stopped working for Potter. In a letter to Choyce dated 13 December 1922, Potter alludes to her lack of sentimental attachment to the farm animals she raises and her recognition that farming is a business. In the letter, Potter announces that she is a "*butcher*," and explains that on her farms, they "have been butchering on the quiet for a long time." They did it on the quiet, she explains, until a professional butcher reported them; then they got licensed. They did the butchering because they could get more meat off an animal they butchered themselves and could thus make more money.[6] Grinstein reports that Potter was involved in butchering rabbits, lambs, and sheep (305), so the lack of sentimental attachment that she showed toward animals when she and Bertram were young and they boiled down animals to get to their bones continued into adulthood.

For all the genuine love she showed toward many of her pets and for all the love she shows toward most of the animals in her books—and the love many of them show to one another—she hardly ever writes about them sentimentally; she hardly ever glosses over the dangers in their lives. Her realistic drawings reveal her understanding of the anatomy of the animals she drew, and that understanding resulted in part from observing those animals carefully and even dissecting some and boiling some down so that she and her brother could get to the bones and reassemble them. As Maurice Sendak writes, "she was unmitigatingly honest about" animals, "sometimes harsh, always adoring, but without any taint of sentimentality" ("Beatrix Potter/1" 67). She did, however, sometimes have them do impossible things in her stories, such as having Peter and Benjamin, two rabbits, walk "hand in hand" in *The Tale of Benjamin Bunny* (20) and having her animal creatures speak human language and wear human clothes that they put on themselves or put on one another. However, she clearly recognized that there are limits to how far this kind of thing can go: in a letter dated 26 June 1842 to Mrs. M.E. Wight, Potter spells out that difference in some things she says about Kenneth Grahame, author of *The Wind in the Willows*. She writes that writers of children's books should "have a sufficient recognition of what things look like" and castigates Grahame, especially for having Toad comb "his *hair?*" She goes on to say that it is all right for a frog to "wear galoshes," but she does not "hold with toads having beards or wigs!" (*Letters* 450). Thus, her own Mr. Jeremy Fisher in galoshes is all right, but Grahame's Toad combing his hair is not.

Potter's preference for what she called "matter-of-fact" over sentimentality appears in her journal entry for 5 June 1891, when she was twenty-five years old. In the journal entry, she writes about meeting Mrs. Hugh Blackburn (Jemima Wedderburn Blackburn) and recalls that her parents gave her a copy of Mrs. Blackburn's *Birds Drawn from Nature* as a present for her tenth birthday and how much she liked the book.[7] Mrs. Blackburn, she writes in her journal, was second only to Thomas Bewick in her ability to paint birds. She was able to meet Mrs. Blackburn because of some kind of family connection Mrs. Blackburn had to Potter's Hutton cousins: her cousin Caroline Hutton's uncle accompanied her to the meeting with Mrs. Blackburn. Mrs. Blackburn, she writes, is not "all matter-of-fact without sentiment," but Potter writes that she sees "no reason why common sense should not foster a healthier appreciation of beauty than morbid sentimentality." Potter praises Mrs. Blackburn's common sense linked with "deep feeling" (*Journal*, complete ed. 215–17). Of course, at twenty-five, Potter would have no way of knowing that she would in future years be praised for the mixture of common-sense and matter-of-fact in her works, works that are full of sentiment but lacking, for the most part, in sentimentality. The words, "for the most part," are important here: it could be argued that many of the happy endings in her books are pure sentimentality. Sentimentality plays an especially large role, for example, at the end of *The Tale of Pigling Bland* when Bland and Pig-Wig cross the bridge "hand in hand" and run "over the hills and far away." The final picture of the book shows the two pigs dancing on two legs to music that some rabbits play. Pigling Bland wears a jacket and Pig-Wig wears a dress (80–81). Here, Potter is clearly both sentimental and untrue to animal nature and capabilities. Also, the love that parents in her books show for their children could also be called sentimentality on Potter's part, especially in light of the relationship she had with her own parents. In *The Tale of Peter Rabbit*, Peter's mother shows concern about Peter when he returns from Mr. McGregor's garden and in *The Tale of Mr. Tod*, Peter's and his cousin Benjamin's willingness to put themselves in jeopardy to save Benjamin's children represents a kind of affection of parent for one's children that Potter apparently never received. This kind of love that she shows so clearly in her books could, in fact, be connected with a wish for a life that as a child she did not lead.

As a farmer, she got quite attached to many of her animals and delighted in winning prizes with her Herdwick sheep and judging at competitions involving Herdwick sheep. She was a member of the Herdwick Sheep Breeder's Association and was one of the few women the members accepted as an equal. She presided at some meetings of the association. In March 1943, she was elected president of the Herdwick Sheep Breeders' Association, to take office in 1944, but she died before her term began. She was, as Lear puts it, "The first woman ever elected to the presidency of this bastion of male sheep breeders," and she felt the recognition the election involved was an honor (436). Nonetheless, she recognized the need to slaughter animals for food and recognized the dangers inherent in their lives, even the lives of domestic animals that she knew from first-hand experience often faced death not only from being slaughtered to provide food but also from sickness, bad weather, predators, and mistreatment by people. Although as an adult she had a pet pig that even slept in her bedroom, she was fully aware of the uses of pigs for food and appears to have not only not objected to this use but also actively participated in it. She even embodies this idea in her books for young children. In *The Tale of Pigling Bland*, when Pigling Bland asks Pig-Wig why Mr. Pipperson stole her, Pig-Wig "cheerfully" answers, "Bacon, hams" (55), recognizing herself what future probably awaits her. In *The Tale of Little Pig Robinson*, Potter matter-of-factly writes of Robinson's Aunt Porcas and Dorcas, "their end was bacon" (25).

Sendak was one of the most honored author-illustrators of children's books in twentieth-century America. He did not hide his love for Potter's works. He published two essays on Potter,[8] and he illustrated Robert Graves' *Big Green Book* with several pictures that he called his tribute to Beatrix Potter. Several places on the Victoria and Albert Museum Website refer to Sendak's debt to Potter. "Sendak's illustrations to Robert Graves's children's story, The Big Green Book (1962)," one Website says, "incorporate several images by Beatrix Potter, including sketches of the bedroom she slept in at Camfield Place, the gabled roof of Bush Hall and the potting shed at Bedwell Lodge, immortalised as Mr. McGregor's potting shed in The Tale of Peter Rabbit."[9]

In "Beatrix Potter/2," Sendak recounts a time he served on a panel discussion of what he calls "experts" in the field of children's literature. The audience voiced "a lack of seriousness and a proper attitude on the part of artists and writers now writing books for children." One person in the audience complained about *The Tale of Peter Rabbit*, insisting, "it seemed to him to be 'neither fact nor even fancy'" ("Beatrix Potter/2" 71–72). Sendak then adds, "To my horror, there were some murmurs of approval" from the audience and "even applause" ("Beatrix Potter/2" 72). Apparently considering himself what he calls "a loyal Potterite" ("Beatrix Potter/1" 69) and part of the group he calls "true-blue Potterites" ("Beatrix Potter/2" 73), Sendak found the statement and the audience's reaction to it disturbing. What, the questioner wanted to know, "had that silly rabbit to do with the hard facts of life or even the dream facts?" Sendak says one of his impulses was to defend Potter's "honor" by smashing the questioner "in the nose" ("Beatrix Potter/2" 73).

Sendak argues that although *The Tale of Peter Rabbit* is not a factual book, it cannot "be easily defined as fantasy," but both factual and fantasy books "should properly come under the heading (if we must have a heading) of imaginative writing" ("Beatrix Potter/2" 72). In fact, he declares, "*Peter Rabbit* transcends all arbitrary categories" ("Beatrix Potter/2" 73). Especially in his use of "arbitrary," Sendak does seem to be correct: *Peter Rabbit* and most of Potter's other works transcend labels. That helps explain the difficulty people have explaining Potter's way of blending fantasy and reality. *The Tale of Peter Rabbit*, according to Sendak, achieves "an imaginative synthesis of factual and fantastical components." Peter, he writes, "is both endearing little boy and expertly drawn rabbit" ("Beatrix Potter/2" 74). He calls it a "fantastic, realistic, truthful story" ("Beatrix Potter/2" 75), a label that clearly reveals Sendak's difficulty explaining the kind of synthesis he finds in Potter's works.

Lear writes that in *The Tale of Mr. Jeremy Fisher*, Potter describes and illustrates nature "truthfully"; Potter, Lear writes, shows it as being "beautifully tranquil" and "unpredictably aggressive" (213). These words could easily apply to nature as Potter depicts it in almost all of her books: Potter creates a nature that is both "tranquilly beautiful" and "unpredictably aggressive" simultaneously and does the same with the human world, that is, if readers see the cat Simpkin in *The Tailor of Gloucester* and the rat Samuel Whiskers in *The Tale of Samuel Whiskers* as human and animal simultaneously, something Potter's words and illustrations demand readers do. The potential for aggression lies within the tranquil beauty, and that tranquility can be and is disrupted in her works at any time without warning in her depictions of both natural and domestic life. Even in her books not set in a natural surrounding, such as *The Tale of Two Bad Mice*, and in ones that involve both natural and domesticated settings, such as *The Tale of Peter Rabbit*, the aggression lies just beneath the surface and erupts spontaneously from the animals or humans. And of course, in books that involve interaction of wild animals and humans or domesticated animals and humans, such as *The Tale of Pigling Bland*, the aggression, mostly carried out by humans, leaps to the surface, giving the stories their centers of interest. As Humphrey Carpenter points out, writers "find in her a sense of the way that the grotesque and unmentionable may lurk behind any domestic façade, particularly the most respectable." She had, Carpenter writes, "the power of creating archetypes that remain with her readers for the rest of their lives" ("Excessively Impertinent Bunnies" 275, 277).

Potter also does not create works that can be summed up in a simple moral. To do so would be to distort nature and human life. Many parents and many undergraduate students in children's literature classes, however, try to tack simple morals onto her works. They say, for example, that the moral of *The Tale of Peter Rabbit* is, always obey your mother. That is a complete distortion of the work. Flopsy, Mopsy, and Cotton-tail obey their mother: they are dull, flat characters indistinguishable from one another. Peter disobeys his mother, has a magnificent and frightening adventure, but emerges victorious. Humphrey Carpenter takes strong exception to critics who say Potter writes things that could be called moral tales: "there is nothing in her work that resembles the moral tale. In fact, it might be argued that she is writing something pretty close to a series of immoral tales [...]." He sees her tales as subversive rather than reinforcing usual adult mores and manners, especially subverting ideas of "acceptable social behavior." Instead, the voice in her works is that "of a rebel, albeit a covert one, demonstrating the reward of nonconformity, and exhorting young readers to question the social system into which they found themselves born," and adds, "Her whole life was dedicated to rebelliousness" ("Excessively Impertinent" 279). In this last assertion, Carpenter clearly exaggerates. In her own life, for example, Potter did not entirely reject the social system of her time, Victorian and Edwardian England and even modern England. She especially did not reject many of the parts of it that privileged her own position as a person of wealth. Still, she made fun of even that in works like *The Tale of Mr. Jeremy Fisher* and *The Pie and the Patty-Pan*.

Yet realistic as her works are, they still are magical. According to W.R. Mitchell, anyone who reads her works "discovers there is magic in ordinary things—in rabbits and ducks, rhubarb patches and water butts, white-washed cottages and lily-covered tarns, roadside flowers, pigs and goats and, of course, in Herdwick sheep" (125). Thus, readers recognize her uncanny ability to portray a world peopled by realistic animals that often dress like human beings and act like human beings but also become pure animals.

As numerous critics show, part of Beatrix Potter's ability to create enthralling stories involves her use of concrete objects in her settings, both inside houses and out.[10] She provides information about her settings in a response to John Stone, who asked her about her settings so he could visit some of the places she uses in her books, telling him in a letter for 19 August 1939 about the settings and inviting him to come to Tom Kitten's house so she can meet him and show it to him. She even gives him directions of how to get there. She goes on to list a number of her settings and to tell Stone where to find them (*Letters* 406).

Most of her animals as well as her gardens, dwellings, and interiors were drawn from real objects and animals. She based the detailed reproductions of clothing in *The Tailor of Gloucester* on originals in the South Kensington Museum (now the Victoria and Albert Museum). Even the dollhouse in *The Tale of Two Bad Mice* is based on a real dollhouse that Norman Warne built for one of his nieces. The clothing in *The Tale of Mr. Jeremy Fisher* reproduces (and satirizes) the fashions of the period in English history just before Potter's day. The examples could go on and on. Like most good producers of fantasy works, she realized that one of the things that makes fantasy interesting and enjoyable for adults and children is its being firmly rooted in reality.

Potter recognized that she did not draw people very well. Critics agree with her. Perhaps her problems drawing people stemmed from her being unable to dissect them as she could do with animals.

Her use of rebirth is also realistic. The changes that come over her animal characters are, in the context of her works, believable. None change into superheroes; none become completely reformed. No creature like Mighty Mouse appears anywhere in her works. The changes her animals undergo are incremental rather than total. Although her central animal characters often face terrible threats and successfully get through them, many do not change, and some, like Tom Kitten in *The Tale of Samuel Whiskers*, lose a good deal as a result of their adventures.

Fairies, Fairytales and Beatrix Potter

Many books involving children's literature just assume that people know what a fairytale is. In modern usage, fairytales have been consigned to the nursery. Many things now considered tales for children, such as "Little Red Riding-Hood" and "Hansel and Gretel," were once not intended for children. Even what was once considered a clear distinction between folk fairytales and literary fairytales has become less clear, especially with recent discoveries about the way the brothers Grimm, especially, shaped and revised the tales that scholars once believed they recorded faithfully from their sources who were believed to be people they interviewed in cottages and fields. Still, there have been many scholarly and popular studies about what constitutes a fairytale. Many scholars insist that the moment a tale is written down, it ceases to be a folk fairytale and becomes a literary invention. In *The Folktale*, Stith Thompson points to the problem of making distinctions between different kinds of tales, simply stating, "Sometimes the expression 'wonder tale' or 'fairy tale' is applied to stories filled with incredible marvels," but then contrasts such tales with legends, which are supposedly "based upon fact" (21). Obviously, Beatrix Potter's tales, with their animals that wear clothes and talk, fit under the rubric of "wonder tale" or "fairy tale"; for all of their grounding in reality, they usually make no claim to being about things that actually happened in what is usually called "the real world"; however, they do claim reality within the context that each tale creates.[1]

J.R.R. Tolkien, a scholar of medieval literature and an author of a number of literary fairytales, in his essay entitled "On Fairy-Stories," joins a number of other scholars and popular authors in pointing out the obvious fact that many works classified as fairytales do not involve fairies at all, writing, "fairy-stories are not in normal English usage stories *about* fairies or elves, but stories about Fairy, that is *Faërie*, the realm or state in which fairies have their being" (9).[2] Stith Thompson also points out that although the label fairytale "seems to imply the presence of" fairies, most of the tales labeled this way "have no fairies." Thompson prefers the German term *Märchen* to describe the tales English authors classify as fairytales since each of them involves some length and what Thompson calls "a succession of motifs or episodes," things that he says are necessary for a *Märchen* (8). Even Potter's tales for very young children, such as *The Story of Miss Moppet*, easily fit such a description. Many of her "miniature letters"—short letters sent to individual child readers usually in response to particular questions about her published works—would also fit this description when they involve a series of such letters, and sometimes her miniature letters do involve such series.

Tolkien says that *Faërie* involves "the Perilous Realm itself, and the air that blows in that country," but then adds that he "will not attempt to define that, nor to describe it directly. It cannot be done" (10). Still, what he calls a "fairy-story" is "one which touches on or uses Faërie," a word that he writes can "most nearly be translated as Magic—but it is magic of a peculiar mood and power," not at all like that "of the laborious, scientific magician." He also asserts what seems to be fairly obvious: many writers, even scholars, "have used the term 'fairy-tale' very carelessly" (11).

Yet for Potter as a child, the realm of *Faërie* was synonymous, she insisted, with the world in which she lived—or at least the part of that world that human beings had not reshaped for their own purposes, what could be called the natural world. While still in the nursery at Bolton Gardens, she loved fairytales, a love that lasted throughout her life. Potter claimed that she learned to love fairies from one of her nurses, Ann Mackenzie. In an essay published in *Horn Book* in 1929, entitled "'Roots' of the Peter Rabbit Tales," Potter writes that she got from the nurse "a firm belief in witches, fairies and the creed of the terrible John Calvin (the creed rubbed off, but the fairies remained)" (69). Margaret Lane quotes Potter that she could not think of ever being unable "to invent pictures" and create for herself "a fairyland amongst the wild flowers, the animals, fungi, mosses, woods and streams, all the thousand objects of the countryside […]" (*The Tale of Beatrix Potter* 32). In her journal for 1884, in one of her recollections of the summers she spent in Dalguise House in Scotland, Potter writes that at that time in her life, for her, the woods really contained "the mysterious good folk." Her "fancies" were so clear that they became real for her, so much so that she inhabited "a separate world" (*Journal*, complete ed. 85).[3]

Linder quotes part of a passage from Potter's journal from 17 November 1896 (*History* 350), when Potter was thirty years old. The journal passage, which has been quoted often since Linder first quoted it, involves her memories of Esthwaite. For her, when sitting on Oatmeal Crag, the "fungus people" sang and bobbed and danced below her, she claimed, so much so that she believed that she knew "something about them." She then adds that "they laugh and clap their hands, especially the little ones […]." She remembers, she writes, that as a child, she "used to half believe and wholly play with fairies" (*Journal*, complete ed. 435).[4]

Her belief in fairies and fairy-like creatures seems to have in some way accompanied her into later life. *The Fairy Caravan* grew, she writes, from her seeing "footmarks of a troop of fairy riders, riding [...] away into Fairyland [...]." Seeing "those little fairy footmarks" caused her to become "aware of the Fairy Caravan" ("The Lonely Hills" 155), thus implying that the caravan itself is a part of the real world in which she lives. For Potter, then, fairyland was in some sense part of her idea of reality, an idea that stayed with her from her early childhood into her adult years. The wonder she saw in that world, the idea that the realm of what Tolkien terms *Faërie* has a real verifiable existence that involves not just fairies but all parts of the natural landscape, is the kind of wonder that clearly exists in her stories for children.

Another of Tolkien's assertions about what he calls "a genuine fairy-story" (14), is also an attribute of Potter's tales, though Tolkien himself seems to deny it. A "genuine fairy-story" must, Tolkien asserts, "be presented as 'true.'" It cannot, he writes, "tolerate any frame or machinery" that suggests it is not true: it cannot suggest it is a dream or even, within itself, a kind of literary invention (14).[5] Potter's knowledge of animal behavior and even animal anatomy, both based on close observation and even dissection, helps create the air of verisimilitude in her tales. Even her entering into some of the tales herself as both narrator and character adds to this atmosphere of verisimilitude. In *The Tale of Samuel Whiskers*, for example, Potter vouches for the reality of the tale when she writes that she in her role as narrator "saw Mr. Samuel Whiskers and his wife on the run" as they moved from the house where Tom Kitten lives to Farmer Potatoes' barn, with Anna Maria pushing their belongings on a wheelbarrow "which looked very much like mine," adding, "I am sure *I* never gave her leave to borrow my wheelbarrow!" (66). Also, in *The Tale of Pigling Bland*, Potter as narrator interacts with Aunt Pettitoes and the other pigs in matter-of-fact ways, helping Aunt Pettitoes drag Alexander out of a pig trough's hoops, in which he has gotten stuck (9), whipping the piglings who get into the garden and leading them from the garden, adding that Cross-Patch, one of the piglings, tries to bite her (12). She even tells Aunt Pettitoes that she must get rid of all her piglings except Spot (15). After Aunt Pettitoes sends the other pigs away, two in a wheelbarrow and three in a cart, the narrator joins Aunt Pettitoes as she brushes the coats, curls their tails, washes their faces, and says good-bye to two of the piglings who remain behind, and the narrator gives those two—Alexander and Pigling Bland— some advice concerning things to avoid and warns them not to "cross the county boundary," for if they do, they cannot return. She also gives them both licenses that allow them to travel "to market in Lancashire," tells them she had great difficulty getting the papers, and pins the papers inside the pockets in the pigs' waistcoats (20–22). In her other books, Potter as narrator does not interact so actively with the characters in the tales, but her incorporating her own observations of animals into the tales helps give readers no reason to doubt their "truth." And in Potter's conclusion of *The Fairy Caravan*, her narrator says that she "can trace my pony's fairy footsteps, and hear her eager neighing" and "can hear the rattle of the tilt-cart's wheels, and the music of the Fairy Caravan" (225). Thus, the narrator insists that this book's reality is also the reality she actually occupies.

Still, Tolkien strangely asserts that Potter's stories "lie near the borders of Faerie, but outside it," and he claims that *The Tale of Peter Rabbit* is not a fairytale but "a beast fable," something he defines as a tale "in which no human being is concerned; or in which the animals are the heroes and heroines, and men and women, if they appear, are mere adjuncts; and above all those in which the animal form is only a mask upon a human face, a device of the satirist or preacher" (15–16). This reading of Potter's tales seems woefully misguided, especially if Tolkien feels that Potter's animals are truly masks upon human faces. He does, however, claim that *The Tailor of Gloucester* "comes nearest" of all her stories to being a "fairy-story," and *The Tale of Mrs. Tiggy-Winkle* would be "as near," except "for the hinted dream explanation" (16 n. 1); he apparently ignores Potter's immediate dismissal of what he calls "the hinted dream explanation" when she says explicitly in parentheses at the end of the story that "some people say that little Lucie had been asleep upon the stile," but then immediately dismisses the idea, writing that, if it were a dream, Lucy could not find the items she lost "pinned with a silver pin" and asserts that she herself has "seen the door into the back of the hill called Cat Bells" and that she is "very well acquainted with dear Mrs. Tiggy-winkle!" (57). Thus, she insists on the reality of the story. To indicate in Potter's tales, "the animal form is only a mask upon a human face," involves what seems ultimately to be a misreading of Potter's work.

It is true that in the 1890s Potter did illustrate some of Aesop's fables, and she wrote some stories that could be classified as beast fables, modeling them on Aesop's tales. Leslie Linder includes some of the texts of these tales in a chapter in his monumental *History of the Writings of Beatrix Potter* entitled, "The Tale of the Birds and Mr. Tod" (245–50); this is the title given in Potter's final suggestion for a collection of tales based on Aesop that Potter wanted to publish as her book for 1919.[6] Her publisher even announced that *Jenny Crow, or The Tale of the Birds and Mr. Tod* would be ready for the Christmas season. But Potter never finished the illustrations.[7] One of her later books that many critics classify as one her best, *The Tale of Johnny Town-Mouse* (1918), is her version of Aesop's "The Town Mouse and the Country Mouse." It truly is a beast fable. Yet even when she deliberately imitated Aesop, her retellings of the tales "always," according to Lear, "reflected" the animals' "true characteristics," and when she changed Aesop, Lear writes, it involved "more faithfully" interpreting "animal nature" within the imaginary world she was creating (292). However, the only one of these stories to be published during Potter's lifetime was *The Tale of Johnny Town-Mouse*. But to classify most of Potter's works as beast fables seems strange indeed.

In "On Fairy-Stories," Tolkien uses *The Tale of Peter Rabbit* as an example of a tale (presumably a "fairy-story"—otherwise, why mention it?) in which a prohibition is central, commenting, "Even Peter Rabbit was forbidden a garden, lost his blue coat there, and took sick. The Locked Door stands as an eternal Temptation" (33). Thus, Tolkien at least seems to undercut his own assertion about Potter's works not being fairy stories.

Like most fairytales, Potter's books contain almost no actual fairies, but they do contain talking animals who go about their busy, event-filled lives, in parallel to the lives of the human beings with whom many of the animals interact, often to their detriment. One obvious exception is *The Fairy Caravan*, where creatures called fairies appear in several things Xarifa, the Dormouse, says. She even tells a tale called, "The Fairy in the Oak." And many of Potter's stories' plots have fairly clear connections to works universally recognized as fairytales, such as "Little Red-Riding Hood" and "Jack and the Beanstalk." In spite of Tolkien and although Potter's books fit no rigid definitions, it is for good reason that her books have been and still are called fairytales, and it is no wonder that they reproduce a kind of world in which the real and the imaginary interpenetrate each other ultimately creating a world in which the imaginary becomes real, at least within the confines of her stories. Her animal characters—Peter Rabbit, Squirrel Nutkin, even Samuel Whiskers—are at the same time human and animal and have the traits of the real animals they seem to be. And readers have no reason to doubt their reality, at least in terms of the worlds within the tales.

Potter's Vocabulary and Readership Awareness

As many critics recognize, another outstanding attribute of Potter's books is that she does not write down to children. In addition to not glossing over the kinds of threats animals face, Potter also does not avoid what Leslie Linder calls "unusual words," even using them sometimes when her publishers asked her not to (*History of the Writings* 195). She obviously liked the sound of certain words and was concerned about the way they sounded in the context of the other words she used. At times, her pages read like a kind of free verse.

Her vocabulary in her children's books is varied and challenging. She herself obviously felt "children like" what she called "a fine word occasionally," a comment she made in a letter to Norman Warne on 16 June 1904, discussing the use of the word "conversed" (*Letters* 96). Examples of her use of "fine" words include in *The Tale of Peter Rabbit*, when Peter gets caught in the gooseberry net, the sparrows "flew to him in great excitement, and *implored* him to exert himself" (36). In *The Tale of Mr. Jeremy Fisher*, after Mr. Jeremy catches Jack Sharp the stickleback and injures his fingers on Jack's stickles, "Mr. Jeremy sat *disconsolately* on the edge of his boat—sucking his sore fingers and peering down into the water" (39). In *The Tale of Tom Kitten*, when she discovers her children have shed all their clothes, Mrs. Tabitha Twitchit says, "My friends will arrive in a minute, and you are not fit to be seen; I am *affronted*" (47). In *The Tale of Jemima Puddle-Duck*, Jemima complains to the gentleman with sandy whiskers of "the *superfluous* hen" who hatches Jemima's eggs. In *The Tale of the Flopsy Bunnies*, Potter tells readers that "lettuce is '*soporific*'" and then explains what the word means by writing, "*I* have never felt sleepy after eating lettuces; but then *I* am not a rabbit" and adding, "They certainly had a very soporific effect upon the Flopsy Bunnies" (27), an explanation that is bound to amuse children and adults. Also in *The Tale of the Flopsy Bunnies*, readers learn the family of Benjamin and Flopsy is "*improvident*" (8). In *The Tale of Mr. Tod*, Peter says that by falling asleep with a badger in the house, his uncle "has displayed a *lamentable* want of *discretion*" (24). Tommy Brock squeezes "into the rabbit-hole with *alacrity*" (14). Tommy Brock, readers learn, "was an incurably *indolent* person" (49), and his "snores were almost *apoplectic*" (53). Also, "*conversed*" itself appears in *The Tale of Mr. Tod* when old Mr. Bouncer and Tommy Brock "*conversed* cordially" (12). In *The Tale of Pigling Bland*, Potter uses herself as a character in the tale who says that Alexander is "hopelessly *volatile*" (23). She tells readers, "Pigling Bland ate his supper *discreetly*" (44), and Pigling Bland uses to cover Pig-wig an "*antimacassar*" (62), a word that may be less familiar to American children than to English children. As a result, Potter enriches children's imaginations and vocabularies. As Peter Hollindale recognizes, children enjoy Potter, "long words and all […], not least for the uncompromising adult briskness of her prose and the ruthlessness of her imagination" ("These Piglets" 141). Never writing down to children, she inspires them—and the adults who read to them—to reach up to her.

In addition, in Potter's books, American children encounter some concepts that may be foreign to them, such as rabbit pie itself (in *The Tale of Peter Rabbit* [11] and *The Tale of Mr. Tod* [10, 30]), and a fortnight (in *The Tale of Peter Rabbit* [64] and *The Tale of Timmy Tiptoes* [44]) as well as the whole problem of understanding English money, especially in *The Tale of Ginger and Pickles*. Many of the names she gives her animal characters are the same as some she gave to her pets and farm animals, such as *Peter* and *Benjamin* for two of her bunnies, *Tabitha* for one of her cats, and *Jemima* for one of her Puddleducks. Many other names are puns, such as *Bouncer* for the bunny family to which Benjamin belongs (at least in *The Tale of Mr. Tod*), a pun easily accessible to both children and adults. Some, however, are not easily accessible for American children or even adults, such as *Joiner* for a terrier named John Joiner in *The Tale of Samuel Whiskers*, who comes to Tabitha Twitchit's house with a bag full of carpenter's tools.[1] Another name, *Tod* in *The Tale of Mr. Tod*, makes even greater demands on readers since *Tod* in German, a language Potter knew well, means death, so it is a kind of label like those common in fairytales[2]; also, *Tod*, her name for the fox and *Brock*, her name for the badger are both puns since they refer to the animals who bear those names.[3]

Potter is, Humphrey Carpenter writes, "famous, perhaps even infamous," because of the demands "she makes on child readers" ("Excessively Impertinent Bunnies" 280). Obviously, she also makes demands on her adult readers, especially, it seems, on American adult readers.

Many of her adult humans also have names that are puns or allusions, sometimes with very unpleasant associations. The terrible man who steals Pig-Wig and snatches Pigling Bland out of the hen house is named Peter Thomas Piperson, clearly alluding to the nursery rhyme involving Tom Tom the piper's son who steals a pig and runs away. The captain of the ship on which Little Pig Robinson finds himself is named Barnabas Butcher.

At the same time that she writes to a child audience, Potter writes to adults. More than one critic has commented on that ability. Peter Hollindale, for example, writes of "an adult readership which is conscious that something else is going on in Potter's stories—something which is never traceably confided to the adult reader only, yet somehow coexists with the secure, unbroken narrative voice to children" ("These Piglets" 141). Hollindale's words, of course, do not just characterize Potter's works for children: they are also true for many of the other greatest authors of children's literature, such as Lewis Carroll, L. Frank Baum, E.B. White, and C.S. Lewis. Perhaps Potter is different in that she creates this "something else" in works directed at very young children. Perhaps this attribute is merely a matter of knowing her audience. Works for children, especially very young children, in order to sell, must have something in them directed toward adults since adults usually are the ones who buy books for children and, with very young children, do the reading aloud that makes the books available to children. Yet it is instructive also to point to Hollindale's assertion that Potter "was, uncompromisingly and aggressively, first and foremost[,] an artist for children" ("These Piglets" 142).

Potter wrote some things, at least initially, to please individual children. *The Tale of Peter Rabbit* first appeared in a story letter she wrote to a particular child; the version in the letter is radically different from Potter's published versions. In a letter dated 26 September 1905, she writes to Mary Warne that "the secret" of the success of *The Tale of Peter Rabbit* is that she wrote it to a particular child (*Letters* 132). However, in a letter of 12 March 1942, a little over a year before Potter died, she comments to Bertha Mahony Miller, one of her American correspondents and the editor of *Horn Book*, that she wrote stories "to please" herself because she "never grew up" (*Beatrix Potter's Americans* 177). Readers, of course, will probably never know why Potter wrote; she may not have known herself exactly why she wrote; however, part of her motivation was surely to make money. Still, that Potter did not grow up may be an accurate statement but in a fairly complicated way: although she became a very mature adult and was certainly grown up in the eyes of society, she never really grew up because she never had a chance to be a child. Perhaps her story letters and her books gave her an opportunity to enjoy the childhood she never was able to experience, much less enjoy.

In another letter to Bertha Mahony Miller, published in *Horn Book* in 1929, Potter comments on her own writing, saying that she was inspired to create Peter Rabbit because of her "matter-of-fact ancestry" and an incredibly good memory (*Beatrix Potter's Americans* 207), and later adds that she thinks she writes because she enjoys writing and enjoys "taking pains over it," but she dislikes "writing to order." She concludes that she writes "to please" herself. In the same letter to Miller, she describes her method of writing as "to scribble and cut" repeatedly, adding, "The shorter and plainer the better." She also sees in the Bible the model for her style, and she finds justification for her use of dialect words in the Bible and Shakespeare (*Beatrix Potter's Americans* 209).

As her works make obvious, Potter was very concerned with getting the right word in the right place. In a letter to Fruing Warne, dated 7 October 1923, she shows this concern in some comments she makes about a Christmas play Jean Sterling Mackinlay wrote based on *The Tailor of Gloucester*. Mackinlay's husband, E. Harcourt Williams, sent a draft of the play to Potter asking for permission to publish it. In the letter to Fruing Warne, Potter insists that the words in the play need to be changed before she "*would consent to its production.*"[4] Potter writes toward the end of the letter that she prefers the Tailor to Peter, probably referring to the books rather than the individual characters, so if the people creating the play are going to print a version of it, she needs to have the right of revising it (*Letters* 283).[5] In a letter dated 21 February 1929 to Alexander McKay, the American publisher of *The Fairy Caravan*, *Sister Anne*, and *The Tale of Little Pig Robinson*, Potter writes that she is sure children learn her tales by heart because of the "trouble" she took "with words" (*Letters* 314). Thus, she was consciously concerned with the language of her books, just as she was with the pictures and as she was with the realistic attitude toward animals that she displays in her fairytales.

Just as Potter's writing seems to combine an adult and a child point of view, so the adult reader of her work ideally should engage—preferably simultaneously—in two kinds of reading: the adult should try to read the works as children read them, bringing a freshness and wonder to the works not easily available to an adult, and at the same time, the adult should read them as an adult, seeing many things, such as allusions, irony, and other kinds of figurative language, that a child probably would not recognize, appreciate, or understand, especially one as young as the intended audience in most of Potter's works.

Really good writers of children's literature usually have both a child and adult audience in mind, especially if they want to make money from their books. They tend to know that for the most part adults, not children, make decisions about publishing children's books and reviewing them. There remains one other very practical reason authors include both a child and adult point of view in their works for young children: they know that children often want the works they like read to them repeatedly. Adults who get bored rereading the works by a particular author may not desire to buy another of that author's works.

All of these things make it appropriate for authors of books for children to aim their works toward both audiences at once. It seems especially important for adults to approach Beatrix Potter's little books with both of these points of view in mind, since her little books are in many ways fairly complex pieces of literary art. Adult readers of Potter's works may easily recognize the excellence of her illustrations. They may easily recognize the exceptional detail and realism of many of the aspects of nature in her paintings and sketches. However, one serious problem for the adult reader is recognizing that the illustrations are important parts of the meanings of the work. Children seem to have no problem finding meanings in both the pictures and the words. It seems as though it is the adult reader who has trouble of this sort, especially with "reading" the pictures. These are then some reasons why the teacher of children's literature to adults would do well to encourage the students to read the works to their children or, if the children are capable of reading them to themselves, to encourage the children to read them, and then discuss the works with the children.[6] Children often have insights into works that adults do not have, and usually young children are ready to share those insights with adults.

As this introductory chapter tries to show, adults often have a difficult time comprehending Potter's view of nature, her amazing combination of realism and fantasy, her ability to put animals in human clothing without completely anthropomorphizing the animals, that is, without ever losing sight of the very real animal beneath the clothes. Potter can switch seamlessly from a fully clothed Peter Rabbit who walks on two legs and wears realistic shoes to one who is all rabbit with no clothes at all. She can move from an uncomfortably dressed Tom Kitten to one without any clothing at all and from a ridiculously clothed Jemima Puddle-duck to one that looks natural with no clothes at all. Enjoying Potter becomes a little easier for adults if they understand that they need to read the works with a child's view as well as their usual adult preconceptions.

The Tale of Peter Rabbit

In several of Potter's works, the protagonists go through a series of events that roughly correspond to processes of initiation in which a kind of rebirth occurs. These tales include, among others, *The Tale of Peter Rabbit*, privately printed in 1901 and published by Frederick Warne & Company in 1902[1]; *The Tale of Jemima Puddle-Duck*, published in 1908, and the tale originally named *The Roly-Poly Pudding* when it was first published in 1908, and later, in 1926, renamed *The Tale of Samuel Whiskers or The Roly-Poly Pudding*. In the course of their adventures, each protagonist escapes from what looks like certain death. Peter grows as a result of his experiences. Jemima Puddle-duck grows in no discernable way. In *The Tale of Samuel Whiskers*, Tom Kitten, who is the protagonist, has adventures that change him, but not entirely for the better.

Graham Greene classifies *The Tale of Peter Rabbit* as one of Potter's "great comedies" (235) and classifies *The Tale of Jemima Puddle-Duck* and *The Tale of Samuel Whiskers* as two of her "great near-tragedies" (239). Yet *The Tale of Peter Rabbit* is also a near tragedy. Humphrey Carpenter writes of "the blackly comic themes" he finds in Potter's stories (141). "Darkly comic" might be a clearer term because of its association with Shakespearean drama; "problem tales," as compared to Shakespeare's "problem plays," might be an even better label. In 1894, in order to combat sleeplessness and depression, Potter memorized "about six Shakespeare plays" (Lear 95).[2] From Shakespeare, she learned that true comedy must border on tragedy. Thus, all three of these tales by Potter are more precisely classified as tragic comedies or tragicomedies, that is, tales that blend tragic and comic elements, that border on tragedy but end happily. They seem more like Shakespeare's late, dark comedies, such as *The Winter's Tale* and *The Tempest*, than his earlier comedies, such as *Two Gentlemen of Verona* and *Love's Labor Lost*. They are fairly serious in tone and involve real dangers that threaten to result in their protagonists' deaths. It is thus easy to understand why rebirth should play a role in them: in anthropological terms, they all involve a threshold passage, a journey from one kind of life into least a symbolic death, and then back to life. If the journey has been successful, the final phase of this journey ends in a life that is in some way markedly different from the earlier life. A change of this sort occurs for Peter Rabbit. Tom Kitten changes also, but his threshold passage does not seem successful in any way except that he survives; in fact, he deteriorates. But no changes occur for Jemima Puddle-duck.

In *The Tale of Peter Rabbit*, Peter's mother's warning to him not to go into Mr. McGregor's garden sets off the series of adventures. One of the best introductions to students and teachers to the study and teaching of *The Tale of Peter Rabbit* is *A Curriculum Guide to* The Tale of Peter Rabbit by Sonia Landes.[3] Some of Landes' readings seem slightly stretched, such as when Landes compares the whiteness of the cat[4] that Peter sees in the garden to the whiteness of Moby Dick and comments, "There is nothing cute about this cat" (*Curriculum Guide* 33). Maurice Sendak apparently agrees: he speaks of the "innocent-looking cat who, on closer observation, turns out to be fearful in color; that is, its innocent whiteness becomes a dreadful *absence* in color." He adds that the cat's "taut, twitching tail and the murderous tension of muscle under the plump, firm exterior betray the untamable cat nature." He feels sorry for the fishes at which the cat gazes: they "haven't got a chance" ("Beatrix Potter/2" 76).[5] Still, some readers look at the cat and see a beautiful cat who is, like all cats, a predator.

The picture letter Potter sent to Noel Moore on 4 September 1893 is, as far as scholars can tell, the first incarnation of the Peter Rabbit found in the story, except perhaps for the real rabbits Potter owned, one of which she called Peter. The picture letter is markedly different from the version of the tale Warne published. In the Warne version, Mrs. Rabbit tells her children about the garden, "your father had an accident there; he was put in a pie by Mrs. McGregor" (11). The information that Peter's father had "an accident" in the garden is a euphemism, if not an outright lie. As Mrs. Rabbit immediately indicates, it was not an accident but something that happened on purpose, at least as far as Mr. and Mrs. McGregor were concerned: Mr. McGregor caught Peter's father and killed him. Then, he gave Peter's father to Mrs. McGregor, and she put him in a pie. Although Potter does not mention it, the McGregors then must have eaten the pie. Peter thus faces real danger: if Mr. McGregor captures Peter, the bunny that seeks food will become food. Mr. McGregor is clearly a predator, and Peter is clearly prey.

In the picture letter, Mrs. Rabbit just says to all four of her children, "Now, my dears, [...] you may go into the field or down the lane, but don't go into Mr. McGregor's garden" ([Emerson] 12). She does not even mention any pie. Thus, the published version sets up a kind of suspense and tension the picture letter does not. Readers of the book are aware from the start of Peter's adventure that real danger awaits him in the garden.

Again, in an episode not in the picture letter, Mrs. Rabbit, apparently afraid Peter does not hear the warning, in effect takes him by the throat as she buttons his jacket and says, "Now run along, and don't get into mischief. I am going out" (12). As the picture accompanying these words indicates, Peter already has his eyes on the direction he will go: straight to Mr. McGregor's garden. He is hell-bent on getting into mischief, on having an adventure, on doing exactly what his mother tells him not to do, and perhaps on seeing whether he can succeed where his father failed. Readers know Peter's mother has good reason to suspect he will get into trouble since, when he returns, he is without his clothes: "It was the second little jacket and pair of shoes that Peter had lost in a fortnight!" (64), words clearly indicating that he has gotten into trouble before.

When Peter enters the garden, he finds himself in what seems to him an Eden-like place, with its abundant food and apparent lack of danger. But it is also a place of real danger in which, as readers know and Peter has been told, death lurks. Peter faces and almost meets the same kind of death his father met in the garden. It is anything but the unfallen Eden it initially seems to Peter. For in the garden lurks a terrible creature that in effect plays the role of a devouring serpent, Mr. McGregor, who resembles the ogre in "Jack and the Beanstalk." Both Mr. McGregor and the ogre are huge compared to their adversaries, and both eat the kinds of creatures their adversaries are. Since many modern American children may not know what a rabbit pie is, it may help to compare it to a chicken potpie. Those more interested (usually adults) may desire to look at Mrs. Beeton's recipe for rabbit pie from 1861, the very recipe Potter may have had in mind. The illustration of the pie that Potter eventually deleted from the published version of *The Tale of Peter Rabbit*[6] and Mrs. Beeton's recipe may help readers understand that in the garden, Peter faces real danger: if Mr. McGregor captures Peter, the bunny, who seeks food and gorges himself on it, will become food.

In spite of his knowledge of the dangers of the garden, Peter acts very foolishly once inside it. His greed seems to overcome his intelligence. Potter writes, "First he ate some lettuces and some French beans; and then he ate some radishes; And then, feeling rather sick, he went to look for some parsley" (23–24). As he stuffs himself with food and hunts for a remedy for his upset stomach (the parsley), he does not pay attention to his surroundings. Potter's illustration shows that as Peter stuffs himself with radishes, Peter's legs are crossed, and his eyes look up rather than around.[7] He looks like anything but a rabbit that is aware of being in dangerous surroundings though Potter's illustration shows the handle of a shovel very near Peter, a clear indication that the garden is a place where people come. In fact, Peter looks like and acts like a little child. Peter must stop behaving like a little child if he is to survive in the garden. Incidentally, the details discussed in connection with this picture are entirely omitted from the picture of Peter in the garden in the picture letter.[8]

When Peter starts feeling sick from having eaten so much, he wanders through the garden without paying any attention to the fact that it is obviously a garden that a human being works. He pays so little attention to his surroundings that he almost walks into the very dangerous Mr. McGregor. Running on two legs and wearing human clothing, Peter seems to have little chance of escaping Mr. McGregor.

Running from his adversary and not paying attention to where he is going, Peter gets caught in a gooseberry net. Once in the net, Potter writes, "He gave himself up for lost, and shed big tears [...]" (36). His death at the hands of Mr. McGregor appears inevitable. The position in which Peter is first caught seems important: the picture shows that in the net, Peter is upside down and slightly curled over (34). In the original story letter, Peter is not nearly as inverted as he is in both Potter's privately printed edition of the book and in the book as published in the Warne edition of 1902.[9] When all three pictures are put together, readers can see that as she changes the picture, Potter makes Peter look more and more as though he is in the usual position of a human fetus getting ready to exit head-first from the birth canal. This position hints that he may escape and that a kind of rebirth is possible. As the picture of Peter in the net indicates, there is something terribly wrong. Unlike a normal fetus, Peter is fully dressed in *human* clothes. He must first shed every vestige of his human clothes and thus his little-boy status for the process of rebirth to occur. Moreover, unlike a normal mammalian fetus in a normal womb, no fluid surrounds Peter. Peter now desires to leave this false Eden, and to do so, unlike Adam and Eve leaving Eden, he ironically has to shed his clothes.

Potter's words about Peter's giving himself up for lost and shedding big tears make it clear that he will probably, like his father, become rabbit pie, roast rabbit, boiled rabbit, or some other form of foodstuff. There is a kind of justice in his becoming foodstuff for the McGregors, since he steals food from them, but it is doubtful that many adults or children would be satisfied to see that kind of justice done. Thanks largely to Potter's manipulation of point of view, readers' sympathies are with Peter, not Mr. McGregor. Even readers who know what pests rabbits can be and how they can destroy gardens, even those who know how good rabbit meat tastes, still sympathize with Peter.

Since he gives up, Peter on his own would not escape. But some "friendly sparrows" come to his aid. They "flew to him in great excitement, and implored him to exert himself!" (36). These words emphasize the importance of the sparrows in Peter's escape. The sparrows "implore" Peter to keep fighting for his life. Hearing them, Peter acts on what they say: Mr. McGregor tries to "pop" a sieve on Peter, but "Peter wriggled out just in time, leaving his jacket behind him" (30). Fittingly, the sparrows are present in Potter's illustration that shows Peter finally escaping from the garden (58). Ironically, the jacket that traps Peter in the net is the one that his mother so carefully buttons in the picture connected with the words, "Now run along, and don't get into mischief. I am going out" (12). Her care to keep Peter out of trouble almost causes him to lose his life. Her insistence that he at least appear to be a good little boy includes his wearing the jacket that makes it much more difficult for him to escape: Potter's writing that the jacket has "large buttons" and again that it has "brass buttons" (35) emphasizes the importance of the buttons, even though the illustration (34) shows no buttons. The buttons get him caught in the gooseberry net in the first place, thus terribly endangering his life. It is interesting that Potter entirely omits the sparrows from the picture letter. They are not present in the text or in the pictures. In the privately printed versions and the Warne version, they act as helpers to Peter, encouraging him to continue to fight. In the picture letter, "Peter wriggled out just in time," with no help from anything ([Emerson] 6). The published version, then, implies that without the encouragement of the sparrows, Peter would probably have died; it also indicates that Peter is not alone in the garden: the encouragement the sparrows give him involves selflessness on their part, something that contrasts markedly with Peter's selfish actions when he gorges himself when he first enters the garden.

Peter's being caught in the net upside down puts him in a position that makes him appear ready to enter the birth canal. His very difficult path to rebirth is about to begin. But the birth canal he has to traverse turns out to be a very long one, involving additional dangerous events.

When Peter escapes from the net, he is, as Potter's picture indicates, all rabbit. He now has the speed and strength to escape from his ogre. His powerful hind legs thrust out behind him; his head is tucked down into his body; his front legs reach out (38). In a fair race, he could easily beat Mr. McGregor. But Peter runs blindly, that is, with no particular destination in mind, and the race is not fair since Mr. McGregor has all kinds of garden implements he can use to help him catch Peter. In addition, Mr. McGregor is still on his own home ground, an area he is much more familiar with than Peter is.

Not thinking, Peter runs into Mr. McGregor's tool shed and jumps into a full watering can (40–41). The picture letter completely omits the tool-shed episode and thus the watering can episode: in the letter, Peter runs right from the gooseberry net to the garden gate and escapes from Mr. McGregor. Thus, the picture letter is much less suspenseful and much less exciting than the Warne edition. In the Warne edition, Peter picks a very unpleasant place in the shed to hide from his adversary. First, it is located in an area that is, in a very real sense, Mr. McGregor's turf. It is a human construct designed for human purposes. Peter is terribly out of place there. Fortunately, Mr. McGregor is not very bright: he yells at a rabbit, "Stop thief!" (28), and he hunts for Peter in places where the little rabbit could not possibly hide: underneath the flower-pots in his shed (42–43). Potter later in this tale emphasizes Mr. McGregor's lack of intelligence in a picture that shows the ineffectiveness of the scarecrow he builds with Peter's clothes (61). Peter, however, does a poor job of hiding since his ears stick out of the watering can (41). He hides here as he does in the frontispiece, where he hides from someone whom, toward the end of the story, he apparently considers another ogre, his mother, who gives him chamomile tea. In both cases, he hides the way a little child hides, thinking that if he cannot see his adversary, his adversary cannot see him. In the watering can, Peter is still not safe. He is not in a liquid that is comforting and comfortable: since the water is not warm, it is very uncomfortable for Peter. On the contrary, in his bed, hiding from his mother, even though Peter is not safe from discovery, he is safe. Incidentally, it is easy for the child viewer of both pictures to see the rest of the rabbit the ears signify.[10]

To emphasize Peter's discomfort in the water, Peter sneezes, "Kertyschoo!" (43). Hearing the sneeze, Mr. McGregor begins the chase again. As Mr. McGregor tries to put his hob-nailed-boot-clad "foot upon Peter," Peter jumps "out of a window, upsetting three plants." "The window was too small for Mr. McGregor, and he was tired of running after Peter," Potter writes, so, "He went back to his work" (44). It seems that Peter now manages to escape from Mr. McGregor. Peter's jumping out of the window that is much too small for Mr. McGregor to follow him seems symbolic of escape from the womb. Peter's process of rebirth finally seems over. But it is not. He still must get out of the garden. In psychological terms, he still must finish passing through the birth canal.

After the escape from the window, he combines the attributes of a real rabbit with the thinking ability of a human being. He rests. He wanders around the garden, "going lippity—lippity—not very fast, and looking all round" (48). Yet he still retains enough of the *little boy* to cry when he discovers he cannot escape through a door he finds in the garden wall. He sees the cat looking at some fish in a pond. As the picture indicates, unlike his first encounter with Mr. McGregor, Peter sees the cat but cannot be seen: "Peter thought it best to go away without speaking to her; he had heard about cats from his cousin, little Benjamin Bunny" (52). Peter now thinks his way through potentially dangerous situations. Thus, he is still a little boy, who cries over trouble, but thinks his way through problems, and he is also a rabbit using rabbit instincts and rabbit speed and strength to escape from problems.

Finally, his condition of being part rabbit, part little boy pays off. He approaches Mr. McGregor, as he can tell from the sound of his "hoe—scr-r-ritch, scratch, scratch, scratch." Hearing the noise, he "scuttered underneath the bushes" (55) instead of walking right up to Mr. McGregor as he does earlier. "But presently, as nothing happened, he came out, and climbed upon a wheelbarrow, and peeped over" (56). As he was with the cat, Peter can now see but not be seen. His perch on the wheelbarrow allows him to look over the whole garden, a position that works well for Peter: "The first thing he saw was Mr. McGregor hoeing onions. His back was turned towards Peter, and beyond him was the gate!" (56). Peter now sees the place he enters the garden and recognizes the entrance as a possible place of escape.

Again, combining his rabbit instincts and speed with his human brain, "Peter got down very quietly off the wheelbarrow, and started running as fast as he could go, along a straight walk behind some black-currant bushes" (59). From Potter's picture of this scene, it is clear that Peter gets to the gate long before Mr. McGregor can reach it (58). Comparing this picture with the earlier one in which Mr. McGregor chases Peter is instructive. In the earlier one, Mr. McGregor is much closer to Peter, who runs on two legs like a little boy. He also has on his shoes that slow him down as well as his jacket that eventually traps him in the gooseberry net. Mr. McGregor's rake is so long that it seems as though he can easily reach out and hit the little rabbit. Fortunately, Peter loses his shoes so that he runs faster, but he ends up in the gooseberry net. In this later picture, Peter is much closer to the gate than he is to Mr. McGregor. He is, in fact, in the course of scrunching down to get under the gate. Fittingly, the three sparrows, that earlier "implored him to exert himself," are present at Peter's final moment of triumph. He scrunches under the gate, a kind of exit from the birth canal. He thus outwits *and* outruns his adversary. The McGregors will not eat Peter-Rabbit pie today.

Peter's being chased by Mr. McGregor and his rake symbolically reenacts the ritual in which someone must run the gauntlet. In some Native American cultures, when someone—often a captive—successfully runs the gauntlet, that person is adopted into the tribe,[11] leading to a very real kind of rebirth. Actually, once he encounters Mr. McGregor, Peter's entire journey through the garden may easily be seen as a kind of running the gauntlet leading to his successful return home.

Once Peter goes under the gate, that is, once he leaves the garden, he is free from danger from Mr. McGregor: as Potter writes, he is "safe at last in the wood outside the garden" (59). In the garden, Mr. McGregor has a good chance of catching Peter; in the wood, he has none.

Peter returns home to the ministrations of his mother, who puts her sick little bunny to bed and gives him "a dose of" chamomile tea to help make him better. Several critics see the dose of tea as a punishment.[12] But Potter makes it clear that it is medicine rather than a punishment by using the word "dose" in connection with it and writing, "one table-spoonful to be taken at bed-time" (67), clearly directions for administering medicine, not punishment. In the picture letter, Potter writes of Mrs. Rabbit's giving him a "dose" of tea, but omits entirely the words, "one table-spoonful to be taken at bed-time,"[13] instructions that clearly indicate the tea is medicinal. Sipe insists that Peter is not punished, other than receiving "the natural consequence of not feeling well and missing his supper" (10). That Peter is not punished seems very different from the kind of reception Potter herself would probably have gotten after such a series of adventures. If Potter was sure her father was ashamed of her after her hat blew off at the International Inventions Exposition, think how much more she would fear that both parents would be ashamed of her if she came home dirty and lacking some articles of clothing.

But since readers know that this is the second adventure Peter has had in a fortnight, they know there is a good chance he will have other adventures, having proven to himself that he can escape from his mother, have a good time, at least initially, have an exciting adventure, and survive.

Peter goes into the garden for selfish reasons: to gorge himself and perhaps measure himself against his father. His sisters take the berries they pick home with them. But unlike them and unlike the mouse, who busily gets food for her family (51), Peter shows no desire to take home any of the food he gets. Nonetheless, in the course of his adventures, he changes from being all little boy to being all rabbit to being combination of much more mature little boy and rabbit, and the details Potter adds as the story goes from picture letter to Warne edition make this process clear. In the original picture letter, in fact, no maturation occurs—just an escape. As combination boy and rabbit, Peter mixes the best attributes of both: the speed, agility, strength, and instincts of a rabbit with the intellect of a little boy. Potter thus uses imagery of rebirth to show Peter's transition to a much more mature rabbit than he is when he leaves his home in search of food and adventure. At the end of the book, he is certainly not an adult rabbit ready to leave his mother and establish a home and even a family of his own. But he takes some major steps in that direction.

According to Gillian Avery, a formidable critic of children's literature and of Beatrix Potter in particular, "By the end of *The tale [sic] of Peter Rabbit* we know Peter is a wimp, certainly not the sort of person to whom we would care to trust our destinies" (198). She bases these words not only on her reading of the tale itself but especially on a comparison of Peter and his cousin Benjamin Bunny as they appear in later books. She calls Benjamin "a poised man of the world, even though apparently the younger of the two" (198). Matthew Dennison seems to agree with this idea when he writes that Peter Rabbit in Potter's tales resembles her pet Peter Rabbit (Dennison calls him "the real Peter") who "was more timorous than Benjamin" (67).[14] Potter seems not to have agreed with this idea. In *The Tale of Benjamin Bunny* (1904), Peter really is a much more timid rabbit. In a later book, *The Tale of Mr. Tod* (1912), he no longer blithely searches for adventure and thus wanders into danger. But when he must encounter danger, he does so though he understands what he is up against. In both of these later books, Peter's cousin Benjamin initiates the journey into danger, but Peter goes along and, especially in the latter, helps make the journey successful. In fact, in the ending of *The Tale of Mr. Tod*, Benjamin seems far more timid than Peter, who without hesitation joins his cousin Benjamin to rescue Benjamin's babies and has to urge Benjamin to run into Mr. Tod's house to rescue the baby bunnies while Peter keeps watch. Keeping watch keeps Peter outside Mr. Tod's house; thus, Peter's position is probably more dangerous than Benjamin's inside the house since Mr. Tod and Tommy Brock are at this time in the story both outside the house. Peter also comes up with the plan to shut the oven door so Tommy Brock will not miss the babies, and Benjamin asks Peter, "Can we get away? Shall we hide, Cousin Peter?" Apparently, Peter decides not to hide, since Potter writes, "Five minutes afterwards two breathless rabbits came scuttering away down Bull Banks, half carrying half dragging a sack between them, bumpetty bump over the grass" (77). Peter, it seems, has become the more decisive (and more thoughtful) cousin, even though the bunnies in the sack are Benjamin's, not Peter's, children.

Also, in an undated miniature letter, sent to Hilda Moore (one of Noel's sisters), Potter creates an exchange of letters between Peter, Mr. McGregor, Mrs. McGregor, and Benjamin. Peter asks Mr. McGregor whether his spring cabbages are ready. Mrs. McGregor replies that her husband has a cold and is in bed, but he sends a message that if Peter comes into their garden again, "we will inform the Polisse" and adds that she has a new pie dish. Peter then writes to his cousin Benjamin saying he has just received a letter from Mrs. McGregor saying her husband has a cold and is in bed; and Peter then asks Benjamin to meet him that evening at the garden (*Letters to Children* 91). Here, Peter clearly uses his head and initiates the action.

Potter changes *The Tale of Peter Rabbit* markedly as it metamorphoses from picture letter to published book. It goes from being a relatively simple tale of escape to a much richer tale of character development and rebirth. In the picture letter, Peter is almost as much of a cardboard figure as his sisters are. He has interesting adventures and an exciting escape that he achieves rather quickly. In the published version, he goes through a learning process. He faces and overcomes several adversaries, including Mr. McGregor and a white cat, by ultimately outwitting them. He emerges victorious, with his victory cheered on by some helpful sparrows that earlier become his helpers by encouraging him not to give up. The most important adversary he faces seems to be Peter Rabbit himself. He needs to grow beyond his unthinking selfishness when he first enters the garden into a more mature rabbit who thinks his way through his problems and comes up with sound solutions to them and, more important, who finds ways to avoid them.

In general terms, *The Tale of Peter Rabbit* follows the pattern of home-away-home. This pattern is so prevalent in children's literature that Perry Nodelman has labeled it the generic or no-name pattern of children's literature. In it, a child or small creature finds home safe but boring, so the creature goes away in search of adventure. Away is exciting and fun but dangerous, so the small creature returns home where the creature is safe (Nodelman 188–91, 265). This basic form occurs in many of Potter's books. Peter Rabbit himself is involved in two more books that follow this pattern: *The Tale of Benjamin Bunny* and *The Tale of Mr. Tod*. This kind of circular pattern (home-away-home) works especially well for authors of children's books that want to take the same character on different journeys in each book, as happens in Potter's books that involve Peter. The form can involve all kinds of variations, including leaving one home and establishing a new home elsewhere; this pattern occurs in *The Tale of Little Pig Robinson:* Robinson leaves his home in Devonshire and is shanghaied onto a boat. He ends up far away from his original home on an island where "the Bong tree grows," a location Potter gets from "The Owl and the Pussycat" by Edward Lear (*The Tale of Little Pig Robinson* 22). In *The Tale of Pigling Bland*, the story ends with PigWig and Bland leaving the county (80–81). Every indication is that they too will establish a new home for themselves once they cross over the county line.

The pattern also can involve something that when viewed from the top is a circle and when viewed from the side is a spiral. The spiral form usually involves a character's growing significantly in the course of the adventure but sometimes the character can deteriorate. Jemima Puddle-duck in *The Tale of Jemima Puddle-Duck* is unchanged by her adventures. Even if Peter does not grow during his first series of adventures in *The Tale of Peter Rabbit*, he certainly has grown by the time he gets to the adventures in *The Tale of Mr. Tod*.[15] In *The Tale of Mr. Jeremy Fisher*, Mr. Jeremy deteriorates. He vows he will never go fishing again. In *The Tale of Samuel Whiskers*, Tom Kitten also deteriorates. He becomes a much more timid, fearful kitten and adult cat.

The Tale of Peter Rabbit involves a kind of hero-quest of the sort Joseph Campbell describes in *The Hero with a Thousand Faces*. Peter defeats his ogre and returns triumphant. He completes many of the episodes that Campbell writes are central to the hero-quest. He certainly goes through what Campbell calls "separation—initiation—return" (*Hero* 30). He experiences a "Call to Adventure" when his mother prohibits him from going into Mr. McGregor's garden and says that his father got put in a pie there. He has a "Helper" in the three sparrows who encourage him to escape from the net. He even has two kinds of experiences that resemble that of being in the "Whale's belly" when his is caught in the net and then tries to hide in the watering can. He undergoes a series of "Tests." He achieves a kind of "father atonement" when he survives where his father failed. More important may be his mother atonement since his mother receives him at home with care and love even though he disregards her instruction not to go into Mr. McGregor's garden. He obviously goes through a "Flight" when he escapes from Mr. McGregor, gets out of the garden, and runs home. The return home is his experiencing the part of the quest that involves a "Return." In what Campbell calls the "monomyth," the hero's return "restores the world." By returning, Peter achieves no such universal triumph; instead, his is more domestic: by not being eaten by Mr. McGregor and returning home, he restores the family to its status before he left.[16] It seems important to remember that Campbell did not invent the hero-quest; he codified what had been embodied in myths and fairytales through the ages. Although Campbell's book did not appear until 1949, he and Potter (and so many other authors) relied on many of the same sources to find their structure for the adventures of their heroes. Moreover, many scholars in addition to Campbell argue that this structure is somehow basic to human life. It would be difficult for someone as broadly read as Potter to have somehow missed it, but even if she had, that would make little difference, since it seems, Campbell and others argue, to be an essential part of what it is to be human.

At any rate, Peter Rabbit seems to have attained what in some way corresponds to something within thousands of readers (and listeners) when *The Tale of Peter Rabbit* first appeared and still corresponds to something within many readers during the twenty-first century. Many years after it first appeared, Potter's little book continues to entertain readers, indicating that it must correspond to something basic to what those readers are.

The Tailor of Gloucester

The Tailor of Gloucester is based on a fairytale and on what Beatrix Potter seems to have believed is a true story. What resulted is a book Potter herself considered her favorite work.[1] The brothers Grimm collected the fairytale on which she based her tale. Translations of it are usually entitled "The Elves and the Shoemaker" or just "The Elves."[2] It tells of a poor shoemaker who cut the material for a pair of shoes and then went to bed. During the night, some elves found the shoes and finished them. The shoemaker was able to sell them for more money than he usually got and then was able to buy and cut out enough material for two pairs of shoes. That night, he went to sleep, and when he awoke, he discovered two more pairs of finished shoes. He sold these shoes for enough money to buy material for four pairs of shoes. This continued for some nights, with his discovery on waking that all the material had been made into fine shoes. The shoemaker made a great deal of money. Just before Christmas, the shoemaker and his wife decided to stay up during the night to see how the shoes were made. Two little naked men, who were elves, finished the shoes. The shoemaker and his wife decided to make some clothes for the little men, including shirts, coats, waistcoats, stockings and shoes. When the elves came into the room, they found the garments and were delighted. They then disappeared, never to return.

Leslie Linder explains that the supposedly true part of the story involves a tailor in Gloucester named John Prichard who, on a Saturday, laid out the material for a waistcoat but did not sew it together and then closed his shop for the weekend. On Monday, he returned to his shop and found the suit finished except for a single buttonhole. Pinned to the waistcoat was a note saying, "No more twist" (*History* 111). According to Prichard's wife, Prichard was making waistcoats for the mayor and the City Corporation to walk in a procession for the Root, Fruit, and Grain Society Show. Prichard was extremely busy since he was on good terms with many of the city councilors. On this occasion, he was overwhelmed with orders, so he asked one of the councilors if he could do without his waistcoat so that Prichard could make a special waistcoat for the mayor. The waistcoat that was laid out was the one for the mayor. Prichard was worried, for the show was coming very soon. Prichard's two assistants went into the shop and worked until they had finished the waistcoat, except for one buttonhole that they could not finish because they were out of thread.[3] Potter combines these two tales, substituting mice for the elves and tailoring for shoemaking. She adds touches of her own, such as the tailor's great poverty and illness and, perhaps most important, the role of Simpkin the cat.

Potter originally wrote out the story and sent it to Freda Moore, a sister of Noel, on Christmas 1901. This version of the story has more rhymes than the Warne version does. In the letter accompanying the story, Potter writes that she wanted to put additional pictures in the story, "only Miss Potter was tired of it! Which was lazy of Miss Potter."[4] Potter's comments about herself here indicate her insight into the mind of a child who would certainly appreciate the things she says about herself.

Like *The Tale of Peter Rabbit*, *The Tailor of Gloucester* originated in a story for a particular child. Also like *The Tale of Peter Rabbit*, Potter published *The Tailor of Gloucester* privately before Warne published it. Linder writes that, fearing that Warne would not publish this work so soon after the publication of *The Tale of Peter Rabbit* and that Warne would cut some of the rhymes in it, Potter decided to publish her own version of the story. Just as she did with the story letter that eventually became *The Tale of Peter Rabbit*, Potter asked for the original back from Freda so that she could use it in connection with the book she wanted to make and from it created her own edition of the tale (*History* 113–14).

The text is longer than most of Potter's other little books and clearly aimed at an older audience than *The Tale of Peter Rabbit* and *The Tale of Squirrel Nutkin*. As she feared, Warne did make her shorten the work by eliminating some of the verses and songs in it and shortening others and shortening the text itself.[5]

Using the fairytale and the story that was told in Gloucester, Potter creates her own tale, in part by making the tailor very ill and giving him a cat named Simpkin, who is potentially the villain of the piece. The tailor lays out the coat and waistcoat except for the twist, which he sends his cat Simpkin to buy for him along with bread, milk, and sausages using the last of his money. When Simpkin leaves, the tailor hears noises and discovers many mice that Simpkin trapped under teacups, hoping to eat them later. The tailor sets the mice free. Simpkin buys everything, but hides the twist from the tailor because Simpkin is upset that the tailor set free all the mice he caught. The tailor, feeling ill and sure he is "undone" (31), goes to bed. The tailor is ill for several days. In the meantime, the mice leave the tailor's room and travel though several houses into the tailor's shop where they finish the coat. Where the buttonhole was meant to be, the mice leave a note saying, "No more twist," words that the mice repeat several times in the story. When the tailor awakens feeling well on Christmas morning, Simpkin, "ashamed of his badness" (48), gives the tailor the twist. Still thinking he is ruined because he does not have time to finish his work, the tailor and Simpkin enter the shop and discover the coat and waistcoat finished beautifully except for the buttonhole. The tailor finishes the work and subsequently grows stout and rich.

This story too involves one of Potter's usual patterns: the tailor becomes extremely sick and thinks all is lost. Even when he gets well, he thinks he has no chance to finish making the clothes. Yet he finds the mice have almost finished the work for him, and he easily finishes it in time. From what seems to be certain defeat, he finds victory. Instead of failing, "he grew quite stout, and he grew quite rich" (54). The tale ends on an ironic note: "The stitches of those button-holes were so small—*so* small—they looked as if they had been made by little mice" (57). Yet the tailor achieves the victory only indirectly as a result of his own actions. Because he frees the mice Simpkin intends to eat, the mice finish the mayor's suit for him. And because Simpkin "felt quite ashamed of his badness compared with those good little mice" (48), the cat gets the "skein of cherry-coloured twisted silk" from the teapot where he hides it and puts it where the tailor can see it when he awakens (48). Thus, as in so many fairytales and Potter's fairytales, good triumphs, and the central character is reborn, in this case as a much more successful, prosperous person.

The Tale of Squirrel Nutkin

The Tale of Squirrel Nutkin follows the same general pattern as *The Tale of Peter Rabbit* and many of Potter's other tales: a small prey animal puts his life into a danger that involves a larger predator. The prey animal eventually escapes from the danger. However, in many ways, *The Tale of Squirrel Nutkin* is radically different from Potter's other works.

Although Potter was brought up in a Unitarian family with ties to Unitarian clergymen, her own relationship with organized religion was very tenuous. In her journal, she shows doubts about organized religions, especially those that claim to have some kind of monopoly on truth. In an often-quoted journal passage for 30 September 1884, when Potter was eighteen, she voices some of the ideas about organized religion that seem to have stuck with her for the rest of her life. She begins by saying she is upset about the people in Hatfield not giving Christian burial to a child if the child has not been baptized. She asks how anyone can believe what she calls "the power above us" to be "just and merciful," but will "consign" a child "to eternal torment?" She then gives what seem to be her own beliefs: "a power silently" works "all things for good" and people should "behave" themselves, "and never mind the rest" (*Journal*, complete ed. 107–08). The ideas she expresses here are not that different from the orthodoxy of the Unitarianism of her day as Clifford M. Reed describes it in "Beatrix Potter's Unitarian Context." She was, Reed argues, as a child, "immersed" in a religion that left her free "to believe according to her own insight and conscience, and encouraged that independence of mind and spirit that became her most distinguishing characteristic" (160). While she experienced nature "in a profoundly spiritual way," Reed writes, "she also viewed it practically" (159). Her cousin by marriage, Ulla Hyde Parker, says, "Religion as such meant little to Cousin Beatie. At least, she attended no church" (15).

However, a kind of religion lies at the heart of *The Tale of Squirrel Nutkin*, the second of Potter's books that Warne published, a religion involving the Owl as a tutelary deity presiding over the island he inhabits, a deity that must be propitiated, the squirrels believe, if the squirrels are to successfully achieve their goal of harvesting nuts. The squirrels' religion is certainly not a religion that Potter practiced. Nonetheless, it appears to be a religion that makes just as much sense—or perhaps even more sense—to Potter than the religions some of her neighbors believed or at least claimed to believe, and certainly more sense to Potter than the religion Potter describes the people of Hatfield believing.

Like *The Tale of Peter Rabbit*, *The Tale of Squirrel Nutkin* also originated in a picture letter, actually several picture letters. In what seems to be an early intimation of the tale, she writes on 8 August 1896 to Eric Moore, Noel's brother, about what she has seen and done while visiting Lakefield, Sawrey, Ambleside. Among other things, she tells of a tame owl eating mice and sitting "with a tail hanging out of his mouth." She ends the letter with an illustration showing the owl on a perch with the tail hanging from his mouth (*Letters to Children* 43). In a letter written from Lingholm, Keswick, Cumberland, dated 26 August 1897, she writes to Noel about minnows, other fish, otter dogs, and otters. She also tells him of a woman who tells her about squirrels that come to an island when the nuts are ripe, but the woman says she never saw them come to the island. Potter than tells Noel about what she calls "an American story" about squirrels that travel on a river on "little rafts," using their tails as sails (*Letters to Children* 50). In a letter written on 25 September 1901 to Nora Moore, Noel's sister, Potter narrates the basic elements of *The Tale of Squirrel Nutkin*, including offerings the squirrels make to Old Mr. Brown so that they can be allowed to collect nuts on Brown's island, Nutkin's riddles, and Nutkin's narrow escape (*Letters to Children* 71–76).

The squirrels regard Old Mr. Brown as a kind of silent deity who must be propitiated if they are to successfully gather nuts from his island. In the book, as in the letter, they offer sacrifices to Brown that he accepts in silence: "three fat mice," "a fine fat mole," "seven fat minnows," "six fat beetles," "wild honey," and "a new-laid *egg*." The sacrifices all seem appropriate to an owl: they are things an owl might eat instead of eating the squirrels. The squirrels also ask Mr. Brown's permission to gather nuts on his island. Then, the squirrels industriously gather nuts. But Nutkin impertinently asks Mr. Brown riddles, taunting him, and after the other squirrels leave to gather nuts, Nutkin plays. Fortunately for readers, especially adult readers, Potter, in the published text, has Nutkin imitate the answer to the riddles through his actions and italicizes in her text the answers to the riddles; she even comments on the idea that the answers are in the text by writing, "old Mr. Brown took no interest in riddles—not even when the answer was provided for him" (31), referring to Nutkin's actions that provide the answers to Mr. Brown. After the first riddle, Potter comments that it "is as old as the hills," giving adult readers an indication of the seriousness of riddles and riddling games and giving the riddles a kind of primeval quality, hinting that some kind of very serious consequences are involved.

Riddles are an important part of folklore and mythical history. In twenty-first century America, they are mostly thought of in terms of harmless children's amusements, but at one time, they held great importance for various cultures. One of the best-known literary manifestations of this fact is found in J.R.R. Tolkien's *The Hobbit*, where the riddling game Frodo Baggins plays with Gollum is a matter of life and death. In fact, the history of riddles is full of instances in which the correct answer is a matter of life and death. In *Turandot's Sisters*, Christine Goldberg deals with that kind of riddle, focusing on the riddles in *The Thousand and One Days: A Companion to the "Arabian Nights,"* by Julia Pardoe, published in 1857. In this tale, Turandot (sometimes spelled Tourandocte) is a beautiful princess. In order to win her hand in marriage, a suitor has to answer correctly three riddles. If he does not answer correctly, he dies. Many have died. Khalaf desires to marry Turandot, so he is willing to risk the test of the riddles. The answer to the first is the sun; the answer to the second is the sea; the answer to the third is the year. Khalaf answers correctly. He then poses a riddle of his own, the answer to which is his name. If Turandot answers it correctly, she need not marry him. Through trickery, Turandot is able to answer it, but they get married anyway. On the answer to these riddles, the fate of kingdoms lies, since Turandot is a princess and Khalaf is a prince.[1]

In mythology, perhaps the best-known riddle is that of the Sphinx, who asks people who want to go to Thebes, what creature walks on four legs in the morning, two at noon, and three in the evening. Anyone who does not solve the riddle dies. Until Oedipus approaches the Sphinx, none had solved it, and all died. Oedipus properly answers the riddle with "man," thus avoiding his own destruction by the Sphinx so that he can ironically go on to meet what he eventually considers a much more terrible fate involving killing his father and marrying his mother and thus bringing ruin on his kingdom of Thebes and himself. He himself then is in a way an answer to the riddle the Sphinx proposes. In many cultures, riddles are extremely important, being intimately connected to things like the changing of the seasons, things which are of utmost importance to people living in societies that depend on the regular cycle of the seasons to enable them to get things like food and water so that they can survive.

Nutkin, however, "who had no respect" (23), does not take riddling seriously. He does not realize that it has life and death implications for him. He reverses the roles of those in the tale of Oedipus and the Sphinx, asking the riddles himself. The only answer he gets from Mr. Brown is silence, until Nutkin asks his last riddle, and then Mr. Brown responds not with words but with action.

Since the squirrels recognize Mr. Brown as a kind of deity ruling over Owl Island, they treat him with great respect and courtesy. They recognize that if they are to gather nuts from the island, they must in some way propitiate Mr. Brown, for he is a predator who can easily kill them. The last gift, an egg, is a symbol of new life, an appropriate "parting present" (43) for a deity, especially one who presides over an island from which they get nuts that enable them to survive the winter. The new life the egg symbolizes may also refer to the whole seasonal cycle that is so important to the squirrels since to survive, they may have to return to the island the next year, and for the group to survive, they have to reproduce. Potter further emphasizes the egg by making it one of the gifts that make their way into one of Nutkin's riddles. It elicits a reaction from Mr. Brown of a sort that the others do not: Potter writes, "Now old Mr. Brown took an interest in eggs; he opened one eye and shut it again. But still he did not speak" (44). Nutkin accompanies the egg with three riddles. The one before the presentation of the egg had "egg" (43) as its answer. The answers to the other two riddles are "sunbeam" (47) and "wind" (48). The answers to the earlier riddles are "cherry" (16), "nettle" (23), "smoke" (24), "plum-pudding" (32), and "bees" (37), as well as "sunbeam" (47) and "wind" (48). It is easy to make too much of the symbolic import of the answers to each of the riddles. Still, the sunbeam and the wind are elemental forces of nature. They resemble Mr. Brown in a way since he rules over the island and allows the squirrels to gather nuts instead of eating the squirrels, making him also a kind of elemental force of nature that the squirrels must propitiate if they are to have enough nuts to get through the winter.

As though the words of the story do not in themselves show how foolishly Nutkin is acting, the pictures make his danger very clear. Especially telling is the illustration involving nettle. Nutkin stands very close to Mr. Brown, "tickling" Mr. Brown with a nettle; Potter's illustration of this act shows Nutkin poking the nettle near Mr. Brown's face (22–23). Nutkin's poking a nettle near Mr. Brown's face clearly shows how foolish Nutkin is, since nettles have hair-like growths on their stems and leaves that sting whenever they are touched and since Mr. Brown can do real harm to Nutkin. When Nutkin tickles Mr. Brown with the nettle, the owl could easily reach out and catch Nutkin. Another illustration shows Nutkin peering into Mr. Brown's house. Mr. Brown sits at the table eating the honey the squirrels have just given him. As a touch of humor, Potter has Brown use a spoon to eat the honey off a plate he holds in his talons (38). Potter writes, "Old Mr. Brown turned up his eyes in disgust at the impertinence of Nutkin" and adds, "But he ate up the honey!" (39). Nutkin apparently does not connect Brown's eating with the possibility of Nutkin's being eaten.

After Nutkin asks his last riddle, he imitates the noise of the wind, which is the answer to the riddle (48). He then "took a running jump right onto the head of Old Brown!" Potter writes, "Then all at once there was a flutterment and a scufflement and a loud 'Squeak!'" (48). The squeak is, of course, the noise Nutkin makes as Mr. Brown catches him. The other squirrels wisely "scuttered away into the bushes" (48). When the other squirrels "very cautiously" peep around the tree Mr. Brown inhabits, they see Old Brown "sitting on his door-step, quite still, with his eyes closed, as if nothing happened" (51). Brown's seeming indifference adds to the horror of the scene, for Nutkin, Potter writes, "*was in his waistcoat pocket!*" (51). Potter's italics emphasize these words and thus emphasize Nutkin's danger. The illustrations in the book, however, show Brown wearing no waistcoat. Instead, they show what looks like a real owl with one large exception. In the illustration showing Mr. Brown eating the honey, Potter certainly deviates from any kind of scientific depiction of nature: her owl apparently has two arms in addition to his legs and wings (38). Perhaps in the words about where Mr. Brown has Nutkin, Potter plays on one of the meanings of having someone in one's pocket: when someone has someone in one's pocket, the person has control over the one who is said to be in the pocket.

Things look very bleak for Nutkin, but Potter relieves some of her readers' anxiety by writing, "This looks like the end of the story, but it isn't" (52). Brown takes Nutkin inside his house, holds him up by the tail, and prepares "to skin him; but Nutkin pulled so very hard that his tail broke in two, and he dashed up the staircase, and escaped out of the attic window" (54). Thus, Nutkin comes close to losing his life and does lose part of his tail. The illustration accompanying these words shows several squirrels watching with their paws folded in front of them (55)—perhaps reminiscent of hands folded in prayer.

Potter wrote several tales that could be classified as pourquoi or origin tales, that is, tales that supposedly, usually fancifully, explain why things are the way they are. Some of the most familiar tales of this sort are Rudyard Kipling's *Just So Stories*, first published in 1902, the year before *The Tale of Squirrel Nutkin* first appeared. Kipling's book supposedly explains such things as "How the Whale Got his Throat," "How the Camel Got his Hump," "How the Leopard Got His Spots," and how the elephant got its trunk (in "The Elephant's Child").[2] Earlier than *The Just So Stories for Children* was Kipling's "How Fear Came," first published in *The Second Jungle Book* in 1895.

At the end of *The Tale of Squirrel Nutkin*, Potter tacks a kind of mock conclusion, making the tale into a kind of pourquoi tale about why squirrels act the way they do:

> And to this day, if you meet Nutkin up a tree and ask him a riddle, he will throw sticks at you, and stamp his feet and scold, and shout—
> "Cuck-cuck-cuck-cur-r-r-cuck-k-k!" [57].

In the letter sent to Nora Moore from Lingholme, Keswick, on 25 September 1901, Potter begins the story with her seeing a squirrel with a tail one-inch long chattering and throwing acorns onto her head. In the illustration of this material, she even shows a view of part of herself with her back turned to the reader and her arms raised toward some acorns falling through the air towards her.[3] She thus becomes a part of the tale she tells. In the finished work, Potter gives no illustration of a human being. The illustration accompanying the words about Nutkin's throwing sticks at a general "you" shows no person and no throwing of sticks. Instead, it shows five squirrels in a tree. One of them has a large part of his tail missing, making it easy for readers to identify which one is Nutkin (56–57). The published tale is thus much less personal than the tale in the picture letter, and Potter holds off until the end the idea that she is writing a kind of pourquoi tale, at least one that tells why squirrels act in a certain way and how Nutkin got the way he is. She thus makes the tale more exciting, for she does not give away the ending at its start. She also does not anchor it at a particular time—that is, a particular time in the life of one person—and gives it the kind of universality that readers associate with fairytales. Nonetheless, as numerous scholars have noticed, Potter does anchor it to reality through the scenery she paints in her illustrations.[4]

In the illustration showing Mr. Brown eating honey (38), Potter certainly deviates from any kind of scientific depiction of nature. Still, her animals face some of the kinds of dangers real wild animals face. Just as Peter Rabbit risks being made into a meal by Mr. McGregor, the Flopsy Bunnies risk being skinned and having their heads cut off, and Tom Kitten risks becoming a roly-poly pudding and being devoured by Samuel Whiskers, so all the squirrels face the danger Mr. Brown poses. They do so not for their own momentary pleasure, but so that they can survive through the winter, and their actions show that they are well aware of the danger they face. But through his foolishness, Nutkin almost becomes a meal for Old Mr. Brown. He has to sacrifice part of himself in order to escape, but he does escape. He gets out of Brown's house, where he seems doomed to die, but loses part of himself in the process.

Nutkin, then, is another of Potter's protagonists who faces what seems to be certain death, in this case by acting extremely foolishly, even more foolishly than Peter does in *The Tale of Peter Rabbit*. Like Peter, Nutkin survives his ordeal and, apparently, learns at least one trick of survival, that is, to avoid creatures that pose a threat to him: human beings clearly pose such a threat, and on the final page of the book, readers learn that Nutkin keeps his distance from human beings. Thus, Nutkin grows in a significant way. With all of its differences from *The Tale of Peter Rabbit*, *The Tale of Squirrel Nutkin* is, then, in some important ways similar to *The Tale of Peter Rabbit*. Both books have protagonists who do not follow the crowd; neither cooperates with others the way Mopsy, Flopsy, and Cotton-tale do and the way the other squirrels do. One of Potter's illustrations in *The Tale of Squirrel Nutkin* makes this similarity clear. It accompanies the words: "The squirrels filled their little sacks with nuts, and sailed away home in the evening" (19). It shows the squirrels at work gathering nuts on their first day on the island. It shows three squirrels on the branch of a tree. One is climbing onto the branch; another holds what looks like a bag of nuts; another lowers a bag to a squirrel on the ground. Two squirrels on the ground work with other bags that are full. Some squirrels in the background appear to be on their way home across the water (18). Like Mopsy, Flopsy, and Cotton-tale, the squirrels work together to put food on the table. Yet Nutkin, the one who does not cooperate and who seems concerned only with himself, is by far the most interesting squirrel in the story and the only one who is individualized. In *The Tale of Benjamin Bunny* and especially in *The Tale of Mr. Tod*, readers see Peter cooperating with others and see that such cooperation can achieve great rewards. But to read *The Tale of Squirrel Nutkin* as a tale with a moral about the glory of cooperation is a mistake.

Peter's individual journey does lead to discomfort: he has a stomach ache and looks as though he is developing a cold. Nutkin's adventures also lead to discomfort: the loss of his tail. Only in later works involving Peter do readers learn that Peter grows significantly from his adventures in Mr. McGregor's garden and has no lasting ill-effects. Squirrel Nutkin's adventures end with what seems to be a kind of mock moral when Potter tells what happens if "you meet Nutkin up a tree and ask him a riddle": Nutkin's throwing sticks, stamping his feet, scolding, and shouting, "Cuck-cuck-cuck-cur-r-r-cuck-k-k!" (57) really shows no growth on his part except for his keeping a potential predator at a distance, something he did not do with Mr. Brown. The whole idea of a squirrel's reacting in this way to a riddle is, of course, absurd, though the actions are things a squirrel could do and even the sounds Nutkin makes are noises that a squirrel can make.[5] In this tale, too, then, to narrow it down to a simple moral cannot possibly do justice to the tale.

The Tale of Benjamin Bunny

The Tale of Benjamin Bunny contains one of the further adventures of Peter Rabbit. The story's impetus comes from Peter's cousin Benjamin seeing Mr. and Mrs. McGregor in a gig with Mrs. McGregor wearing "her best bonnet" (7). Benjamin assumes from what he sees that they will not be in Mr. McGregor's garden for a while. He goes to the home of his cousins, Flopsy, Mopsy, Cotton-tail, and Peter, and his aunt, who is Peter's mother. A picture early in the book shows Mrs. Rabbit hard at work in her kitchen, with Flopsy, Mopsy, and Cotton-tail nicely standing at the table where she is working (10). Just as it is in *The Tale of Peter Rabbit*, in *The Tale of Benjamin Bunny*, it is impossible to tell Peter's siblings apart. In this picture of the rabbits at home, Mrs. Rabbit and two of Peter's siblings seem to be staring directly at the reader. In the first picture in *The Tale of Peter Rabbit*, all five rabbits appear. They are unclothed; they are completely realistic rabbits. Four—three of the bunnies and the adult—seem to be staring at the reader. Some readers do not count four rabbits in this picture. But the bunny's tail that sticks out at the left of the picture cannot belong to the bunny that stares. If it did, the bunny would be exceptionally long. What really seems to be happening is that readers see only the tail end of one of the rabbits. The other four, including the adult rabbit who is probably their mother, look at the reader, or, as some readers assume, at the author who has come upon them in the woods. The rabbits in this first picture in the first book are without clothes; they appear to be realistic rabbits in a realistic wood. Some readers guess that the rabbit not looking at the reader is Peter since he does not do what his siblings do. In *The Tale of Benjamin Bunny*, when they first appear, Peter's mother and siblings are domesticated; they are anthropomorphized. Mrs. Rabbit wears clothes and is doing some kind of work at a table. Her daughters stand on their hind legs with their paws on the table. Mrs. Rabbit and two of the bunnies stare toward the front of the picture. They may be looking at the author since Potter herself enters the story as a character, writing in parentheses that she once bought "rabbit-wool mittens and muffetees" from Mrs. Rabbit at a bazaar, where Mrs. Rabbit sold many things, some of which in this picture hang above and behind her. There is also a sign behind her (10–11). In the frontispiece of the book, Mrs. Rabbit sits knitting, probably one of the muffetees she sells; at least, what she is knitting certainly looks like a scarf. Her four children sit to her left, with one barely visible peering out of some kind of doorway. It seems probable that the rabbit barely visible is Peter since he again goes away from his siblings to have an adventure. On the frontispiece, the sign is clearly visible: it says, "Josephine Bunny, licensed to sell TEA and TOBACCO." The sign helps give validity to Potter's statement in parentheses. As readers learn from Potter's text, the tea is rosemary tea, and the tobacco is rabbit tobacco, which Potter explains in parentheses "is what *we* call lavender" (11). A bunny's being licensed to sell things is probably one of Potter's jokes in the story, a joke directed toward adult readers who easily see the absurdity of such an idea.

When Benjamin goes to his aunt's home, he does not "much want to see his Aunt" (12) for fairly obvious reasons: now that the McGregors are going away, he wants to get Peter to accompany him into the garden, and he probably senses that Peter's mother would not agree to such an idea. When Benjamin finds Peter, Peter seems to still be suffering from the after-effects of his earlier trip into Mr. McGregor's garden: "He looked poorly, and was dressed in a red cotton pocket-handkerchief" (15). Peter tells Benjamin that Mr. McGregor's scarecrow now has his clothes. Benjamin tells Peter that he knows the McGregors have gone out "certainly for the day, because she was wearing her best bonnet." "Peter said he hoped that it would rain," thus spoiling the McGregors' outing. Then, Old Mrs. Rabbit calls out, "Cotton-tail! Cotton-tail! Fetch some more camomile!" (19). Immediately after she says these words, Peter, no doubt remembering about chamomile from what happened after his recent trip into Mr. McGregor's garden, tells his cousin "he might feel better if they went for a walk" (19), apparently wanting to escape from another dose of chamomile tea. The two bunnies walk "hand in hand" (20) (something impossible, of course, for bunnies to do but indicating their close friendship) to Mr. McGregor's garden where Benjamin shows Peter how to get in by climbing down a pear tree instead of squeezing under a gate, the way Peter does in his previous foray into the garden, for, Benjamin says, "It spoils people's clothes to squeeze under a gate" (23). Potter's ability to write about two bunnies walking holding hands and still have them appear to be real rabbits is something critics find amazing and to a large extent unexplainable. As the two bunnies stand on the garden wall, they see the scarecrow Mr. McGregor built, complete with Peter's blue jacket and shoes and "topped with an old tam-o-shanter of Mr. McGregor's" (20–21). Peter then manages to fall down on his head but does not hurt himself since the garden bed he falls in "was newly raked and quite soft" (23).

Benjamin seems in charge of the foray, saying first they should get Peter's clothes so Peter can get dressed. Then, they can use Peter's pocket-handkerchief (the one he is wrapped in), Benjamin says, to fill with onions to give to Peter's mother. Although the gathering of onions for Peter's mother should probably be seen as a peace offering, it indicates that unlike Peter in *The Tale of Peter Rabbit*, Benjamin is concerned about something other than satisfying his own immediate desires. After Peter and Benjamin take Peter's clothes down from the scarecrow, Peter puts on his jacket and shoes (26–29), and Benjamin tries on the tam o' shanter, but it is, as seems logical, too big to fit Benjamin (27). The words of the story say nothing about Peter's shoes, but the pictures show him barefoot when Peter is putting on his jacket (26) and with shoes as Benjamin begins collecting onions (29), so he must have taken them off the scarecrow and put them on.

At Benjamin's suggestion, the two bunnies start gathering onions. In this book, Peter seems very timid. Potter writes, "Peter did not seem to be enjoying himself; he kept hearing noises" (28). Benjamin, however, who is "perfectly at home" in the garden, says that "he was in the habit of coming to the garden with his father to get lettuces for their Sunday dinner" (31), information that prepares readers for what happens when Benjamin's father later enters the garden and, incidentally, words that help explain how Benjamin was able to tell Peter about cats, a warning that comes in handy for Peter during his adventures in *The Tale of Peter Rabbit*.

Right after Benjamin says he is "in the habit of" entering the garden, Potter interrupts her narrative to tell readers that Benjamin's father's name is "old Mr. Benjamin Bunny" (31). In *The Tale of Mr. Tod*, the father's name becomes old Mr. Bouncer; thus, she gives Benjamin's family two entirely appropriate surnames for rabbits.

In the garden, Benjamin eats, but Peter does not; he says he wants to go home. Soon, he drops half the onions. Benjamin then decides that, when they want to leave the garden, they cannot carry onions up the pear tree and starts "boldly" leading Peter toward the garden's other end (35). Peter drops the rest of the onions (36). Apparently, however, the bunnies collect the onions again, for the next picture shows Peter in front of Benjamin carrying the full handkerchief as the bunnies walk through a place with "flower-pots, and frames and tubs" where Peter hears "noises worse than ever, his eyes were as big as lolly-pops!" (38–39).

Potter interrupts the narrative again to write: "This is what those little rabbits saw round that corner!" (40). The picture shows the two bunnies peeping around a corner seeing a cat lying on its side with its head up, looking away from the rabbits (41). This cat is not all white, like the one in *The Tale of Peter Rabbit*, and it has some kind of ribbon or collar around its neck, making it look not nearly as fearsome as the cat Peter encounters in the earlier book. Still it is a predator, the kind of predator that kills bunnies.

Benjamin quickly hides Peter and the onions and himself under a large basket (40). Benjamin clearly knows just what to do in the garden and acts upon what he knows. The cat approaches the basket and sniffs it. Potter then facetiously interjects, "Perhaps she liked the smell of onions!" (43). Even fairly small children, however, recognize the joke: the cat smells the bunnies.

The cat then sits on the basket for the next five hours (43–44). After communicating this information, Potter again interrupts the narrative, again playfully explaining, "I cannot draw you a picture of Peter and Benjamin underneath the basket, because it was quite dark, and because the smell of the onions was fearful; it made Peter Rabbit and little Benjamin cry." It became "quite late in the afternoon, but still the cat sat upon the basket" (44). The picture accompanying these words shows an alert looking cat atop the basket staring down where the rabbits hide (45).

Eventually, Benjamin's father comes "prancing along the top of the wall of the upper terrace." He smokes a pipe, has "a little switch in his hand," and looks for Benjamin (47). The picture accompanying these words shows Mr. Bunny, dressed in a jacket and waistcoat, with a scarf around his neck, and a pipe in his mouth. His hands are behind him holding the switch. He looks as though he is anything but uncomfortable as he stands on the garden wall (47); thus, the picture reinforces the idea that Mr. Bunny is at home in the garden. Readers have no sure way of knowing whether Mr. Bunny always carries a switch when he goes into the garden or is carrying the switch to use on his son when he finds Benjamin, but Potter's words certainly imply that the switch is to be used on Benjamin, an idea the rest of the story reinforces, since Potter writes, "He was looking for his son" (47). Mr. Bunny, who had "no opinion whatever of cats," jumps off the wall onto the cat, cuffs it off the basket, drives it into the greenhouse, and locks the door. He then takes Benjamin from under the basket and uses the switch to whip his son. He then pulls Peter from under the basket. Potter here writes simply, "Then he took out his nephew Peter" (51). Although the text does not say so, one of the pictures makes it clear that Mr. Bunny also whips Peter (50). Peter's uncle takes the onions from Peter and marches Peter and Benjamin out of the garden (52). Another picture accompanying this marching shows proud Mr. Bunny carrying some lettuce, the switch, and the handkerchief carrying the onions as a pair of very unhappy looking bunnies—Peter and Benjamin—walk ahead of him. Benjamin visibly sheds tears; Peter's paws seem to be up to his eyes, indicating he too may be crying, from the onions, from remorse, or because of the whipping, or because of all three. The picture also shows a cat with its forepaws up against the glass of the window of the greenhouse looking out, watching as the three rabbits walk toward the gate that leads out of the garden (53).[1]

When Mr. McGregor returns to the garden, he again shows that he is not too bright, just as he does in *The Tale of Peter Rabbit*. His not understanding where the little footprints in the garden came from and "how the cat could have managed to shut herself up *inside* the green-house, locking the door upon the *outside*" (54), show his inability to reason carefully. He stares at the scarecrow, which is now a pair of sticks with the tam o' shanter on top. Six rabbits stare over the garden wall at Mr. McGregor as the cat rubs against his leg (54–55). This part of the story involves Potter's being able to have her animal characters do things real animals cannot possibly do and still remain real animals. Part of the joke here involves there really being no way a rabbit could lock a cat into a greenhouse. No wonder Mr. McGregor cannot understand the situation. The adult reader will probably understand this joke; the child reader may not but will still be able to see the humor in the situation.

As she does in *The Tale of Peter Rabbit*, Peter's mother shows love for her son When he gets home: she forgives him "because she was so glad to see that he had found his shoes and coat." Old Mrs. Rabbit hangs the onions from the ceiling of the kitchen with the herbs and rabbit tobacco she has drying there (57). The final illustration in the book indicates that order has returned to the world of the rabbits. It shows Mrs. Rabbit in a rocking chair cuddling two little rabbits on her lap as Peter and one of his sisters stand in front of her folding the handkerchief.[2] The illustration makes it clear that Peter now looks at his mother while the other bunny folding the handkerchief looks at what she is doing. Hanging from the ceiling are the onions Peter and his cousin bring back from the garden as well as other vegetables. Vegetables also lie on the floor next to a bowl that has vegetables in it (56). Mrs. Rabbit's cuddling the bunnies on her lap indicates the love she has for her children, and the abundance of vegetables shows that she is a good mother who nurtures and nourishes her children. And Peter's looking at his mother rather than trying to hide from her, as he does in *The Tale of Peter Rabbit*—shows perhaps that he is maturing in his view of her. Peter's mother shows the kind of love Potter's own mother apparently never did show for her children.

The symbolism in this story is not as stark as it is in *The Tale of Peter Rabbit*. The garden itself is still a kind of Eden, but Peter knows from the beginning that it is a dangerous place. The bunnies still face the possibility of death if the cat or Mr. McGregor catches them, but Benjamin has much more experience of the garden than Peter, so he knows what to do: he knows the McGregors will be away when the bunnies enter the garden, and he knows how to avoid the cat, saving Peter and the onions in the process. Although the bunnies are uncomfortable under the basket, mainly because of the onions, they are still relatively comfortable when compared to Peter in the gooseberry net or the watering can full of water. Unlike Peter in his earlier adventure, the bunnies do not save themselves. Benjamin's father, who is also familiar with the garden and knows how to handle cats, saves and punishes his son and his nephew. He rescues both of the bunnies and calmly leads them from the garden. And Peter's mother again is glad to have her son home unhurt.

There are still threats of death in the story, and the entry into the basket and eventual release from it are a kind of symbolic death and resurrection. The basket is a womb-like object, but much more comfortable than the watering can is in *The Tale of Peter Rabbit*. Still, the story is much tamer than are stories like *The Tale of Peter Rabbit*, *The Tale of Squirrel Nutkin*, *The Tale of Mr. Jeremy Fisher*, *The Tale of the Flopsy Bunnies*, and especially *The Tale of Samuel Whiskers* and *The Tale of Mr. Tod*. Again, the pictures help tell the story. In the final picture, Mrs. Rabbit, like a good homemaker, wears her apron, and Peter wears the jacket he and Benjamin rescued from Mr. McGregor's garden. The picture clearly communicates the love Mrs. Rabbit has for her children and the way she is able to nurture them both physically and emotionally. Peter seems to be looking at his mother, not hiding from her the way he does at the end of *The Tale of Peter Rabbit* or looking away from her, as he does when she warns him not to go into Mr. McGregor's garden. The rabbits are united by the warm glow of the fireplace, although in the picture Potter indicates the fireplace itself with only a few lines that suggest it (56). The warmth of the fireplace reinforces the warmth and love Mrs. Rabbit has for her family, illuminating the end of the book; thus, Potter conveys a feeling very different from the feeling Helen Potter conveyed to her daughter. Surely, Beatrix knew what was so sadly lacking in the home in which she grew up and gives that thing to the Rabbit household.

The Tale of Two Bad Mice and *The Tale of Mrs. Tiggy-Winkle*

In creating two works each of which Potter considered "a *girl's* book,"[1] *The Tale of Two Bad Mice* (1904) and *The Tale of Mrs. Tiggy-Winkle* (1905), Potter used several of her pets as models—two mice she had and a pet hedgehog—for the characters in her books, just as she used her pet rabbits as models for the rabbits in *The Tale of Peter Rabbit* and *The Tale of Benjamin Bunny*. In all three works, she manages to blend fantasy and realistic portrayals of animal life to create a seamless whole. In *The Tale of Two Bad Mice*, she seems at first to downplay the dangers real mice face and the kinds of problems they create in a domestic situation. But the mice in the story—even the babies—face a trap the nursemaid sets, and the mice leave a trail of destruction in the doll's-house.[2] The house the mice plunder is based on a real doll's-house Norman Warne made for his niece. The dolls inhabiting the doll's-house are also based on real dolls, as is the policeman doll that also appears in the book. In the story, "The little girl that the doll's-house belongs to" wants the nursemaid to get "a doll dressed like a policeman" (51) to protect the doll's-house. The nursemaid's idea of setting a trap (52) is much more practical. Juxtaposing the two ideas shows Potter incorporating the child point of view and the adult point of view into her tale.

In *The Tale of Two Bad Mice*, Potter creates a fairytale to explore the kinds of damage mice create in houses. That two mice would leave a trail of destruction as terrible as the one Tom Thumb and Hunca Munca create, even in a doll's-house, seems extremely unlikely. Also, Potter surely knew that the reasons real mice create such destruction are not the same as those that motivate Tom Thumb and Hunca Munca. Like little children—and far too many adults—when their desires are thwarted, the two mice destroy the things they blame for thwarting those desires.

The plot of the story is relatively simple. The two dolls—Lucinda and Jane, who is the cook—inhabit the doll's-house. They go for a ride in their "perambulator" (12) or baby carriage, a term American children may not understand. While the dolls are away, two mice—Tom Thumb and Hunca Munca—enter the house hunting for food. When they discover that the things that look like food in the house are artificial and thus they cannot eat the food, they go on a rampage. But then they discover that there are some things in the house they can use, such as the bolster on Lucinda's bed, so they take those things into their mouse hole. Just as the mice are making a final trip from the doll's-house to their hole, the two dolls return. When they see the mess in their house, "Lucinda sat upon the upset kitchen stove and stared; and Jane leant against the kitchen dresser and smiled—but neither of them made any remark" (44). This description of their lack of action is appropriate, since they are dolls. The little girl who owns the doll's-house wants to get a policeman doll, but the more practical nurse decides to set a trap. The mice, however, turn out to be not so bad. Tom Thumb pays for the things he breaks with a "crooked sixpence" he finds (54), and every morning, Hunca Munca sweeps "the Dollies' house" (57).[3]

The ending of this story is in keeping with its fairytale atmosphere. However, it is more sentimental than the endings of most of Potter's stories. That the mice would leave a "crooked sixpence" to pay for the damage they have done is, of course, not true to animal nature, but does involve the kind of thing that could really happen, that is, the appearance of a real sixpence in a place that a child would not expect it. The idea of Hunca Munca's cleaning the house every morning is also sentimental, but an adult could use it to explain to a child how a place gets cleaned before a child wakes up.

E. James Anthony writes that in Potter's works, "an undercurrent of deeper anxieties" propels her tales into "the hearts and minds" of children. This statement is clearly true of *The Tale of Two Bad Mice*, especially connected with the temper tantrums of the mice and the consequent unhappiness of the dolls and of the child who owns the doll's-house, but the tale has none of the imagery obviously connected with death and rebirth that is central to Potter's earlier works: at no time do the dolls face an actual life and death situation; they are, after all, dolls. Still, a threat of death for the mice enters the story in the shape of the mousetrap, and with the deaths of the parents, the babies would also die. But at no time does the mousetrap pose a serious threat for any of the characters involved in the story. On a much more subtle level, the entrance of the mice into the doll's-house and their exit from it unhurt could be construed as imagery of death and rebirth, although this idea seems to be stretching what the story may involve.

The story, however, has a more important undercurrent of anxiety for Potter herself. It is easy to see the mice doing to the doll's-house exactly what Potter would have liked to have done to 2 Bolton Gardens, a place she calls her "unloved birthplace," as she described it in 1942. After telling one of her American friends about the destruction of the house during the war, she adds that she is "pleased" to know that it was destroyed (*Beatrix Potter's Americans* 213). Incidentally, the later destruction of the house the Potter's lived in at 2 Bolton Gardens was undoubtedly much worse than the destruction the mice cause in the doll's-house. However, the Potter of 1942 was much more outspoken than that of 1904. The Potter who wrote *The Tale of Two Bad Mice* was still living in her unloved birthplace and was still the very obedient daughter. The destruction of the doll's-house, perhaps, produced so much anxiety in Potter that she had to invent the far-fetched fairytale ending so that she could overcome her own anxiety. In some miniature letters from Tom Thumb and Hunca Munca to Lucinda Doll, both of the mice become extremely subservient to *Miss* Lucinda Doll. In one, Tom Thumb asks the Doll to "forgive" him for "asking whether you can spare a feather bed," since the feathers are all out of the one they stole. He adds a P.S. that he and Hunca Munca "are grateful to" Lucinda for hiring Hunca Munca to clean the house, and he hopes Hunca Munca will continue to do satisfactory work. In another P.S., he adds that he and his "wife would be grateful for any old clothes […]." In another letter, Tom Thumb writes that he has whipped Hunca Munca for not dusting the mantelpiece, and then begs for "another kettle." In this series of letters both Tom Thumb and Hunca Munca address Lucinda as "Honoured Madam" and sign themselves, "yr obedient servant," terms that are fairly common in letters from the late nineteenth and early twentieth centuries but that go very nicely with the subservience both mice show (*Letters to Children* 86–87).[4]

In *The Art of Beatrix Potter*, Emily Zach touches what is probably another source of anxiety for Potter that probably would not cause anxiety for many twenty-first century readers of the book: the mice disrupt what Zach calls "the Edwardian sense of cleanliness and order" when they enter the house, and they display "terrible table manners" and proceed "to ransack" the house (58). Thus, this tale certainly involves what might have been a source of more anxiety for Potter than for at least most children living in the late twentieth and early twenty-first centuries in the United States. To see the actions of the mice as representing things Potter wished would happen in the house her family occupied in London does not seem like much of a stretch. After all, Potter expressed pleasure in its having later been destroyed.

The Tale of Mrs. Tiggy-Winkle also seems to lack what most people would consider "an undercurrent of deeper anxieties" and *obvious* imagery of death and rebirth, although it does involve some of the kinds of anxieties a very real Beatrix Potter may have faced as a child, and it also involves an underground journey but in a setting that is not very threatening, except, perhaps, since Mrs. Tiggy-Winkle has quills. Still, in *The Tale of Mrs. Tiggy-Winkle*, entering and leaving the door leading into the hill does have overtones of death and rebirth for someone who comes from a background as stifling as Potter's was, especially in connection with Lucy's getting back items of clothing she lost.

There is, however, a very well hidden undercurrent of anxiety in *The Tale of Mrs. Tiggy-Winkle*. In a letter to Norman Warne, dated 8 June 1905, Potter discusses the grammar in the song Lucie hears before she enters Mrs. Tiggy-Winkle's house (*Letters* 119–20); Potter is referring to some correction in grammar to be made to the proofs of the book. Potter writes that Mrs. Tiggy-Winkle is "exorcising" the blemishes on the garment and compares what the hedgehog is doing to Lady Macbeth's actions (*Letters* 120). However, it seems certain that few, if any of Potter's adult readers, much less her child readers, would recognize the allusion. They also would not be aware of Potter's anxiety about grammar that she treats in the letter to Norman Warne.[5]

The central problem of *The Tale of Mrs. Tiggy-Winkle*—the loss of three pocket-handkerchiefs and a pinafore—hardly seems fraught with great anxiety for people as affluent as the Potters were, except for someone like Beatrix Potter, who had such a demanding mother. Lucie's crying about the loss of her "handkins" indicates that she is, in this way, a person at least somewhat like Potter, but the anxiety she shows hardly matches that of Peter in the gooseberry net. Still, Potter's narration in her journal of the episode when her hat blew off at the International Inventions Exposition shows how demanding she felt her parents were. If having a hat blow off can cause her to feel that it shows that the prophecy of her being a "discredit" to her parents is coming true, losing several articles of clothing could also be very disturbing.

The Tale of Mrs. Tiggy-Winkle involves Lucy's search for and ultimate retrieval of her lost items of clothing. It begins with Lucie lamenting the loss of "three handkins and a pinny" and asking Tabby Kitten whether she has seen the lost items (7). She next asks Sally Henny-penny whether she has seen the handkerchiefs. The kitten does not pay any attention to the little girl, and the hen replies, "I go barefoot, barefoot, barefoot" (8), indicating the loss is of no consequence to her. She next asks Cock Robin, who flies over a stile and away (11). Thus, Lucie finds herself in a world that seems basically indifferent to what is, to her, a serious problem. She then goes over the stile the robin flies over and sees on a hillside some white things on the grass. Apparently thinking those are her handkerchiefs, she goes way up the hill until she comes to a spring bubbling from the hill and sees a tiny tin can used to catch water and "foot-marks of a *very* small person" (15). The small person turns out to be Mrs. Tiggy-Winkle, a washerwoman who happens to be a hedgehog. Lucie climbs further until she comes to a door in the hill with clothes-props and tiny clothespins in front of it. Lucie hears singing coming from inside the door (16). She knocks on the door and "a frightened voice called out 'Who's that?'" (19). The voice's being "frightened" indicates that Lucie herself is a source of fright to the person beyond the door.

Beyond the door, Lucie finds a kitchen with a very low ceiling and small pots and pans. The place smells as though ironing has been occurring there, and at a table, holding an iron, "stood a very stout short person staring anxiously at Lucie." Beneath the person's cap are "PRICKLES!" (20). The illustration clearly shows that the person is a hedgehog (21). When Lucie asks the person who she is and if she has seen her handkerchiefs, the person replies, "Oh yes, if you please'm; my name is Mrs. Tiggy-winkle; oh yes if you please'm, I'm an excellent clear-starcher!" and she begins ironing clothes. Children and even adults may not understand that a "clear-starcher" is a laundress. First, she irons a waistcoat belonging to Cock Robin and then a tablecloth belonging to Jenny Wren. As these items appear, Lucie inquires whether they are her handkerchief or pinafore (23–27).

Potter observed first-hand the fastidiousness of hedgehogs. As Lear points out, the story is "set in a real place, about a real washerwoman, a real hedgehog named Tiggy-winkle" that was one of Potter's pets, "and a child, Lucie." The tale is set in the Newlands Valley in the Lake District that Potter loved so much (187).[6] Still, Potter recreates the place, the washerwoman, the hedgehog, and Lucie when she puts them into her story. And the story has an atmosphere of anxiety, not just involving the disappearance of the items of clothing but also the indifference of the animals Lucie questions, the long distance Lucie travels by herself to get to the home of Mrs. Tiggy-winkle, and the prickles on Mrs. Tiggy-winkle, as well as the anxiety and deference Mrs. Tiggy-winkle shows when Lucie enters her underground home. Fairytale elements enter the tale, of course, when Mrs. Tiggy-winkle talks and when she interacts with the other animals for whom she does washing. Still, the whole tale can easily be dismissed as a dream when Lucie realizes toward the end that Mrs. Tiggy-winkle did not wait "for thanks or for the washing bill!" Instead. Lucie sees her "running, running, running up the hill—where was her white-frilled cap? and her shawl? and her gown—and her petticoat?" (54). Also, Mrs. Tiggy-winkle has grown very small—returning to the size of a real hedgehog, with the brown color of a hedgehog, "and covered with PRICKLES!" Potter even asserts, "Why! Mrs. Tiggy-winkle is nothing but a HEDGEHOG" (57). Yet Potter ends the story with words in parentheses that anticipate the idea readers will have of its being only a dream; she even includes what a child might take as proof it is not just a dream:

> (Now some people say that Little Lucie had been asleep—but then how could she have found three clean pocket-handkins and a pinny, pinned with a silver safety-pin?
> And besides—*I* have seen that door into the back of the hill called Cat-Bells—and besides *I* am very well acquainted with dear Mrs. Tiggy-winkle!) [57].

Potter's logic here works well on a child's level, especially the eye-witness testimony.

The Tale of Two Bad Mice and *The Tale of Mrs. Tiggy-Winkle* are thus similar to many of Potter's other stories not just in the human-animal association within them but also in the way they treat problems central to Potter's own life. A reader, of course, need not know any of the biographical background of the books to appreciate the books, as millions of child-readers have shown. So it seems that in tapping her own deepest feelings, Potter, possibly without being fully aware of what she was doing, gave her little books universal appeal.

The Tale of the Pie and the Patty-Pan

In several of her stories, Potter satirizes the society of her time. In particular, critics see her as satirizing the lives her parents led. In *The Tale of the Pie and the Patty-Pan* (1905), Potter illustrates how the manners of civilized society can go awry. Critics rightly see *The Tale of Mr. Jeremy Fisher* (1906) as satirizing the life Potter's father led and *The Tale of the Pie and the Patty-Pan* as satirizing the life her mother led.[1] It is also easy to see "The Sly Old Cat" as satirizing the manners of civilized society.[2] All three stories indicate that just beneath the veneer of civilized manners can lie barbarism and that the adult Potter recognized many of the problems involved in the kinds of lives her parents led.

Potter's original title of *The Tale of the Pie and the Patty-Pan* was simply *The Pie*. It was originally published as *The Pie and the Patty-Pan*.[3] Not until 1930 did it get the title, *The Tale of the Pie and the Patty-Pan*. It is a humorous story of a cat who invites a dog to tea. All kinds of misunderstandings occur. At the same time that the animals are extremely polite to one another, the dog, at least, is a glutton who, true to her dog nature, stuffs her food in her mouth and begins to feel ill, but only after she discovers that she has been eating mouse pie. Thus, she is human at the same time she is dog.

Duchess the dog receives an invitation from Ribby, a cat, to come to her house and eat a delicious pie, adding, "You have never tasted anything so good!" (7), and telling Duchess, "*You* shall eat all of it! *I* will eat muffins, my dear Duchess!" (8). Duchess answers her very politely, writing that she will come "with much pleasure," and adding "But it is very strange. *I* was going to invite you to come here, to supper, my dear Ribby, to eat something most delicious" (8), but Duchess ends her original response with the words, "I hope it isn't mouse" (8), referring to the pie. But after reflection, she decides the statement about mouse pie does "not look quite polite," so she writes instead, "I hope it will be fine" (10). Here, Potter hints at what she later makes more explicit. By writing, "I hope it will be fine" instead of something like, I'm sure it will be fine, Duchess indicates her snobbery. Nonetheless, she frets about being served a mouse pie, saying to herself, "I am dreadfully afraid it *will* be mouse!" and adds, "I really couldn't, *couldn't* eat mouse pie," but she knows that to be polite she will have to eat whatever Ribby serves "because it is a party" (10). Most dogs, of course, would not hesitate to eat and enjoy a mouse pie—if they could get one. But Potter attributes to Duchess the finicky taste of a human. Potter here also foreshadows some of the class consciousness that permeates this work: in Duchess's mind, cats eat mouse pie; dogs do not. Duchess's name clearly indicates that Duchess at least considers herself to be of a class superior to Ribby, as does at least one other character in the book who sees Ribby as engaging in social climbing when she invites a dog rather than a cat to her party.

Duchess decides to bake a ham and bacon pie of her own, sneak into Ribby's house, and substitute her own pie for the one Ribby is baking. Duchess has the same kind of dish Ribby says she is baking the pie in, so she decides to put her pie in the dish and use a patty-pan to hold the crust up (12).[4] She bakes her pie and sneaks into Ribby's house when Ribby goes out to shop (18–21).[5] In the meantime, Ribby puts her pie in her upper oven because the lower, she thinks, will cook it too quickly. Duchess tries to open the top oven door but cannot turn the handle, so she puts her pie in the lower oven. She wonders why, when she opens the oven door, there is no pie already in it. Hearing Ribby returning home, she quickly exits the back door. She still wonders why she could not find Ribby's pie. As Ribby enters, she hears noises and wonders whether someone is in her house. She remembers she locked the spoons before she left, so she is sure they were not stolen. She also finds nothing amiss (22).

Duchess goes home to get herself ready for the party. She brushes "her beautiful black coat" and then picks flowers from her garden for Ribby (25). The picture that accompanies these words shows a happy-looking Duchess before a mirror brushing her beautiful coat and looking very pleased with herself (25).

After Duchess carefully gets ready for the party, she runs through the village so fast that she arrives at Ribby's house too early, so practicing good manners, she waits a while, wondering whether Ribby "has taken *my* pie out of the oven yet?" and wondering where Ribby's pie is (28). When the dog gets ready to enter, she gives "a most genteel little tap-tapppity" at the door and asks, "Is Mrs. Ribston at home?" Ribby replies, "Come in! and how do you do? my dear Duchess," adding, "I hope I see you quite well?" to which Duchess replies, "Quite well, I thank you, and how do *you* do, my dear Ribby," adding, "I've brought you some flowers; what a delicious smell of pie!" Ribby replies, "Oh, what lovely flowers! Yes, it is mouse and bacon" (30). By putting this greeting ritual in the mouths of a dog and cat, Potter clearly satirizes it.

Ribby feels her pie needs to bake for five more minutes, so she serves tea first, even placing a lump of sugar on Duchess's nose the way the dog asks her to do and complementing Duchess on how prettily she begs (32). Thus, Potter mixes animal and human traits in the making of her dog and cat at the same time that she shows the ridiculousness of their manners.

Duchess comments that the pie cooking smells wonderful, and she loves "veal and ham," quickly correcting herself to say, "I mean to say mouse and bacon" (33). The narrator tells the readers that when Ribby puts the pie on the table, there is "a very savoury smell" (34). Adding to the comedy, while Ribby gets the pie out, Duchess drops the sugar that is on her nose and hunts for it under the table, so she does not see Ribby getting the pie out of the lower oven (34). Potter here makes fun of the manners the dog and cat exhibit, thus making fun of the manners people exhibit.

Ribby says, "I will first cut the pie for you; I am going to have muffin and marmalade." Duchess then asks, "Do you really prefer muffin? Mind the patty-pan!" (35), words that cause Ribby to reply, "I beg your pardon?" (36). The little dog quickly changes the subject, asking, "May I pass you the marmalade?" (36). Beneath the politeness of this conversation lies the fact that the two animals are not really communicating with each other and that Duchess is trying to fool Ribby so that the little dog will not have to eat mouse pie. She even admires what she believes is her own pie, thinking, "What very small fine pieces it has cooked into! I did not remember that I had minced it up so fine ..." and guesses that Ribby's oven is quicker than her own oven (36). Earlier in the story, Ribby comments to herself about the rapidity of Duchess's eating (14). Duchess then predictably wolfs down four servings of the pie. She then hunts for the patty-pan, not knowing that there is none in the pie she devours so quickly. Instead, when she cannot find the patty-pan, she thinks she has swallowed it, even though Ribby assures her, "There most certainly is not one, my dear Duchess. I disapprove of tin articles in puddings and pies. It is most undesirable ..." (37–40). And she adds as an aside to herself, "especially when people swallow in lumps" (40), as Duchess has just done. Duchess, however, continues to hunt for a patty-pan. Ribby continues to try to convince Duchess that there is no patty-pan in her pie, saying her Great-Aunt Squintina "died of a thimble in a Christmas pudding. *I* never put any article of metal in *my* puddings or pies" and tells Duchess she owns only four patty-pans, all of which are in her cupboard (41). Nonetheless, the little dog begins howling, thinking she has devoured her own pie along with a patty-pan, and she begins to feel ill. She sets "up a howl" and says, "I shall die! I shall die! I have swallowed a patty-pan. Oh, my dear Ribby, I do feel so ill" (41). Ribby then goes to fetch Dr. Maggoty. Dr. Maggoty is, as his name implies, a magpie. Having a magpie as the doctor is, in a strange way, appropriate and may involve one of Potter's jokes that most children and adults would not understand but some might. Magpies peck ticks and other insects off of mammals, often drawing blood. Bloodletting was once a very common way to treat various kinds of illnesses. The widespread practice of bloodletting continued into the nineteenth century. Some illnesses are still treated using bloodletting, a practice called phlebotomy. Although Magpies have a reputation for eating small birds and causing damage to mammals, their bloodletting clearly associates them with doctors who also used to let blood, and who, incidentally, had a reputation for killing many of their patients. That Dr. Maggoty is not capable of curing Duchess becomes very obvious after Ribby summons him, but, of course, Duchess has nothing wrong with her except an upset stomach from eating too much too quickly.

When Ribby leaves, Duchess realizes that something is still baking in the oven and discovers it is her own pie. Realizing the pie she just ate is mouse, she says that must be why she feels so ill, obviously not realizing (or admitting) that her imagination that she has eaten a patty-pan may be what is making her ill or even her gulping down so much food may be responsible. Thinking she feels so ill because she has been eating mouse, she realizes she would perhaps feel even worse if she had swallowed a patty-pan (49). In order to hide the trick she tries to play on Ribby, she decides to put her pie in Ribby's backyard and fetch it after she leaves for home. By the time the doctor and Ribby arrive, Duchess feels much better; Potter thus indicates that Duchess's imagination has been a major cause of her distress.

Dr. Maggoty, a magpie, is a comic figure, as his name indicates, since it plays on magpie and maggot. When Ribby first sees him, he is engaged in a magpie-like ridiculous activity, "putting rusty nails in a bottle of ink" from the post office and saying, "Gammon? Ha! HA!"[6] When Ribby explains that Duchess has swallowed a patty-pan, Dr. Maggoty replies with the words, "Spinach? Ha! HA!" (44). The doctor hops so quickly through the village that Ribby has to run to keep up with him, making a spectacle of herself. Earlier, when Ribby's cousin, Tabitha Twitchit, hears that Ribby is having Duchess to her house for a tea party, she thinks, "A little *dog* indeed! Just as if there were no CATS in Sawrey! And a *pie* for afternoon tea! The very idea!" (21–22), insinuating that Ribby is social climbing. As Ribby and the doctor rush through the village, Tabitha remarks, "I *knew* they would over-eat themselves!" (46), arriving much closer at the truth than Duchess apparently does. In the story, Ribby herself indicates that she is social climbing. Right after Ribby puts her pie in the top oven, Ribby comments to herself, "It is a pie of the most delicate and tender mouse minced with bacon. And I have taken out all the bones; because Duchess did nearly choke herself with a fish-bone last time I gave a party. She eats a little fast—rather big mouthfuls." However, Ribby adds that Duchess is "a most genteel and elegant little dog; infinitely superior company to Cousin Tabitha Twitchit" (14).

Before Ribby and the doctor arrive at Ribby's house, Duchess returns to the house, sits by the fire, and shuts her eyes. When the two do arrive, Duchess seems "fast asleep." In fact, she really is fast asleep, as her waking "with a jump" indicates (50). The doctor again speaks nonsense, saying, "Gammon, ha, HA?" (50). However, the word gammon makes more sense here than it does earlier since gammon is a kind of ham or bacon. Duchess says she feels "much better," but Ribby asks her to take the pill the doctor has brought. Duchess says she would "feel *quite* well if he only felt my pulse," but Ribby encourages her to take the pill and drink some milk. Apparently, Duchess does take the pill and the milk, since she coughs and chokes while the doctor says, "Gammon? Gammon?" (51). Ribby loses her temper and tells the doctor, "Don't say that again!" and adds, "Here, take this bread and jam, and get out into the yard!" to which Dr. Maggoty responds, "Gammon and Spinach! ha ha HA!" (52).

The name Duchess for the dog in this story is itself part of the satire, since Potter knows that no matter how impolite, vain, and foolish a duchess is, she will be above the Potters in the strata of English society near the turn of the twentieth century. If a duchess were to rush under the table, people like the Potters would probably not complain, at least to the duchess's face. When Tabitha Twitchit's comment is put into the context of the little dog's name, it becomes clear that she views her cousin as a social climber. Ribby's words about Duchess being "infinitely superior company" to her cousin indicate that Tabitha is probably right.

Duchess clearly has terrible manners, as her chasing under the table for the piece of sugar, her sneaking her own pie into Ribby's house, and her wolfing down her food indicate. Potter indicates that just beneath the façade of polite society that this dog and cat create lies a kind of barbarism indicated by their interaction with one another. As Tabitha indicates, Ribby is social climbing. Duchess, on the other hand, shows what a barbarian she truly is. At the same time, Potter expertly mixes dog and human characteristics in her little dog. The illustrations of the dog show a very real dog who wears human clothes and ornaments and engages in the kind of activities that a dog could not engage in, and elements of the dog's behavior are quite realistic for a real dog, such as her gobbling down her food. Duchess, in her role as a human, at the end of the story runs "home feeling uncommonly silly!" and Ribby, when she gets a "pailful of water to wash up the tea-things," discovers the smashed pie dish in her yard and a "patty-pan [...] under the pump where Dr. Maggoty had considerately left it" (56). The words about Dr. Maggoty's considerateness are clearly sarcastic since Dr. Maggoty shows no real considerateness at all. In fact, he also never "considers" anything.

Ribby herself seems chastised when she says to herself at the end of the story, "Did you ever see the like! so there really was a patty-pan? ... But *my* patty-pans are all in the kitchen cupboard. Well I never did! ... Next time I want to give a party—I will invite Cousin Tabitha Twitchit!" (56, ellipses in the original).

Thus, Potter clearly satirizes the manners of people like her mother and their social climbing, yet in the end, she reinforces the social strata of her times, indicating that Ribby has learned the lesson of staying within her own social class. Potter thus clearly is subversive of social mores, but does not subvert the whole idea of class distinctions. That Potter is not as consistently subversive as some people would have her should not be surprising. As Robert Leeson has shown in "Beatrix Potter: One of Nature's Conservatives," Potter's views of society were more complex. Her views of her place in society were also complex: she did seem to feel that her wealth entitled her to certain kinds of respect that she demanded from others. But the idea of keeping in one's place, as Ribby refuses to do, remains fairly firm. Like Tabitha, Potter sees Ribby as a social climber who should have invited a cat to tea rather than a dog, as she simultaneously reveals that absurdity of social climbing and of social distinctions.

The Tale of Mr. Jeremy Fisher

The Tale of Mr. Jeremy Fisher (1906) is another of Potter's tales that deal with predator and prey relationships, with the twist that the central character, who is a predator who goes after fish for his dinner, becomes prey. It seems to be one of her finest tales. However, Graham Greene calls it her "only one failure" of the period from 1904 to 1908, a period of what Greene calls Potter's "vintage years in comedy" ("Beatrix Potter" 243). When Margaret Lane comments about Greene's calling it a failure (*Magic Years* 152), she writes of Greene—surely, with tongue-in-cheek: "Perhaps he is not a fisherman?" (152). It is difficult to imagine what he may have had in mind.[1] It involves an ogre—in this case not a human but a trout—that desires to devour the protagonist, Mr. Jeremy. Peter manages to escape from Mr. McGregor by getting rid of his clothes and using his head. Mr. Jeremy escapes from his ogre as a result of the ridiculous outfit he wears: the fish spits him out because it is "displeased with the taste of the macintosh."[2] When he escapes, he is almost all frog: he wears only the now-tattered mackintosh (46). For modern readers, Mr. Jeremy wears clothes that are comic in and for themselves; put on a frog, they become even more comic. Never in *The Tale of Mr. Jeremy Fisher* does Mr. Jeremy appear without clothing. Small children might find the clothing attractive because of its colors; they may not recognize how absurd Mr. Jeremy appears. Most adults probably do recognize the absurdity of his costumes. This is, then, one aspect of the tale about which Potter may have had an adult readership in mind.

Like *The Tale of Peter Rabbit*, *The Tale of Mr. Jeremy Fisher* had a fairly long prehistory. In July and August of 1883, Potter made several entries in her journal that involve observations of amphibians, especially frogs (*Journal*, complete ed. 50–51). She also had a pet frog named Punch that lived with her for five or six years (Linder *History*, 175). The first sure beginning occurs in a picture letter Potter sent to Eric Moore, Noel's brother, on 5 September 1893, the day after she sent the picture letter involving Peter Rabbit to Noel. Writing in 1992, Judy Taylor says the last time the letter "was seen in public" was 1947 (*Beatrix Potter's Letters to Children* 17). However, Lloyd Cotsen purchased the letter, and his wife published it in *The Beatrix Potter Collection of Lloyd Cotsen*, as part of the celebration of his seventy-fifth birthday. In addition, a frog appeared in a series of nine line drawings that Linder implies involved her work on Mr. Jeremy Fisher embodied in the picture letter (*History* 175). Ernest Nister, publisher, used the drawings in 1894 in a book entitled *Comical Customers;* however, the text accompanying the drawings was not by Potter but by Clifton Bingham.³ The drawings present the barest outline of the adventures of a frog who goes fishing in the rain in what looks like a real boat, catches a fish that nips his fingers, and as he goes home, the fishes laugh at him. He eats a meal consisting of a grasshopper. In the antepenultimate drawing, the frog sits alone at his table, a knife and fork in his hands with which he is about to begin carving the grasshopper. In the last drawing, the water is full of fishes who are laughing at the frog. Obviously, *The Tale of Mr. Jeremy Fisher* is much more developed than these nine drawings. Potter's finished tale brings the frog to life and adds many details that seem to involve Potter's satirizing the kind of life her father lived.

In the picture letter to Eric Moore, Potter treats mostly the material in *Comical Customers*, except that she names the frog—Mr. Jeremy Fisher—and calls him "Mr. Fisher." His boat is still not a lily pad but what looks like a real rowboat. As the stickleback gets away, a very unhappy looking Mr. Fisher sucks the fingers of his right hand. The galoshes Mr. Fisher wears, Potter writes, are "immense"; however, they do not look so immense although they are clearly too big for Mr. Fisher. After the stickleback gets loose, Mr. Fisher is "too cross" to fish anymore, so he goes home, walking on the land as the fishes laugh at him. The final picture shows him alone at his table getting ready to carve his "roasted grasshopper with lady-bird sauce," something Potter writes that she thinks is "nasty."⁴ Obviously, the published book is much more detailed than the letter and much more exciting. Of more interest is the fact that the letter shows the frog as being merely uncomfortable; *The Tale of Mr. Jeremy Fisher* shows him almost losing his life.

On 11 October 1995, Potter wrote to Molly Gaddum a letter that included in it pictures of a frog that fishes and catches a fish but loses it. The frog wears a mackintosh and slippers that are too big for him and carries a basket for fish. Here, too, the frog uses a regular boat rather than a lily pad. After losing the fish, he uses a butterfly net and catches a grasshopper for dinner. In this tale, one of the pictures shows a tortoise, using a walking-stick, coming to dinner. The final picture shows the tortoise and the frog at a table with the frog carving a large grasshopper that sits on a plate in front of the frog (*Letters to Children* 98–99). Here, too, Potter produced just a bare outline of the finished book.

Margaret Lane writes that throughout *The Tale of Mr. Jeremy Fisher*, Mr. Jeremy wears the clothing of "a Regency buck" (152). Ruth K. MacDonald recognizes that Mr. Jeremy's clothing is that of "a Regency-period dandy" (96). Putting a frog in the kinds of outfits Mr. Jeremy wears shows how ridiculous the outfits are. MacDonald calls using Regency outfits "particularly felicitous," since "Regency dress focuses on dainty feet and the tight-fitting trousers that show off footwear" (97). Even without being on a frog, the outfits look extreme to twenty-first-century readers, even more extreme than they may have looked to readers of Potter's own time. The slippers Mr. Jeremy wears are dainty, greatly distorting Mr. Jeremy's real feet, which appear only after Mr. Jeremy escapes from the trout that almost devours him.

Mr. Jeremy is not a member of the nobility but of the middle class, as is shown by his being labeled *Mr.* Jeremy Fisher, yet he does have at least one friend who has been knighted—*Sir* Isaac Newton—whose cravat, blue dinner jacket, and speckled waistcoat rival Mr. Jeremy's clothing for gaudiness (53). His other friend in the book—Alderman Ptolemy Tortoise—wears only his badge of office on what looks like an ornamental ribbon around his neck in addition to his natural shell (55).

MacDonald recognizes that Potter's depiction of Mr. Jeremy and his activities satirizes "males-only entertainments" while corresponding to "the natures of these pond inhabitants." Like the gentlemen of leisure of Potter's own time as well as the Regency period, Jeremy goes fishing "more as an interesting sport and hobby than a livelihood" (97). In part, Potter seems here to be satirizing her own father, who spent most of his time in male-only environments and enjoyed fishing as recreation but certainly not as a means to gain a livelihood or as a necessity. Potter also seems to have modeled Mr. Jeremy's predation on her own father's and even her own predation, since she sometimes joined her father on his fishing trips and she often killed animals in the course of studying and painting them.

When Mr. Jeremy fails to bring any fish home with him, he furnishes his friends with a beautiful roast grasshopper in place of the fish he fails to catch. Thus, readers see that Mr. Jeremy does not fish for need: he has plenty to eat and to feed his friends. His ornate clothing, his cottage, and his dishes and silverware (depicted on 56) show that Mr. Jeremy does not need to catch fish in order to feed himself or his guests. According to MacDonald, "The elaborate details and copious quantities of the provisions all indicate the passion with which elegant cuisine is pursued among leisured gentlemen" (98). Potter's father certainly did not fish out of a need to feed his family and would probably have been offended had anyone suggested he fished primarily for anything other than recreation.

Mr. Jeremy's magnificent clothing also is an indication of his class status. He clearly is able to pay close attention to his wardrobe. It is difficult to distinguish between his striped pants and his natural skin color. Also, Sir Isaac Newton's waistcoat matches his skin. Potter shows the natural coloring of both creatures at the same time that she shows how ridiculous they look with such ornate clothing. When readers first see Mr. Jeremy, he lounges on his windowsill, leaning back and reading a newspaper, while a dragonfly looks on. One side of his double window is open, but it does not frame Mr. Jeremy. He leans back beyond the frame, his coat and right leg extending below it, as do his right knee and his left leg and slipper. He has on exquisite black slippers that cover his frog feet. He lounges against the window-frame as his right toe hangs nonchalantly in the water as does the tail of his magnificent red jacket, and his left foot extends to the top of the widow-frame. A white cravat is around his neck. Lush vegetation—"buttercups" the text says—grow at the edge of the pond where Mr. Jeremy lives (8–9). His house and his clothing and his apparent need not to work for a living emphasize his status as a person of leisure.

"The water," in Mr. Jeremy's house, Potter writes, "was all slippy-sloppy in the larder and in the back passage," thus creating an excellent environment for a frog, except that it contrasts markedly (and humorously) with the ornate clothes Mr. Jeremy wears and, incidentally, with the interiors of the houses in which the Potters lived and spent their vacations. He apparently has no idea how ridiculous he looks, but he does come across as a comic character who comes very close to meeting a tragic end. As he tiptoes through the water inside his house carrying an ornate dish and pitcher, he bends to look at a fairly ordinary snail climbing down an inside wall (9). Thus, for all his gentlemanly aspirations, he seems content to share his home with ordinary creatures. "Mr. Jeremy," Potter writes, "liked getting his feet wet; nobody ever scolded him, and he never caught cold." As he tiptoes through the house, the reader can see his waistcoat that picks up the colors of his pants and skin. His cuffed pants show that he wears very tight pants over his similarly colored skin (8–9). Seeing it is raining, he decides to engage in the gentlemanly pastime of fishing in hopes of providing "a dish of minnows" for Sir Isaac Newton and Mr. Jeremy himself.

Like a true person of leisure, Mr. Jeremy provides a nice roast for himself and Sir Isaac. The carving of the roast grasshopper at the table echoes and satirizes the carving of roasts at tables that characterizes middle-class dinners. However, the Alderman brings his own meal in a string bag since the alderman "eats salad" (12), again showing how realistic Potter is able to be even with animal characters as silly-appearing as Mr. Jeremy, Sir Isaac, and Alderman Ptolemy Tortoise. The appropriateness of the characters' names adds to the satire, as does the use of an important scientist's name as the newt's name and the name of an ancient Egyptian who was also a scientist as the tortoise's name. Children should be able to recognize the appropriateness of Newton and Tortoise. Adults may recognize the humor in Sir Isaac Newton and Ptolemy.

The picture of Mr. Jeremy digging bait also is a caricature. He wears his ornate clothes while digging daintily with a shovel and has a can nearby that matches his skin color labeled with the word "BAIT," in the midst of green vegetation. Part of a worm sticks out of the ground (13). This is the reader's first indication that Mr. Jeremy is at least successful in one aspect of his role as a predator. He catches his prey—worms—and hopes he will be able to use them to catch more prey.

Putting "on a macintosh, and a pair of shiny goloshes,"[5] he gets his fishing rod and basket, and hops to where he keeps his boat (14–15). Again, the picture shows just how ridiculous Mr. Jeremy looks with his creel bouncing on his back as he jumps with his mackintosh flapping behind him. Even when going fishing, he wears his tight pants (14).[6] Unlike the boats in the earlier versions of the tale, the boat in the book is itself a lily leaf in the pond, surrounded by other leaves and water lilies in bloom (14–15), thus making it a more natural part of the scenery than Mr. Jeremy's clothing is. He uses a reed pole to push the boat to the open water where he will fish (19). Once in the proper location, he gets out his tackle and attaches his float. He then ties a wriggling worm on his line, made of "a fine long white horse-hair" (20). He fishes for about an hour in the rain. The picture of Mr. Jeremy huddled over in his mackintosh reminds readers of how pathetically small Mr. Jeremy is in spite of his fancy clothes and in spite of Potter's always referring to him as "Mr." Since fishing is "getting tiresome," he decides to have his lunch (23), consisting of a butterfly sandwich (another indication of Mr. Jeremy's predatory nature), and to wait until the shower he is in is over (24). While Mr. Jeremy eats, "A great big water-beetle" tweaks the toe of one galosh, so he crosses "his legs up shorter, out of reach" (27), words that, when combined with the illustration for this action (26), remind readers again just how tiny Mr. Jeremy is: from his point of view, the water-beetle really is huge: its front legs easily span the tips of Mr. Jeremy's galoshes, which are the only parts of Mr. Jeremy visible in the illustration. Potter stresses Mr. Jeremy's vulnerability, not only with the water-beetle but also when Mr. Jeremy hears a noise and thinks, "I trust that is not a rat," and "I had better get away from here" (28). The picture accompanying these words lets the reader know what Mr. Jeremy does not: there are at least two rats nearby (29). Thus, according to what Mr. Jeremy himself implies, the place is dangerous. Before the story is over, Mr. Jeremy will get into grave danger.

After he begins fishing again, Mr. Jeremy gets a bite and experiences "a horrible surprise": he hooks "little Jack Sharp the stickleback, covered with spines" (32), a fish that is almost as big as Mr. Jeremy (34). The fish gets away but not before Mr. Jeremy hurts his fingers on Jack Sharp's stickles. In the meantime, "a shoal of other little fishes put their heads out, and laughed at Mr. Jeremy Fisher" (36), again emphasizing how vulnerable the frog is and how ridiculous he appears.

Potter foreshadows in words and picture what happens next to Mr. Jeremy. The words say, "And while Mr. Jeremy sat disconsolately on the edge of his boat—sucking his sore fingers and peering down into the water—a *much* worse thing happened; a really *frightful* thing it would have been, if Mr. Jeremy had not been wearing his macintosh" (39). The picture shows what looks like a monstrous fish with sharp teeth approaching one of Mr. Jeremy's feet (38). "An enormous trout," Potter writes, "seized Mr. Jeremy with a snap, 'Ow! Ow! Ow!' and then it turned and dived to the bottom of the pond" (40). The picture accompanying these words shows Mr. Jeremy's thin legs spread so that the galoshes are plainly visible with the rest of his body inside the trout's mouth while tiny fish, who seem smarter than Mr. Jeremy, get out of the trout's way (41). Mr. Jeremy the predator becomes Mr. Jeremy the prey who appears to be about to lose his life. However, the trout dislikes the taste of the mackintosh, so it spits Mr. Jeremy out and just swallows his galoshes (43). The picture illustrating this event shows tiny Mr. Jeremy swimming for the surface. Much more clearly depicted than Mr. Jeremy, the trout is shown in all its beauty. Mr. Jeremy is, after all, a frog, so the picture showing him without his galoshes shows regular frog feet that would enable him to swim much more swiftly than he could with galoshes on his feet. The picture also helps show how ridiculous it is for a frog to wear galoshes. The most important part of the picture belongs to the trout that is depicted in great detail with glowing colors while a much smaller Mr. Jeremy is depicted in muted colors. "Mr. Jeremy bounced up to the surface of the water, like a cork and the bubbles out of a soda water bottle" (44), words that emphasize Mr. Jeremy's passiveness in getting to the surface. The picture accompanying these words shows the frog's head and parts of what would be his hands above the water with the rest of him vaguely depicted beneath the surface. Beside him are bubbles rising toward the top of the water (45). Thus, through the accident of his wearing a mackintosh, Mr. Jeremy avoids death, and what saves him is ironically part of his ridiculous, ornate outfit.[7]

Mr. Jeremy then swims "with all his might to the edge of the pond" (45). The next picture clearly shows Mr. Jeremy in great detail with "his macintosh all in tatters" as he climbs from the pond (46). Hopping toward home, Mr. Jeremy says, "What a mercy that was not a pike" (48). Had it been a pike, the reader assumes, Mr. Jeremy would not have escaped alive. The reader learns just how timid and vulnerable Mr. Jeremy is when Mr. Jeremy says, "I have lost my rod and basket; but it does not much matter, for I am sure I should never have dared to go fishing again!" (48).

Mr. Jeremy puts "sticking plaster on his" sore fingers, and his friends do come to dinner. Sir Isaac Newton is clothed as gorgeously as Mr. Jeremy, but the only thing the alderman wears is his badge of office hung on a ribbon around his neck, and he carries his salad "in a string bag" (55). Mr. Jeremy serves Sir Isaac and himself "a roasted grasshopper" instead of minnows (56). The final picture shows Mr. Jeremy, seated at the head of the table, about to carve the roast in front of his guests (56). Potter thus continues throughout the book the idea that Mr. Jeremy, like Potter's father, is a member of the wealthy upper middle class, again participating in a decidedly middle-class activity.

The story contains one of Potter's usual patterns: a central character goes for an adventure. The adventure turns out to be more dangerous than the character anticipates. He comes near to getting devoured, much nearer than Peter comes in *The Tale of Peter Rabbit*. When the trout grabs Mr. Jeremy, he finds himself in an enclosed space: the mouth of the fish. Yet he manages to survive—to get out of the water and to continue to live. In symbolic terms, the womb Mr. Jeremy finds himself in is not at all nourishing or comforting. Mr. Jeremy, of course, achieves no great victory, but he does manage to survive. Yet he loses something in the process, for he vows he will never go fishing again.

Unlike Mr. McGregor in *The Tale of Peter Rabbit*, who almost captures Peter, the ogre in this story actually captures Mr. Jeremy and begins the process that seems will inevitably lead to devouring him, only to spit him out because of the taste of his mackintosh. Unlike Peter Rabbit, who at the urging of the sparrows refuses to give up and who later manages to get himself out of Mr. McGregor's garden, Mr. Jeremy escapes from the trout through a fortunate accident involving his choice of clothing. Although critics disagree about whether the adventure with Mr. McGregor destroys Peter's bravery, Potter leaves no doubt that Mr. Jeremy, who was never very brave, loses whatever bravery he may have had but still puts on a good face. Unlike Peter, Mr. Jeremy is no hero. Being spit out by the trout allows him figuratively to be reborn, but no growth occurs as a result. Peter Rabbit in his tale is certainly no predator. He steals vegetables but attacks no animals. Mr. Jeremy, however, is a predator who actually attacks worms and fish and eats insects. In turn, he becomes prey himself, not to a human being but to another animal—a fish that is in no way humanized—and he lives in a world with other predators he fears—the rats. Thus, in this work of fantasy, Potter realistically depicts some important aspects of animal life and the very real dangers they face.

The Story of a Fierce Bad Rabbit,
The Story of Miss Moppet,
and "The Sly Old Cat"

Beatrix Potter wrote *The Story of a Fierce Bad Rabbit* and *The Story of Miss Moppet* for very young children, even younger than the intended audience of most of her other books. Both books were written shortly after Norman Warne's death in August 1905 and published in 1906 in a format different from Potter's other books: instead of being her usual small books, they were published as fold-out books. Leslie Linder describes the original publication as involving for each book pictures and text arranged in pairs and using a wallet that folds out to show the pages. Linder adds that Potter projected three stories for this form, the third being "The Sly Old Cat," but only the two were published during Potter's lifetime (*History* 183). In *The History of the Writings of Beatrix Potter*, Linder has an illustration of the wallet both closed and open for "The Sly Old Cat" and provides a facsimile of its manuscript (beginning opposite 182); thus, Linder makes it clear that Potter had in mind the same kind of fold-out book that *The Story of the Fierce Bad Rabbit* and *The Story of Miss Moppet* originally were. In 1916, both *The Story of a Fierce Bad Rabbit* and *The Story of Miss Moppet* were reissued in Potter's usual small-book format because booksellers felt the original fold-out format was too difficult to keep in proper form (Linder 183).

All three of these stories are of interest for purposes of this study. The title of *The Story of a Fierce Bad Rabbit* is obviously humorous, although a child may not see any humor in it. Potter wrote it in response to a request from Louie Warne, one of Harold Warne's children, who thought Peter Rabbit was too nice and wanted a story of a rabbit that is not so nice (213). But the rabbit of the title is not just "naughty"; he's "fierce" and "bad." Can a rabbit really be bad and fierce? Probably not. The rabbit in this tale, however, is a bully. He steals a carrot from a good rabbit and scratches the good rabbit so that the good rabbit hides. The bad rabbit then sits on the bench he drove the good rabbit off of and begins eating the carrot. Then, a man creeps up behind the bad rabbit, thinking it is some kind of strange bird, and shoots his gun at it. Potter describes what happens next more in pictures than words. She writes, "This is what happens" (27). The picture accompanying these words shows a carrot, two paws of the rabbit, the rabbit's ears, and its tail, with its whiskers all around the picture (26).

When the man goes to the bench, he finds only the tail and carrot. Again, Potter uses the words simply to say, "this is all he finds on the bench" (28). The picture shows the carrot, the tail, and the bench with the man, rifle in his arms, running toward the bench (29). The good rabbit sees the man running by, an action again not said in the text but illustrated in the picture (30–31). The text says, "And it sees the bad Rabbit tearing past—without any tail or whiskers" (33). The illustration accompanying these words shows a rabbit minus tail and whiskers running (32). The bad rabbit thus narrowly escapes death, surviving only because the man does not hit it fatally. But the story ends before anything else happens. One of the ironies of the story is that the most fierce and bad character in the book is not the bad rabbit but the man.

The Story of Miss Moppet involves a kitten named Moppet, whose name probably identifies her as one of the three kittens that appear in Potter's book published in 1907, *The Tale of Tom Kitten*. She wears a pink bow tied around her neck. Potter identifies the other character in the story as the Mouse.[1] The Mouse is dressed in a green jacket and a red bowtie. The story involves an encounter between Miss Moppet and the Mouse. Miss Moppet thinks she hears "a mouse" (7).[2] The Mouse is not afraid of her. The Mouse peers out from a cupboard, and Miss Moppet jumps at him, hitting her head on the cupboard. To attract the Mouse, Miss Moppet pretends to be sick, "ties her head in a duster, and sits before the fire" (16). The illustrations in the book indicate that the *duster* is simply a cloth used to dust furniture. The Mouse comes close to Miss Moppet, and Miss Moppet catches the Mouse. Then, Potter writes, "because the Mouse has teased Miss Moppet—Miss Moppet thinks she will tease the Mouse; which is not at all nice of Miss Moppet" (27). Here Potter clearly refers to the way cats have of apparently teasing and playing with animals they catch. Miss Moppet ties the Mouse in the duster, "and tosses it about like a ball" (28). However, the picture that accompanies these words shows the Mouse peering out of a hole in the duster (29). Forgetting the hole, Miss Moppet unties the duster, apparently expecting the Mouse to still be there, but when she unties the duster, the Mouse is gone (30). The picture accompanying these words shows a very puzzled looking Miss Moppet (31). The Mouse, Potter writes, "has wriggled out and run away; and he is dancing a jig on the top of the cupboard" (33). The final picture shows the Mouse dancing on the cupboard, celebrating his escape from the cat and thus his victory (32).

This story again has a pattern that readers are familiar with in Potter's

Fierce Bad Rabbit, Miss Moppet, and "The Sly Old Cat" 103

works: a small creature finds him- or herself in an enclosed space. Although being enclosed in the duster presents potential death for the Mouse since after they play with mice, cats often kill them, Potter, possibly with very young readers in mind, does not even hint at such an eventuality. The Mouse then escapes from the closed space, and, after Miss Moppet discovers he is gone, he dances in celebration.

The Story of Miss Moppet is unusual for Potter in several ways. The child readers of Potter's day live in a world without Mickey Mouse and the mice of Disney's *Cinderella*. Their tendency would thus be to side with the cute kitten rather than the Mouse. But Potter makes it clear that both animals tease each other. Since neither is really hurt by the encounter, the child reader probably finds the ending satisfactory. Potter sympathizes with the cat, and, as she does in *The Tale of Two Bad Mice*, Potter sympathizes with a mouse, an animal that most parents would find unsympathetic and a pest.

The final of these stories for very young children is the one not published during Potter's lifetime, "The Sly Old Cat." It is a tale of a cat that invites a rat to a tea party. From several things that occur during the party, the rat learns that the cat probably intends to eat him "for dessert." When he realizes what is happening, he escapes. Potter calls the rat "poor Mr Rat."[3] However, the label for the rat and the title of the story are ironic since the rat ends up outsmarting the cat. He proves slyer than the cat, who hopes to devour the rat.

The rat dresses nicely for the party, wearing a jacket, a top hat, slippers, and a fancy outfit with a fancy collar. He enters and greets the cat very politely, bowing to the cat and removing his hat in the cat's presence. The cat greets the rat politely and offers him a chair. As Potter's illustration shows, however, the chair the cat offers him is much smaller than the one she sits in. When the rat sits in the chair, his head is much lower than the cat's head; when he tilts his head up, the tip of his nose barely goes as high as the table. The cat's polite words barely cover over the cat's real intention. The way she actually treats the rat contrasts markedly with her polite words. Potter seems to be commenting here on the kind of "polite" society that she encountered repeatedly as a child.

The cat then announces that she will eat the bread and butter first, leaving the crumbs for the rat. The rat begins to see through what is happening, recognizing that the cat treats visitors rudely.

The cat announces that she will have her tea and the cat can have the drops the cat leaves, and then, she says, she will eat dessert. It is at this point that the rat thinks that the cat will probably try to eat him for dessert and wishes he had not come to the tea party. The cat then begins to drink out of the milk jug itself, and the narrator comments that the cat tried to not leave any milk for the rat. The illustration accompanying these words shows the rat jumping on the table as he looks at the cat with her head tilted back and the milk jug covering her head up to the level of her eyes so that she can get every drop of milk to go into her mouth. This illustration foreshadows what will happen next: jumping "on the table," the rat pats the jug, so the jug slips completely over the cat's head. The rat then sits and drinks from the mug, eats some bread, puts a muffin in a bag, and leaves. Thus, Potter shows that the rat can act just as barbarically as the cat.

When the rat gets to his home, he takes off his hat and slippers, devours the muffin, and puts his feet on the table. Potter communicates these last pieces of information through the picture, not the words. The picture shows a very satisfied looking rat with his hands folded over his fat belly. Potter comments, "that is the end of the Rat." The cat, meanwhile, breaks the jug against the table leg. The final picture shows what looks like a human maid looking horrified at the cat who is in the middle of the mess the cat and rat have created. Potter ends the story writing, "that is the end of the Cat." By "the end," Potter probably does not allude to their deaths but instead just refers to their story.

The cat and rat are involved in what is supposed to be a civilized ritual with rules of its own: a tea party, something Potter treats at much more length in *The Tale of the Pie and the Patty-Pan*. In that story, she uncovers some of the barbarism that lay beneath some of the rituals of the society in which she grew up. In "The Sly Old Cat," the cat is the one that finds herself enclosed in a physical object. But she is at no time in danger of death and escapes by simply breaking the milk jug against the leg of the table at which the cat and rat sat earlier. The rat, however, realizes that he is in danger of losing his life, but by using his head, he manages to escape. Thus, the idea of escape is central to the story for both the rat and the cat, but the rat alone escapes from probable death. Here too Potter treats both cat and rat fairly sympathetically, but most adults would not view rats with sympathy.

In these three stories aimed at very young children, Potter uses simple terms and pictures to convey amusing tales. Still, she treats what are for her some serious topics: the very real dangers small animals face, some from humans and some from other animals, and the way that danger lurks beneath—and even within—the very manners that supposedly make a civilized society.

The Tale of Tom Kitten

The Tale of Tom Kitten deals with domesticated animals: cats and ducks. In it, Tabitha Twitchit tries to prepare her house and her three kittens for visitors who are coming over for tea. She cleans and combs the kittens and dresses them nicely. Tom looks especially uncomfortable in the tight-fitting clothes his mother puts on him (18). After dressing the kittens, Tabitha rather foolishly sends them outside to play in the garden, telling them to "walk on your hind legs. Keep away from the dirty ash-pit, and from Sally Henny-penny, and from the pig-stye and the Puddle-ducks" (20). The last prohibition Tabitha gives to her kittens turns out to be especially important. Still, she demands of her kittens much more than most little children can achieve. As is to be expected of mischievous kittens, they quickly find ways to mess up and lose their uncomfortable clothes.

Grinstein wonders whether the actions of Tabitha Twitchit are in some way a reflection of the way Beatrix Potter's mother treated her children. She gives the children almost impossible commands to fulfill and then is "affronted" when they do not fulfill them. Then, she lies to her visitors about what has happened to them (139). Grinstein is probably correct. However, it is difficult to imagine the Potter children having to be sent to their room or, after being sent to their room, creating the kind of chaos the kittens create once they are punished. Again, it seems important for readers to keep in mind the harshness of both Potter's parents upon occasion, especially Beatrix's recounting of the episode in which her hat blows off, something that reinforces her idea that she was destined to bring shame to her parents. For children to act the way Tom and his sisters do should not upset an understanding parent who would recognize how difficult it is for children not to get dirty when sent into a garden to play and who might at least be concerned about why her children no longer have their clothes. The story has overtones of *The Tale of Mrs. Tiggy-Winkle* with its anxiety about losing some items of clothing. Readers might prefer to have Tabitha Twitchit treat her kittens the way Peter Rabbit's mother treats him when he returns from his adventure in Mr. McGregor's garden, showing concern for him and for his well-being.

The command to walk on their hind legs, that is, to act in a way that is unnatural for the kittens, leads to the first mishap: Moppet and Mittens walk "unsteadily," step on their pinafores, and fall "on their noses." Consequently, their pinafores end up with "several green smears" (23). When they decide to climb on the rockery and sit on the garden wall, Moppet's "white tucker fell down onto the road" (24). Tom, who "was very fat" (19), had trouble jumping on the rocks and climbing on the wall. As he approaches the wall, he breaks ferns and loses his buttons (27). By the time he reaches the top of the wall, "He was all in pieces." His sisters attempt "to pull him together," but he loses his hat and all his remaining "buttons burst" (28).

The Puddle-ducks, about whom their mother had warned them, then come "doing the goose step" and walking in single file, "along the high road" (31). When they get to the wall where the kittens are, Rebecca and Jemima Puddle-duck put on the hat and tucker (35). Mittens then laughs so hard she falls onto the road. Her siblings follow her, and the rest of Tom's clothing falls off. The sisters ask Mr. Drake Puddle-duck to help them dress their brother (36). He picks up Tom's clothes and puts them on himself and says, "It's a very fine morning," and the three ducks walk down the road. The illustration shows that they walk through the barnyard (39–43). The Puddle-ducks look even more ridiculous in the clothing than the kittens do. The story ends with the Puddle-ducks going into a pond and losing the clothes they stole from the kittens: "And Mr. Drake Puddle-duck and Jemima and Rebecca have been looking for them ever since" (57). Thus, the tale becomes a humorous pourquoi tale telling why ducks often appear to be looking under the water with their rumps pointing to the sky.

In the meantime, the kittens' mother finds the kittens: "She pulled them off the wall, smacked them, and took them back to the house" (47), clearly demonstrating how angry she is at them for not keeping commands that seem to many readers overly harsh. At this point in the story, she utters one of Beatrix Potter's most impressive sentences: "My friends will arrive in a minute, and you are not fit to be seen; I am affronted" (47). She sends her kittens upstairs and lies to her friends, saying the kittens are "in bed with the measles" (48). Potter's text mentions all kinds of noises coming from overhead that "disturbed the dignity and repose of the tea-party." The illustration accompanying the words shows the kittens having a grand time messing up the bedroom (50–51). The next illustration shows Mrs. Twitchit with a surprised look on her face entering the bedroom which is a terrible mess. Two of the kittens hide while the third stands clearly in front of their mother with a hat on (53). The words accompanying this illustration only say, "And I think some day I shall have to make another, larger, book, to tell you more about Tom Kitten!" (52), something Potter does in *The Tale of Samuel Whiskers*. These words help contribute to the idea that, at least from the narrator's point of view, Potter's little books are part of one larger work and thus may be treated as such by readers and critics. These words about Potter's future work end the main action of the story. Yet Potter continues the book, writing about the Puddle-ducks losing the clothes and hunting underwater for them.

Some critics insist that Mr. Drake Puddle-duck is a villain. I doubt that children see him in that way. Instead, he just seems another funny character in a story full of funny characters.[1]

Potter's interruption saying that she has to tell more about Tom some day needlessly interrupts the narrative. The ending seems inappropriate since the tale focuses on the kittens rather than the ducks. Still, the tale is full of fun and whimsy and seems to be very popular with children and adults alike. The kittens act like little children, and Mrs. Twitchit acts very much like a slightly foolish, vain mother who demands too much of her children and administers punishment very foolishly. The story also shows that though she smacks her kittens, she still loves them since she imposes no additional punishment on them. Earlier, when the "very naughty" Tom scratches her, apparently while she combs him, the accompanying picture indicates that she does not punish him but simply licks her own paw where it hurts (14–15). Incidentally, Potter's dedication of the book "...TO ALL PICKLES /—ESPECIALLY THOSE THAT GET / UPON MY GARDEN WALL," indicates that her sympathies are with the three kittens.[2]

This tale has many similarities to *The Tale of Peter Rabbit*. The Twitchit family has three siblings, two girls and one boy, rather than the four of *The Tale of Peter Rabbit*. The male child is "naughty." Both mothers are very interested in putting their children into what, at least in the case of the male children, look like inappropriate, uncomfortable clothes. And both mothers warn their children against certain real danger; however, *The Tale of Peter Rabbit* is much more specific in terms of the danger involved—being caught by Mr. McGregor and put into a pie—than the danger in *The Tale of Tom Kitten*, which simply has a list of things to avoid. Peter it seems is much naughtier than Tom is, deliberately going where his mother warns him not to go, and the danger he faces turns out to be much greater than that Tom faces. Peter also gets into a situation in which it looks as though he cannot possibly escape death; Tom gets into no such situation. Unlike Peter, Tom doesn't seem to be in grave danger in the course of his and Moppet's and Muffin's adventures, and unlike Peter, Tom seems to enjoy all aspects of his adventure except his mother's catching him and smacking him. Nor does Tom suffer any of the consequences Peter suffers (feeling ill and having to be put to bed). And Tom shares his adventures with his sisters while Peter faces his demon alone. In fact, in *The Tale of Tom Kitten*, Tom faces no real demon. Although both Peter and Tom lose their clothes in the course of their adventures, as do Tom's sisters, Tom's adventure seems to be one of pure fun rather than one involving a life-and-death struggle. In fact, except in the foreshadowing of a later book, *The Tale of Samuel Whiskers*, Tom's adventures do not seem to involve even a hint of serious danger.

However, in *The Tale of Samuel Whiskers*, Tom faces very serious immediate danger, and he confronts an adversary that seems much more terrible than Mr. McGregor. Samuel Whiskers is an out-and-out villain who certainly outdoes foolish Mr. McGregor in his hideousness.[3] He also is a rat, and, as such, readers immediately associate him with a kind of villainy. In that later book, Potter clearly returns to the formula that works so well in her first book, with a few major differences that will be discussed later.

The Tale of Jemima Puddle-Duck

Throughout most of *The Tale of Jemima Puddle-Duck* (1908), Jemima has no idea that she is in danger. She goes through the steps of a rebirth process, and she does survive, but no rebirth in psychological or anthropological terms occurs.

Interestingly, Jemima's experience begins with a desire on her part to hatch her own eggs, since "the farmer's wife would not let her hatch" them (7); that is, she desires to be directly involved in a real birth. So she determines "to make a nest right away from the farm" (11). She climbs a hill, sees a wood, and decides, "it looked a safe quiet spot" (15), but for Jemima, a highly domesticated denizen of the farmyard, the wood turns out to be anything but safe. The picture following these words shows how absurd Jemima, in her cloak and bonnet, looks taking off (16), but once she is airborne, she flies "beautifully" after having "a good start" (19). The picture accompanying these words contradicts them: the flying may be beautiful, but in her cloak and bonnet, she still looks ridiculous (18). She flies over the wood until she finds a clearing where she lands. She wants to build her nest on "a tree stump amongst some tall fox-gloves," but "she was startled to find" on the stump "an elegantly dressed gentleman reading a newspaper. He had black prick ears and sandy colored whiskers" (20). Fox-gloves are, Heather A. Evans points out, "beautiful but poisonous flowers" (605). Their name along with their poisonous nature links them to the glove-wearing gentleman, but Jemima is too stupid to recognize any connections. In the course of the story, Potter even calls her "a simpleton" (39). The flowers' name lets the reader know that no matter how much a fox may dress up, he is still a fox and thus dangerous. He is, in effect, the ogre or serpent in the Eden in which Jemima foolishly thinks she finds herself.

Too stupid to sense danger, Jemima simply asks, "'Quack?' ... 'Quack?'" to the gentleman (20). Potter later appropriately calls Jemima a "simpleton" (39). She thinks the gentleman "mighty civil and handsome" and explains to

109

him that she is trying to "find a convenient dry nesting-place" (23). When she tells the gentleman about her situation and about the hen to which the farmer's wife gives her eggs to be hatched, he replies, "I wish I could meet that fowl. I would teach it to mind its own business" (24), words that Jemima fails to understand. Although they may not know the term *irony*, little children easily recognize Jemima's danger.

Even without the illustrations of Jemima that show how ridiculous she looks dressed in human clothes, the story is wildly humorous, largely because of Jemima's being such a simpleton. She goes through the tale completely unaware of the danger she is in, no matter how obvious that danger may be. M. Daphne Kutzer defends Jemima by pointing out that her "stupidity is not entirely her own fault" and explains that as a result of being a domesticated duck, "her wild instincts about foxes and their predatory natures have been dulled" (206). At the story's beginning and ending, when she is in a domestic setting, she wears no costume, possibly indicating that she is really more at home in a domestic than a wild setting. Jemima's costume alone indicates how out of place she is in the wild. Her unhappiness at not being able to hatch her own eggs indicates that she is also out of place in a domestic setting. She is then a foolish as well as a sympathetic creature. Still, it is doubtful that most of Potter's readers are concerned with excusing Jemima's foolishness. Instead, they laugh at it at the same time that they worry about what will happen to Jemima as a result of it.

As numerous critics have recognized, *The Tale of Jemima Puddle-Duck* is a kind of Little Red Riding-Hood tale. In Jemima's tale, the equivalent of the wolf is the fox. In both the Perrault and brothers Grimm versions of her tale, the Little Red Riding-Hood character is, like Jemima, a simpleton for not recognizing the danger the wolf presents. In Perrault's *Tales of Mother Goose*, she never becomes less of a simpleton. The wolf eats her, and the tale ends. In the brothers Grimm version (often called "Little Red-Cap"), however, Little Red-Cap goes through a symbolic rebirth process when a huntsman cuts open the wolf's belly and thus delivers her and her grandmother from the belly. As a result of their experiences, both she and her grandmother grow significantly, so much so that when Little Red-Cap next encounters a wolf, she and her grandmother work together to outsmart and destroy the wolf. Jemima, however, who does not get eaten by the fox, remains a simpleton from beginning to end. Putting Jemima's tale into the context of the brothers Grimm version of Little Red-Cap makes her lack of development all the more significant.

The wolf that Jemima considers a "gentleman" offers Jemima a place to build her nest. He has, he says, "a sackful of feathers" in his woodshed. He tells Jemima she may "sit there as long as" she likes (17). Still not recognizing her danger, Jemima never wonders where the feathers come from. When the gentleman shows her his "summer residence" (28), Potter indicates that the reader knows much more than poor Jemima: the gentleman leads Jemima to "a very retired, dismal-looking house amongst the fox-gloves" (27), a location that again indicates the danger that silly Jemima does not see and that belies the highfalutin term, "residence." As Jemima enters the shed, Potter's picture showing the fox winking indicates that the fox and the reader share the secret of Jemima's foolishness and her danger (29).

Jemima finds the shed "almost quite full of feathers—it was almost suffocating; but it was comfortable and very soft." Jemima "made a nest without any trouble at all" (31). As the picture accompanying these words shows, Jemima is in a warm, enclosed space (30). Even the feathers set off no alarms for Jemima, so she goes ahead and lays her eggs. Both she and her eggs are in a womb-like setting. But the picture of the fox peering through the slightly open door (30) lets readers know what Jemima does not know: her womb-like space is anything but safe. Jemima constantly misinterprets the fox's motives. As Potter writes, "He was so polite, that he seemed almost sorry to let Jemima go home for the night. He promised to take great care of her nest until she came back next day," and he tells Jemima that "he loved eggs and ducklings; he should be proud to see a fine nestful in his woodshed" (32). Returning every afternoon, Jemima lays nine eggs. "The foxy gentleman admired them immensely. He used to turn them over and count them when Jemima wasn't there" (35). In the picture accompanying these words, Potter lets readers see the fox in all his foxlike glory. He wears no clothes and is pure fox (35). After she lays all her eggs, Jemima says to the fox that the next day she will bring a bag of corn with her so that she can begin sitting on her eggs. The gentleman tells her he will supply her with oats, so she need not bring the corn. But since he intends "to give" Jemima "a treat," he asks her if she will bring "some herbs from the farm garden to make a savory omelet? Sage and thyme and mint and two onions, and some parsley. I will provide lard for the stuff—lard for the omelet" (35–36). Jemima, of course, has no idea that the word "stuff" would, if the gentlemen continues, have an *ing* on its end. Even the idea of an omelet does not upset her. Potter comments, "Jemima Puddle-duck was a simpleton: not even the mention of sage and onions made her suspicious" (39). Incidentally, *Mrs. Beeton's Book of Household Management* tells how to roast duck in recipe 934 and describes how to make the sage and onion stuffing for all kinds of poultry, including roast duck, in recipe 504. Potter makes what is going on even more explicit to her readers when she writes, Jemima "went round the farm garden, nibbling off snippets of all the different sorts of herbs that are used for stuffing roast duck" (39). When Kep, the collie, asks her what she's doing, Jemima tells him the whole story. In this instance, Jemima's being a simpleton helps save her life, since Kep recognizes Jemima's danger while Jemima has no idea what her words convey to the collie. He fetches two fox-hound puppies while Jemima flies to the wood and to the gentleman (40–43). When she lands, she sees him sniffing "the air and [...] glancing uneasily round the wood. When Jemima alighted he quite jumped." He says to her, "Come into the house as soon as you have looked at your eggs. Give me the herbs for the omelet. Be sharp!" He is, Potter writes, "rather abrupt. Jemima Puddle-duck had never heard him speak like that." Now, finally, probably because of the gentleman's abruptness, Jemima feels "surprised and uncomfortable" (47). The readers who look carefully at the picture accompanying these words can easily see why the fox sniffs the air and seems uneasy: Kep and the fox-hound puppies are visible near a large tree (47).

When Jemima is inside, she hears "pattering feet round the back of the shed. Someone with a black nose sniffed at the bottom of the door, and then locked it." Becoming "much alarmed," Jemima hears "barking, baying, growls and howls, squealing and groans" Then, Potter writes, "And nothing more was ever seen of the foxy-whiskered gentleman" (48–51).

Kep then lets Jemima out of the shed, and the puppies run in and gobble "up all the eggs." Kep has "a bite on his ear, and both the puppies were limping" (52). Jemima seems curiously unaware of their wounds. She cries, but for a different reason: "Jemima Puddle-duck was escorted home in tears on account of those eggs" (54). When she lays more eggs, the farmer's wife allows her to keep them to hatch herself, but only four hatch. "Jemima Puddle-duck said that it was because of her nerves; but she had always been a poor sitter" (57). The final picture in the book shows Jemima with her four ducklings near the farmhouse. She is not wearing clothes, and neither are the ducklings (56). As a result, she looks like a real duck with real ducklings in a yard with other animals: chickens and cows.

Jemima cries immediately after she is rescued, but only because her eggs are ruined. Apparently, she never understands the kind of danger she is in, just as she misinterprets the intentions of the foxy gentleman. When she last encounters the foxy gentleman, she realizes something is wrong, but never realizes what it is. She even provides the herbs for her own stuffing. Peter learns and grows from his danger. Jemima remains the same. Her hatching only four of her eggs could, from one point of view, appear to be a tragedy. However, that the foolish duck manages to hatch four could also seem to be wonderful. Although she does not hatch the eggs she lays in the wood, she is able to fulfill her dreams of motherhood, of bringing new life into the world.

It is easy to see sexual overtones in the tales of Little Red Riding-Hood. Several critics see similar overtones in *The Tale of Jemima Puddle-Duck*. Carpenter calls *The Tale of Jemima Puddle-Duck* "a masterly reworking of the Red Riding Hood Theme" ("Excessively Impertinent" 292). Sale writes that the tale of Jemima has in it "beast fable sexuality and innocence of animals of a different species" (153) and writes that Potter's "daring here is …great, because of all that is involved in making one's Little Red Riding Hood a mature female" (155). However, making Jemima not just a mature female but also a duck may undercut some of the "daring."

Sale also writes about Potter and *The Tale of Jemima Puddle-Duck*, "Just once, so far as I can see, did she allow herself to do a book about herself, though," he writes, one need not "see *Jemima Puddle-Duck* in this way, or insist that Potter did" (152).[1] Potter's own comment about what she considers the Freudian readings of Graham Greene indicates that she might not agree with Sale's ideas or might even find them offensive. Humphrey Carpenter points to "Potter's own obvious contempt for Jemima, who surrenders herself trustingly into the hands of 'the gentleman with the sandy whiskers,' a fox whose manners suggest the caddish seducer of a dairy maid [...]" ("Excessively Impertinent" 292). Carpenter's idea that Potter feels contempt for Jemima seems irrefutable, making it difficult but not impossible to believe that her portrait of Jemima is a kind of self-portrait. After all, many people do feel self-contempt, and in some of her journal entries, such as the one about her hat blowing off, Potter does show a degree of self-contempt. Still, she also shows compassion for the duck, giving her a happy ending. However, seeing Jemima as a self-portrait seems to distract readers from what is going on in the work. Still, according to Sarah Gristwood, Potter, in 1940, showed a visitor from New Zealand a picture of Jemima "rushing down the hill," and said, "that is what I used to look like to the Sawrey people. I rushed about quacking industriously" (138).

The Tale of Samuel Whiskers or The Roly-Poly Pudding

In *The Tale of Samuel Whiskers or the Roly-Poly Pudding*, originally named simply *The Roly-Poly Pudding* (1908), Tom Kitten has an experience that brings him to the brink of death. This tale clearly fulfills Potter's saying toward the end of *The Tale of Tom Kitten* that she thinks she will write "another, larger book, to tell you more about Tom Kitten!" (52). However, the tone of *The Tale of Samuel Whiskers* is much darker than the tone of *The Tale of Tom Kitten*.

Unlike Jemima, who is a mature duck in *The Tale of Jemima Puddle-Duck*, Tom, who is just a kitten, becomes fully aware of the terrible danger he wanders into as his adventure proceeds. As Daphne Kutzer points out, *The Tale of Samuel Whiskers* is "even more savage" than *The Tale of Jemima Puddle-Duck* (207). The horrible experience Tom undergoes changes him, but not necessarily for the better. Greene calls *The Tale of Samuel Whiskers* Potter's "masterpiece" (232), and Margaret Lane agrees (*Magic Years* 158). In fact, she calls it, "The finest" story in the group of stories "which Graham Greene, with affectionate mockery, calls her 'great near tragedies'" (*Magic Years* 160).[1] Humphrey Carpenter is a little more hesitant: he calls *The Tale of Samuel Whiskers* "perhaps Beatrix Potter's masterpiece [...]" (*Secret Gardens* 149).

The Tale of Samuel Whiskers involves what are, at least by human standards, really ugly, even horrifying villains and a very cute protagonist. The villains are rats, and the protagonist is a kitten. Readers are thus predisposed to sympathize with the protagonist and not with the villains. When they hear Tom's mother, Mrs. Tabitha Twitchit, tell her neighbor, Mrs. Ribby, another cat, that she has lost her "dear son Thomas" and that she is "afraid the rats have got him" (14), and adds that the whole house is "infested with rats [...]. I caught seven young ones out of one hole in the back kitchen, and we had them for dinner last Saturday" (*Tale of Samuel Whiskers* 19), instead of feeling sympathy for the rats and seeing in the probable devouring of Tom Kitten a kind of justice, most readers feel horror at the prospect of the rats' devouring Tom. Some also feel upset at the reversal of the usual predator-prey relationship: in popular culture, cats are supposed to devour rats; rats are not supposed to devour cats. Incidentally, many critics and biographers point out that the story is based on Potter's real-life adventures with the many rats who infested the farmhouse at Hill Top Farm when she first bought the place.

Yet Carpenter, in "Excessively Impertinent Bunnies," claims that Potter's own "sympathies are clearly with the ingenious, unscrupulous rats." He admires Tom's "enterprise in climbing up the chimney to escape imprisonment on baking day" and finds it preferable "to his sisters' caution" and "to his restraining, socially-conscious mother [...] and to her censorious neighbor Mrs. Ribby" (292–93). As outrageous as Carpenter's assertion about Potter's sympathies may at first seem, Potter provides at least one telling piece of evidence to support it: she dedicates her book:

> IN REMEMBRANCE OF
> "SAMMY,"
> THE INTELLIGENT PINK-EYED REPRESENTATIVE
> OF A PERSECUTED (BUT IRREPRESSIBLE) RACE
> AN AFFECTIONATE LITTLE FRIEND
> AND MOST ACCOMPLISHED THIEF [5]

Thus, she sets the stage for the story's being read on at least two levels: the child will probably come to the story with sympathy for the cats, especially Tom Kitten, because of his helplessness and cuteness. Some adults may sympathize with the rats, especially after Potter praises her real pet, calling Sammy "an affectionate little friend." Telling the reader about Sammy's pink eyes even gives him a kind of cuteness that may help open-minded readers feel more sympathy for the rats in her tale. Nonetheless, In *The Tale of Samuel Whiskers*, the rats are rats—not cute little mice.[2] In fact, the rats in *The Tale of Samuel Whiskers* are certainly not pets and are vicious. They tie Tom up, they debate while Tom hears them how to prepare him for baking, and they do it all in a strangely high-toned diction that makes them even more despicable. It seems inarguable that the rats are the most interesting characters in the story, even admirable in their viciousness, but hardly creatures to be regarded with sympathy. At any rate, Carpenter shows that in this tale, as in others, Potter really does write subversively, perhaps even upsetting what readers think of as the usual relations between cats and rats. Moreover, she puts an adorable, irrepressible, curious kitten into a terrible situation from which most readers are delighted to see him escape. Nonetheless, after the escape, he is still adorable but no longer irrepressible or curious.

Hiding from his mother, who wants to put him in a cupboard and does put his two sisters there to keep them out of trouble while she bakes, Tom wanders up the chimney. Incidentally, Potter puts a mock moral on Tom's going up the chimney: "it shows," she writes, "how very unwise it is to go up a chimney in a very old house, where a person does not know his way, and where there are enormous rats" (29).

Evans points out that the tale begins, "Once upon a time," and claims that these words make readers suspect that "Tom has bravely embarked on an adventure or quest which will provide him with the opportunity to prove his masculine mettle and return home to claim the rewards of manhood." But she goes on to say, correctly, that no such thing happens in Tom's case (604). Instead, he wanders through a series of narrow passages, and he has an adventure that terrifies him and, simultaneously, terrifies a number of readers of the tale. The symbolic journey through the birth canal in the case of Tom ends with a near death from which Tom escapes through none of his own resources.

As he wanders, he comes across some mutton bones and smells a funny smell that is, he says, "something like mouse, only dreadfully strong" (38). Unaware of what he actually smells, he goes through a hole in the wall. The picture that Potter uses to illustrate Tom's squeezing "through the hole in the wall" and dragging "himself along a most uncomfortably tight passage where there was scarcely any light" (40) shows a very uninviting jagged triangular hole in what look like rocks that make up a wall or chimney. Eventually, Tom "fell head over heels in the dark, down a hole, and landed on a heap of very dirty rags" (43), thus symbolically repeating a kind of passage through a birth canal leading not to birth but to probable death. When Tom exits the passage, he finds, "Opposite him—as far away as he could sit—[…] an enormous rat" (43). This rat is Samuel Whiskers, who is the ogre or serpent (or better yet, one of the ogres or serpents) in the anything but garden-like surroundings in which Tom now finds himself.

Samuel Whiskers calls his wife to come catch Tom and doesn't move as she ties him up in "very hard knots" (46). He initially seems a tyrant in his home who need not do any work. But his wife, Anna Maria, is his match.

After the kitten is captured, Samuel Whiskers orders, "Anna Maria, make me a kitten dumpling roly-poly pudding for my dinner." Then Samuel and Anna Maria argue about the recipe to be used:

> "It requires dough and a pat of butter and a rolling pin," said Anna Maria, considering Tom Kitten with her head on one side.
> "No," said Samuel Whiskers, "make it properly, Anna Maria, with breadcrumbs."
> "Nonsense! Butter and dough," replied Anna Maria [46–49].

The two rats thus treat Tom like a thing with no feelings. Apparently, Anna Maria wins, since the story both tells and shows the rats getting a rolling pin and some butter (50–53). Yet the matter-of-fact way the two rats discuss the proper way to make the pudding as Tom listens adds to the horror of Tom's situation.

The Tale of Samuel Whiskers or The Roly-Poly Pudding 117

While the rats are away gathering material to make the pudding, Tom tries unsuccessfully to escape from the knots. He tries "to mew for help," but cannot since "his mouth was full of soot and cobwebs, and he was tied up in such very tight knots, he could not make anybody hear him" (54). Unlike Jemima, he clearly recognizes the danger he is in and wishes to escape. Potter's use of "mew" instead of "scream" or "yell" indicates how helpless and impotent Tom is. The illustration that accompanies the words about Tom trying to "mew for help" shows a spider approaching him, but the spider offers no help. The spider looks at the knots "critically, from a safe distance" but does not say or do anything (54). Like the rats, the spider treats Tom like a thing rather than a person. The presence of the spider indicates that rats are not the only unpleasant thing in Tom's present surroundings, thus adding to the horror of the situation.

Most American readers are not familiar with roly-poly puddings. *Mrs. Beeton's Book of Household Management* recipe number 1291 is for a jam roly-poly pudding. It explains how to put the jam on a suet crust, roll the crust, tie it with a floured cloth, and boil it. Unfortunately, she does not explain how to make any kind of meat roly-poly pudding, much less a kitten roly-poly pudding, but presumably it would be the same as for a jam roly-poly pudding.

After the rats come back, they smear Tom "with butter, and then they rolled him in the dough" that Anna Maria stole from Tom's mother and put into a "borrowed" saucer (52–53). Adding to the horror of the whole situation is that Tabitha herself thus unwittingly supplies the dough in which the rats will wrap Tom.

"Will not the string be very indigestible, Anna Maria?" inquires Samuel Whiskers in coldly polite language. Anna Maria thinks the string's being indigestible is of "no consequence," but she wishes "Tom Kitten would hold his head still, as it disarranged the pastry. She laid hold of his ears" (56–57). Grabbing Tom's ears to make him hold his head still is another indication that the rats regard Tom as a thing rather than as a terrified little kitten. In symbolic terms, by rolling Tom in the dough, the Whiskers are putting him in his winding sheet, something in which he will be buried not in the ground but in their stomachs. The escape from the dough and the string and the rats is a kind of symbolic rebirth for Tom Kitten.

Tom is fully aware of the horror of his plight: "Tom Kitten bit and spit, and mewed and wriggled; and the rolling pin went roly-poly, roly; roly-poly roly. The rats each held an end" (59). The picture accompanying these actions clearly shows the horror on Tom Kitten's face. As the picture also shows, the dough does not cover Tom's tail:

> "His tail is sticking out! You did not fetch enough dough, Anna Maria."
> "I fetched as much as I could carry," replied Anna Maria.
> "I do not think"—said Samuel Whiskers, pausing to take a look at Tom Kitten—"I do *not* think it will be a good pudding. It smells sooty." [58–59].

118   *The Tale of Samuel Whiskers or The Roly-Poly Pudding*

The formality of Samuel Whisker's diction—notice the lack of contractions—adds to the horror just as does the matter-of-fact way he and Anna Maria discuss the proper way to make a kitten roly-poly pudding. Gillian Avery calls "the sinister Samuel Whiskers" "perhaps her [Potter's] greatest character" and compares him with R.L. Stevenson's Long John Silver, who is, Avery writes, "one of the supreme rogues of children's books." She also comments that the "Johnsonian prose" that Samuel Whiskers uses, "even at moments of crisis," increases "his balefulness" (199). It is ironic that Samuel Whiskers is based in part on one of Potter's own pets, a rat named Sammy, to whom Potter dedicates the book. In the dedication, she calls Sammy, "the intelligent pink-eyed representative of a persecuted (but irrepressible) race" and "an affectionate little friend and most accomplished thief." It is interesting that in the book, she does not make Samuel Whiskers' eyes pink. Still, she does make him admirable just as Long John Silver is admirable. Yet she certainly makes Tom's journey up the chimney and through the hole into the rats' den the stuff of nightmare.

Writing in 1977, John Fletcher goes so far as to say that "the modern paterfamilias" who reads this tale "cannot fail to tremble himself at this story. [...] If this did not give Miss Potter's little friends nightmares children must have been made of rather sterner stuff in those days" (71). The polite, overly correct conversations between Samuel Whiskers and Anna Maria probably fit into what Evans writes about the way Potter in many of her works "hints that the conventions of cultivated human society are often little more than a veneer to disguise animal drives, desires, and instincts." Using words that apply well to *The Tale of Jemima Puddle-Duck* and, in a way, to *The Tale of Samuel Whiskers*, Evans adds that in her tales, Potter shows "correspondences between the savagery of the animal world and the truculence of human behavior" as her "characters are [...] in danger of being consumed by animals that in nature would be their predators," and of becoming "a tasty baked good or savory dish fit for consumption by the most discerning human gastronomes" (605). It is difficult to believe that many of Potter's readers would even consider eating a kitten roly-poly pudding, but not many readers would turn down a roast duck dinner, and many would gladly eat rabbit-pie. Thus, readers may find Jemima Puddle-duck's adventures and even those of Potter's rabbits much less horrifying than those of Tom in *The Tale of Samuel Whiskers*.

As Anna Maria is about to argue with Samuel Whiskers about whether Tom will become "good pudding," the rats hear something, and Samuel Whiskers says, "We are discovered and interrupted, Anna Maria; let us collect our property—and other people's—and depart at once." Samuel Whisker's words here are a bit ambiguous: he says he does "*not* think it will be a good pudding"; the word "it" may refer to Tom in particular, continuing to treat Tom as

The Tale of Samuel Whiskers or The Roly-Poly Pudding

a thing, or "it" may be referring to the whole thing that the rats have prepared so far. Samuel adds:

> I fear that we shall be obliged to leave this pudding.
> But I am persuaded that the knots would have proved indigestible, whatever you may urge to the contrary [59–61].

The whole idea of a rat being concerned about his digestion adds to the horror of the situation: most house rats are known to eat almost anything, including electric wires, so having Samuel Whiskers worry about his digestion again humanizes him, increasing his villainy.

Potter adds to the horror of the situation by the things she shows in the first picture showing the two rats with Tom shortly after he falls into their den. In it, Anna Maria "rushed upon Tom Kitten" and begins to tie him up. Samuel Whiskers sits on a pile of rags, watching her. It looks as though he is about the take a pinch of snuff. His huge belly hangs over his knees. Both are unmistakably rats, but wear costumes not usually associated with rats, who in their native surroundings wear no clothes at all. Samuel Whiskers wears a bluish-green coat with tails and yellow and brown pants and a vest. He also wears what look like slippers on his feet. Anna Maria wears a full blue gown, also with what looks like a slipper on the one foot that is plainly visible. Her dress has a white hem at the bottom—or one of her petticoats shows beneath the dress. Her naked tail sticks out and forms an s-like shape behind her and pointing upwards. Thus, the rats' clothing makes them appear to be members of the upper-middle class, the same class to which the Potters belonged (47). Such properly clothed creatures with such impeccable manners add to the horror of the whole situation. They may be Potter's way of showing what she shows in other works, including *The Pie and the Patty-Pan:* beneath the façade of polite manners and polite speech lie all kinds of horrors: rats are still rats no matter how wonderful their diction and clothing are and no matter what part of polite society they belong to. Carpenter's idea that Potter's works are subversive certainly applies to *The Tale of Samuel Whiskers.* The overly polite rats are horrible, and the adult cats with their party manners are no match for the rats. Instead, after trying unsuccessfully to find Tom but hearing a roly-poly noise that gives them an idea of his location, they summon a workman, a "joiner," who is more than up to handling the menace the rats pose. The joiner is also a terrier, and terriers have a well deserved reputation of being excellent rat catchers.

When the rats hear noises and fear they have been discovered, John Joiner is cutting the board over the rats' dwelling, rescuing Tom through a sort of cesarean section, but the rats escape. In true terrier fashion, "Jon Joiner spent the rest of the morning sniffing and whining, and wagging his tail, and going round and round with his head in the hole like a gimlet" (63).

Although Potter shows Tabitha bathing Tom after he is rescued (64), Tabitha uses the dough that the rats put around Tom to make "a bag pudding, with currents in it to hide the smuts" (65). Perhaps Potter thus makes Tabitha herself almost as horrible as the rats since she does not do everything she can to eliminate all vestiges of the horror her kitten has been through. Granted, Tabitha is being a frugal, conscientious housekeeper in using every scrap of the dough, but she does not seem to be acting the way Potter (and many of her readers) might desire a loving mother to act.

When Tom's sisters grow up, they become "very good rat-catchers." They hang rats' tails on their door as a symbol of their prowess (72–74). They become the kinds of hunters that the beginning of the story, with its overtones of the quest, leads some readers to feel Tom will become. But Tom Kitten does not become like his sisters: he certainly does not become a brave hunter.

Although they may not realize it, many children are familiar with the sources of Jemima Puddle-duck and Tom Kitten before they read or have read to them Potter's tales: Many of them have heard "Little Red Riding-Hood." John Fletcher says Jemima "is rescued from a fate worse than death by the timely intervention of a collie dog" (71). Carpenter explicitly recognizes the relationship between Jemima's plight and that of Little Red Riding-Hood: "*The Tale of Jemima Puddle-Duck* ... is, as Beatrix Potter herself pointed out, a reworking of *Little Red Riding-Hood*," but Carpenter adds, "the sexual implications" in Potter's tale "are even clearer than in Perrault's story, with Jemima strongly suggesting an empty-headed maiden and the fox behaving exactly like an elegant, caddish Victorian seducer" (149). However, in *The Tale of Jemima Puddle-Duck*, Potter does not closely follow Perrault's version of the story of "Little Red Riding-Hood" since that tale ends with Little Red Riding-Hood and her grandmother in the wolf's belly.

Potter draws heavily from the versions of Red Riding-Hood's tale, like that of the brothers Grimm, in which an improbable woodsman or huntsman serves as a kind of *deus ex machina* and rescues Little Red and her grandmother. Because of what Jemima foolishly tells him, Kep has a good idea what is happening in the wood. Here, her foolishness becomes a valuable thing for her: it leads to her rescue. So unlike the intervention of the woodman in the Red-Riding Hood tale, Kep's intervention is not at all improbable. In *The Tale of Samuel Whiskers*, Ribby and Tabitha both know that rats are a present danger. So they send for John Joiner; thus, his appearance also is not improbable.

In several versions of *Little Red Riding-Hood*, including the one collected by the brothers Grimm, Little Red and her grandmother both grow from their experiences: another wolf tries to deceive them both, but they are not deceived. Instead, they use their brains and work together to kill the wolf. Unlike Little Red Riding-Hood and her grandmother and unlike Peter Rabbit, Jemima and Tom do not grow. Jemima remains the same; she is still what

Potter calls her early in the story: a simpleton. In *The Tale of Samuel Whiskers*, Tom deteriorates. He changes from being an adventurous, mischievous little kitten to being a grown cat who, Potter writes, "has always been afraid of a rat; he never durst face anything that is bigger than—" (75). Evans claims that Tom here "exhibits a kind of post-traumatic stress disorder" (619). Evans' words may seem to be stretching things a little until readers look more closely at the final illustration of the book and see the look of horror on Tom's face and the hair standing up on his back when he encounters a mouse (75). Still, Tom learns a survival technique from his adventures: if Tom carefully avoids rats, they will do him no harm. The picture accompanying these words shows that, in spite of what Potter writes at the end of the story, then, he is unwilling to face even a mouse. In fact, in this final picture, Tom's face and his body language indicate that a mouse terrifies him.

Thus, the processes of rebirth and initiation are not simple ones in Potter's works. Coming close to death and escaping does not in itself lead to growth. Perhaps for Potter, for true growth to occur, one must in some way be active in one's rescue, that is, at least participate in overcoming one's demon, as Peter does and as Jemima and Tom do not. At any rate, Potter recognizes that rebirth can lead simply to continued living or it may lead to genuine change. It may involve true initiation, or it may involve failed initiation. Potter is, in many ways, unrelentingly realistic in her works of fantasy, and her ideas about rebirth and initiation also seem unrelentingly realistic. They involve no simple formula to be followed in work after work.

The Tale of the Flopsy Bunnies

The Tale of the Flopsy Bunnies (1909) follows a pattern that was familiar to Potter's readers by 1909, the year of its publication. It fits nicely under the category tragicomedy, with bunnies almost getting destroyed. In it, Mr. McGregor is again the predator. His wife is at least as villainous as he is. And just as he is in *The Tale of Peter Rabbit*, here too he is a fool, and he and his wife end up destroying no bunnies at all.

The Flopsy Bunnies are children of Benjamin Bouncer and Peter's sister Flopsy. The book begins with Potter's writing about the supposed soporific effect of lettuce. As Potter states, "*I* have never felt sleepy after eating lettuces; but then *I* am not a rabbit" (7). Here Potter the narrator clearly separates herself from her rabbit characters but not from the story herself, something she shows when she says she cannot remember the names of individual bunnies. Yet her insights into what it is like to be a rabbit help make the story come alive as does the humor of her asserting that she really is not a rabbit.

Early in the story, Potter writes, "I do not remember the separate names of their children; they were generally called the 'Flopsy Bunnies'" (8). The picture that accompanies these words shows an individualized pair of adult rabbits who wear clothes that let readers know the one wearing a red jacket is Benjamin and the one in a blue dress with a baby in her lap and one at her side is Flopsy. The picture also shows four other young bunnies, none of whom is individualized (9). Not giving the bunnies separate names or in any other way individualizing them makes the probability of the bunnies' being slaughtered produce less anxiety for young children than the book would if Potter treated each bunny as an individual. Obviously, this book is not as anxiety-producing as *The Tale of Samuel Whiskers* or even *The Tale of Peter Rabbit*, nor do the bunnies themselves get terrified the way Tom Kitten does.

The action begins when the Flopsy Bunnies go into Mr. McGregor's garden because their family is "large" but "very improvident and cheerful" (8). When the family members have nothing to eat, they borrow cabbages from Peter, but "Sometimes Peter Rabbit had no cabbages to spare" (12). In *The Tale of Peter Rabbit*, as the picture shows when Peter returns after his adventures in the garden, Peter's family has plenty to eat. In *The Tale of the Flopsy Bunnies*, the Flopsy Bunnies go to the rubbish heap in a ditch outside Mr. McGregor's garden because they are hungry. There, they eat lettuce and fall asleep. Potter indicates that their father is most likely with them when they enter the garden by writing, "Benjamin was not so much overcome as his children," so he puts a paper bag over his face to keep off flies and then falls asleep (19). Thomasina Tittlemouse, a long-tailed woodmouse foraging for food in the rubbish heap, accidentally awakens Benjamin in time for Benjamin to see Mr. McGregor put the bunnies in a sack (20–24). It seems as though the McGregors will inevitably slaughter the bunnies.

Many of Potter's animals are almost always polite: when Thomasina wakes Benjamin, she apologizes "profusely, and said that she knew Peter Rabbit" (23). As Peter and Thomasina talk, Mr. McGregor comes and dumps grass he has mowed onto the heap. Peter and Thomasina hide (24), but the bunnies remain sleeping "because the lettuces had been so soporific." Mr. McGregor sees the tips of their ears (27). When a fly settles on one of the bunnies' ears, the ear moves, so Mr. McGregor realizes that he sees bunnies. Then, Mr. McGregor counts the rabbits as he puts them in his sack: "The Flopsy Bunnies dreamt that their mother was turning them over in bed. They stirred a little in their sleep, but still they did not wake up" (28). The picture shows Mr. McGregor's hand carefully putting one of the rabbits in the sack. Part of the head of another rabbit is already in the sack (29). Mr. McGregor then ties the sack up and puts it on the wall. Fortunately, he then goes to put the mowing machine away as Flopsy, who has entered the garden, notices the sack (32). Benjamin and Thomasina then come out from hiding. Benjamin tells Flopsy "the doleful tale." Despairing, Flopsy and Peter cannot untie the sack. But Mrs. Tittlemouse, "a resourceful person," nibbles "a hole in the bottom corner of the sack" (35), allowing their parents to pull them out and pinch them awake. Symbolically, the parents and Mrs. Tittlemouse deliver the babies by a kind of cesarean section, complete with pinching the babies awake instead of spanking them, a procedure many doctors used to practice immediately after delivering a child to help the child start to breathe. The parents then put "three rotten vegetable marrows, an old blacking-brush and two decayed turnips" into the sack (36). Incidentally, a vegetable marrow is a term for several kinds of squash; the term is more commonly used in England than in the United States.

The bunnies and their parents watch as Mr. McGregor carries the sack home to his wife. They follow him and listen as he counts aloud, "One, two, three, four, five, six leetle rabbits!" (44). Mrs. McGregor feels the lumps in the sack and decides they are too old to eat. She wants to use them to line her cloak. Mr. McGregor wants to sell them and buy tobacco. Mrs. McGregor then says, "Rabbit tobacco! I shall skin them and cut off their heads" (48), showing the kind of viciousness necessary for survival if one is gardening to feed oneself since rabbits are pests in gardens who eat food from the garden. Still, it is a viciousness not designed to endear readers toward the McGregors. When Mrs. McGregor learns what is really in the sack, she begins throwing the things in the sack at her husband: "She said that Mr. McGregor had 'done it a purpose'" (51). Though the rabbits in this story are "improvident," they have a loving family; the human beings seem to be well fed, but their family is dysfunctional and even involves physical abuse. Yet the whole episode inside the McGregors' house is humorous, thus eliminating some of the anxiety it might produce in children.

When one of the rotten marrows hits one of the bunnies accidentally, the rabbits wisely decide it is time to go home (52–54). The illustration that accompanies the words about the thrown marrow shows Flopsy carrying one of the bunnies, probably the one the marrow hits, as the rabbits hurry out of the garden (55). Thus, the illustration shows the kind of loving concern the rabbits have for one another in contrast to the anger for one another the McGregors show.

For the next Christmas, Thomasina Tittlemouse receives "a present of enough rabbit-wool to make herself a cloak and hood, and a handsome muff and pair of mittens" (57). She rescues the bunnies apparently without thought of reward. But the rabbits repay her generosity with more generosity, giving her something she can use and they can spare. Ironically, the rabbits give Thomasina a gift that enables her to keep warm in the winter instead of having Mrs. McGregor line her cloak with rabbit fur. Thomasina's creativity harms no one; Mrs. McGregor's creativity and Mr. McGregor's avarice would do great harm to the rabbit family. In addition, the interspecies' cooperation that frees the Flopsy Bunnies contrasts with the conflict of the members of the human family. Moreover, the love the bunnies show one another contrasts with the animosity that characterizes the McGregors. Finally, the ability of the animals to think their way through their difficulties contrasts with the lack of clear thinking the McGregors exhibit.

Thus, a tale that borders on tragedy ends happily for the rabbits. Just when it seems that the McGregors will inevitably slaughter the bunnies, the adult rabbits and Mrs. Tittlemouse manage to rescue them, in large part by using their minds and cooperating with one another. The bunnies not only live but also see how foolish the McGregors are. And readers see how well the cooperation between the bunnies' parents and Mrs. Tittlemouse works out.

There is no clear-cut hero in the story, but Mrs. Tittlemouse is a kind of hero for her role in rescuing the bunnies. Through cooperation and ratiocination, the adult rabbits and the mouse achieve a victory over an enemy who is much stronger and is supposed to be much more resourceful than they are, for the enemy is human and they are animals that humans often consider pests. The Flopsy Bunnies, who are in no way responsible for their own survival, do not grow in the course of this story, even though they are involved in a kind of rebirth. Like several of Potter's other characters who undergo rebirths, they remain the same, at least as far as readers can tell from *The Tale of the Flopsy Bunnies*.

The Tale of Ginger and Pickles

Children love *The Tale of Ginger and Pickles* (1909) in part because it involves so many of the characters in other works by Potter. Many of the creatures in Potter's earlier works come to shop at the store Ginger, a tom-cat, and Pickles, a terrier, run: for example, Lucinda and Jane-Doll-cook shop there (7), as do Mr. Jeremy Fisher, Peter Rabbit and his sisters, and Samuel Whiskers (9).[1] Adults love many of the jokes in the tale that seem to be aimed exclusively at them, such as those involving credit.

Ginger and Pickles offer credit to everyone, and their customers take unfair advantage of that offer, never paying for the items they get. Soon, Ginger and Pickles have to go out of business. Grinstein points out that with its "combination of elements from reality and from fantasy," the tale has a surrealistic quality to it (164). The same kind of combination, of course, can be found in all of Potter's books, with their animals with human traits. However, as Grinstein adds, the "totally unreal type of business policy" Ginger and Pickles follow, especially when compared to the matter-of-fact business policies that the inhabitants of a town like Sawrey would practice, adds to the dreamlike quality of the book (164).[2]

Even in a tale as silly as this one, Potter remains true to animal nature. Ginger, a cat, cannot wait on the mice since they make her mouth water. The rabbits fear Pickles, who is a terrier, and Pickles admits he feels the same way about rats as Ginger does about mice, and adds, "It would never do to eat our customers; they would go to Tabitha Twitchit's." Ginger replies to Pickles, "On the contrary, they would go nowhere" (12). Even fairly young children might be able to understand the humor here. After the store closes, "Ginger is living in the warren. I do not know," Potter writes, "what occupation he pursues; he looks stout and comfortable" (38). Potter's black and white illustration accompanying these words shows him wearing a coat and setting a trap in front of a rabbit hole (39). "Pickles," Potter writes, "is at present a gamekeeper" (41). The color illustration accompanying these words shows him wearing a coat and carrying a rifle as he walks hunched over on two legs alongside a stone wall. A rabbit peers around a corner of the wall as Pickles approaches. Two other rabbits are at the roots of a tree; one looks in Pickles' direction. The reader sees only the tail of the other (40). Pickles' new profession is appropriate for him since terriers were bred to hunt small animals, such as rats and even foxes, and pursue them into their dens.[3]

In this comic tale, two predators have great trouble, in part because they suppress their predatory instincts. They try to be what they are not. For Ginger not to attack mice, for Pickles not to attack rats is contrary to all the realism in most of Potter's books. Both appropriately cannot find happiness running the store since it demands that they go against their animal natures. Both end up following their animal instincts. Doing so leads to Ginger's being "stout and comfortable" (38). Readers have only a picture to use to try to find out how Pickles feels about his new occupation as a gamekeeper, but the picture shows him with a gun stalking rabbits, an occupation in keeping with his predatory instincts. The two animals, then, are in a sense reborn as what they were meant to be, not shopkeepers but predators in the world of Potter's books, a world composed at Potter's best of animals involved in a nature that is extremely dangerous often for both predator and prey. It is possible to read the struggles of Ginger and Pickles to find their true natures and occupations as paralleling those of Potter herself, whose parents wanted her to be dependent on them throughout their lives and who wanted to follow her own desires, finding at least an initial escape when she found her true occupation, not as an illustrator of scientific texts, an occupation unavailable to her as a female without a formal education, but as an illustrator and author of children's books, an occupation available in Victorian England to females without formal educations.

The discussions involving money may present problems to some American readers, both adult and child. However, young child readers (or more likely, auditors) would probably have the same problems if the prices in the book were converted into dollars and cents. Here, adult readers can take a lesson from children: enjoy the work on a child's level and not worry about exactly how much £3 19 11¾ is.

The Tale of Mrs. Tittlemouse

In *The Tale of Mrs. Tittlemouse* (1910), the title character, Mrs. Tittlemouse, is what Potter calls, "a wood-mouse" (7); she is a very tidy housekeeper who is woefully out of place in her home "in a bank under a hedge" (7) because she has so much trouble keeping it clean and neat. Since mice are often treated as nasty, dirty vermin and even wood mice are considered by some to be vermin, the idea that Mrs. Tittlemouse should be clean probably comes as a surprise to some adults. Potter, however, kept pet mice and observed wild mice, so she clearly knew something about their habits. Still, just as Hunca Munca's cleaning the dollhouse in *The Tale of Two Bad Mice* is a little far-fetched, so is the extent to which Mrs. Tittlemouse keeps her house clean. It is almost as though Potter is trying to satirize people with an obsessive-compulsive disorder that involves a cleaning fetish. When insects and spiders inevitably get into her tidy house, she gets very upset because they bring dirt with them. One of her uninvited guests is Mr. Jackson, a toad who "lived in a drain below the hedge, in a very dirty wet ditch" (28). Yet ironically Mr. Jackson ultimately helps Mrs. Tittlemouse keep her house clean, and she figures out a way to keep him out of her house and still maintain friendship with him.[1] Part of the delight of this little book involves the way Mrs. Tittlemouse is at war with her environment, demanding cleanliness in a situation that is full of things that disrupt her attempts to keep her home clean.

Like *The Tale of Mrs. Tiggy-Winkle*, *The Tale of Mrs. Tittlemouse* seems to be more appealing to girls than boys. In fact, Potter herself wrote on 30 June 1910 to Harold Warne, her publisher, predicting the book's popularity with girls (*Letters* 181). The book was published the following month: in July. This tale is similar to *The Tale of Mrs. Tiggy-Winkle* since it does not verge on tragedy but involves a concern for keeping a house cleaner than one would expect such a house to be kept, just as Lucie is more upset by the disappearance of her things than the situation seems to warrant. The main comedy of the tale involves Mrs. Tittlemouse's attempts to keep her house clean and Mr. Jackson's unwittingly helping her succeed.

After Potter describes Mrs. Tittlemouse's "funny house" (8), she shows the difficulty Mrs. Tittlemouse has keeping it clean, especially since she is "a most terribly tidy particular little mouse, always sweeping and dusting the soft sandy floors" (12). When a beetle enters her house, she clatters her dustpan at it and says, "Shuh! Shuh! little dirty feet" (12). The accompanying picture shows that she drives the beetle away (13). A ladybird (more commonly called a ladybug in America) enters the house. Potter describes it as "a little old woman" who "runs up and down in a red spotty cloak" (15). Even without the picture that clearly shows a ladybug, American children might recognize that the English ladybird is a ladybug from the way Mrs. Tittlemouse gets rid of it by saying, "Your house is on fire, Mother Ladybird! Fly away home to your children" (15). In another reference to a nursery rhyme, a spider enters Mrs. Tittlemouse's house to escape from the rain, and asks Mrs. Tittlemouse, "Beg pardon, is this not Miss Muffet's?" to which Mrs. Tittlemouse replies, "Go away, you bold bad spider! Leaving ends of cobweb all over my nice clean house!" (16). Just as *The Tale of Mrs. Tiggy-Winkle* may be read as embodying some of Potter's rebellion against her mother's demands on her to keep track of her things, so *The Tale of Mrs. Tittlemouse* may be read as Potter's reaction to her mother's demands that servants keep the house clean and, more importantly, that Potter herself be sure the servants do their jobs.

The Tale of Timmy Tiptoes

The Tale of Timmy Tiptoes (1911) is one of Potter's stranger stories. Still, it involves some familiar patterns, including a small animal that gets into grave danger, entrance (in this case involuntary) into an enclosed space, and exit from that space. Potter uses animals in the story that were familiar to American readers, who were becoming more and more interesting to Beatrix Potter as a result of her correspondence with some American children and their parents and the visits they paid her. She seemed to have a special kind of admiration for American children and parents, and as she got older, she often thought of them as having more respect for the work she did than her English readers had. Emily Zach goes so far as to write that *The Tale of Timmy Tiptoes* occurs "in the American eastern woodlands" (223), probably because the book includes American animals. Linder writes that Potter wrote this tale "primarily for American children" (*History* 208), probably because of the American animals in it. *The Tale of Timmy Tiptoes*, Potter felt, includes animals that American readers would find familiar: gray squirrels, chipmunks, and brown bears. Yet in Potter's time, gray squirrels were fairly common around Sawrey. On 6 March 1919, Potter wrote letters to two siblings, Neville and Eileen Rowson (British, not American), who wrote to her praising her books. In their letter, Eileen included colored drawings of some of Potter's animals. Potter wrote to Eileen that to draw a chipmunk, she went to a cousin of hers who had one, and for the brown bear, she went to the zoo, presumably the London Zoo (Potter, *Letters to Children* 191). Clearly, she still was very concerned with realistic depictions of the animals in her stories both in terms of their actions and their appearance in her artwork. If the book is set in woodlands in the eastern United States, it is obviously one of Potter's imagining rather than one she actually saw. In addition, even though she says she used a chipmunk belonging to a cousin and went to the zoo to draw the bear, some critics say her animals in this story look stuffed.[1]

The story involves a pair of gray squirrels, Timmy Tiptoes and his wife Goody; and a pair of chipmunks, Chippy Hackee and his wife, who has no name of her own but is simply called, Mrs. Chippy Hackee. When the two wives meet, Potter clearly shows the squirrel larger than the chipmunk (37). Chippy Hackee she describes as "a small striped Chipmunk" (31).

The story begins with Timmy and Goody talking about gathering nuts so they will have something to eat when they wake up in the spring after "being sound asleep all winter" (8).[2] Their nest, Goody says, is "snug" so they can sleep soundly all winter, but there is nothing in it to eat in the spring (8). When they go out to gather nuts, they discover other squirrels are already there. Still, the two squirrels gather nuts, working "quietly by themselves" (11). The illustration that accompanies these words shows Timmy hanging his jacket on a twig, Goody bending down and looking at the ground, and four other squirrels in the background (12). For days, they go out and gather nuts and store them in some hollow stumps near their nest. They fill the stumps and begin to store nuts in a woodpecker hole way up in a tree. When Goody wonders how they will get the nuts out, Timmy says he will be much thinner after winter is over (15), implying that he will then easily be able to get the nuts out.

According to Potter, squirrels that hide their nuts in holes in trees tend not to lose them; ones that bury them "lose more than half" (16). A particular squirrel called Silvertail digs but cannot remember where his nuts are. He then digs up some nuts that do not belong to him, which starts a fight; "And other squirrels began to dig—the whole woods was in commotion!" (16). At the same time, some birds fly by, "twittering different songs." One sang, "Who's been digging-up *my* nuts? Who's-been-digging-up *my* nuts?" Another one sang, "Little bit-a-bread and-*no* cheese! Little bit-a-bread an'-*no*-cheese!" (19). The bird singing about digging up nuts "did not expect an answer. It was only singing its natural song and meant nothing at all" (20), but hearing the song, the squirrels attack Timmy Tiptoes, who runs toward his nest with the squirrels following him (23). They catch Timmy Tiptoes, drag him up the tree where he and Goody store nuts, and force him into the hole. Silvertail, the squirrel that was really digging up other squirrels' nuts, says they will leave Timmy there until he confesses (24). Some of Potter's squirrels, then, are not so different from people. Not knowing what happened to Timmy, Goody goes home. She makes tea for Timmy Tiptoes, but he, of course, does not come. The next day, she tries to find him but cannot (29).

Timmy Tiptoes finds himself "tucked up in a little moss bed, very much in the dark, feeling sore; it seemed to be under ground. Timmy coughed and groaned, because his ribs hurt [sic] him." He hears a chirpy noise and sees Chippy Hackee, who "appeared with a night light, and hoped he felt better." The house, of course, is "full of provisions" because of all the nuts Timmy and Goody poured into it (32). While Timmy is in bed, Chippy "'ticed him to eat quantities" of nuts, so Timmy grows fatter than he was (32), thus making it very difficult for Timmy to get out through the hole in the tree. In the meantime, Goody gathers more nuts and hides them under a root of a tree. "Once when Goody emptied an extra big bagful, there was a decided squeak; and next time Goody brought another bagful, a little striped Chipmunk scrambled out in a hurry" (35). The chipmunk is Chippy's wife. Goody tells her about Timmy's being missing, and Chippy's wife tells her that Chippy has run away. She knows where Chippy is because "a little bird told" her (36) and shows Goody where they are in the tree where Timmy and Goody stored nuts. Though Mrs. Chippy Hackee can fit into the hole, she says she will not go into it because "Chippy Hackee bites!" (40). In the meantime, the two women hear "a fat squirrel voice and a thin squirrel voice" singing (39).

Goody calls into the hole, "Timmy Tiptoes! Oh fie, Timmy Tiptoes!" and Timmy replies, "Is that you, Goody Tiptoes? Why, certainly!" He kisses Goody through the hole, but cannot get out because he is so fat (43). The picture accompanying these words shows Timmy with his head out of the hole and Goody looking up at him (42). Chippy is not too fat, but he just does not want to come out: "He stayed down below and chuckled" (43). Thus, Potter clearly differentiates between the two male animals.

In a fortnight, a big wind blows the top off the hollow tree, opens the hole, and lets rain in. Timmy comes out and goes "home with an umbrella" (44). Only the picture shows that Goody probably brings the umbrella, under which Timmy and Goody walk home (45). Chippy remains in the tree "for another week, although it was uncomfortable" (47), but when he sees a large bear that may be hunting for nuts "sniffing around" (48), he too goes home (51). When Chippy gets home, he discovers he has a head cold (52). As Potter's picture indicates, his wife takes care of him (53). Mrs. Chippy Hackee is thus like Peter Rabbit's mother who accepts Peter back into the house and treats him with love though he has lost some clothing and clearly been doing what he was not supposed to do.

From that time on, Timmy and Goody fasten their nuts "up with a little padlock" (54). The picture accompanying these words shows Timmy locking a small door in the tree where they live and Goody with three little squirrels, one nestled in her arm and two in a little cloth swing that she holds (55). Timmy thus appears as the thrifty father who provides for his family and Goody as the caring mother. Incidentally, the story also illustrates love of husband and wife and children, and in the case of Mrs. Chippy Hackee, forgiveness as a part of love.

Strangely, the story ends not with Timmy Tiptoes but with Chippy and his wife: "And whenever that little bird sees the Chipmunks, he sings—'Who's-been-digging-up *my*-nuts? Who's been digging-up *my*-nuts?'" The picture accompanying these words shows a bird heading for Mrs. Hackee, who wears what looks like a blue housecoat and looks up at the bird while she holds up a tattered umbrella to fend off the bird (56). The final words of the book are, "But nobody ever answers!" (57).

This book seems more careless than most of Potter's books. Zach goes so far as to call it Potter's "least pleasing" story because it deals with a setting with which Potter was unfamiliar (223). Lear calls it Potter's "least satisfactory" tale (237). Especially puzzling is the title's referring to Timmy and the interaction between the birds and the Tiptoes that leads to Timmy's being stuffed in the tree, but the book's ending focusing on the Hackees involving their interaction with "the bird" since no interaction between the bird and Chippy occurs earlier in the story. In the course of the book, Chippy seems to become more interesting and thus perhaps a better focal character. Still, Timmy's descent underground and reemergence seems more important than that of the chipmunk, who for no reason Potter gives stays away from his wife and then returns when he is afraid to stay away any longer, who accepts his wife's care when he returns, and who watches as his wife fends off the bird. When Chippy is away, his wife cannot even visit him because he bites. The squirrels, however, have a warm, loving relationship throughout the book. Timmy cannot return to his wife because he is too fat to squeeze through the hole. He only gets into the hole because the other squirrels force him in, and he suffers great pain as a result. As soon as he is able, he returns to his wife.

Timmy goes through some of the classic steps of rebirth that occur in many of Potter's little books: he enters a confined space and then leaves it. As a result of his adventure, he and his wife seem to have gained some knowledge, learning to lock up his nuts, thus ultimately becoming a better able to care for their family.

The Tale of Mr. Tod

Many readers, from Graham Greene to Roger Sale, consider *The Tale of Samuel Whiskers* (1908) and *The Tale of Mr. Tod* (1912) to be among Beatrix Potter's best, most mature, darkest works. They use the word "masterpiece" in describing them.[1] Like so many of her works, both *The Tale of Samuel Whiskers* and *The Tale of Mr. Tod* deal with predator-prey relationships, and both involve narrow escapes from what looks like certain death. In the earlier work, the central character, Tom Kitten, escapes certain death through none of his own actions: when his aunt, Mrs. Ribby, who is visiting Tom's mother, and Tom's mother cannot find Tom, when Mittens tells of the big rat she saw stealing butter and a rolling-pin, and most of all, when Ribby and Tabitha realize they heard a "roly-poly noise" "under the attic floor," Mrs. Ribby tells Tom's mother, "This is serious," and says they "must send for John Joiner at once, with a saw" (26–28); thus, the rescue is set in motion. John Joiner, a terrier, then comes and rescues Tom. In *The Tale of Mr. Tod*, the Flopsy bunnies also face what looks like certain death, but that story contains little of the kind of horror that *The Tale of Samuel Whiskers* does. As the bunnies do in *The Tale of the Flopsy Bunnies*, the ones in *The Tale of Mr. Tod* escape through none of their own actions: their uncle, Peter Rabbit, and their father, Benjamin, rescue them. In *The Tale of Mr. Tod*, the baby rabbits do not even appear in the illustrations as individuals or as a group in the part of the book that deals with their kidnapping and rescue. Instead, they are inside a sack into which Tommy Brock, a badger, puts them and later, while still in the sack, inside an oven in Mr. Tod's house. They are in no way individualized or humanized. Only before their kidnapping and after their rescue do readers see pictures of the baby bunnies themselves. In the first illustration in the book, five rabbits peer over a wall at a fox (7); the rabbits appear too old to be the offspring of Flopsy and Benjamin that are kidnapped in the book. Also, before their abduction, four bunnies appear as a group huddled together in their "shallow burrow"; an adult rabbit, who may be their mother, sits outside the burrow facing not the bunnies but the reader (12); these rabbits also appear to be too old to be the helpless babies that get kidnapped. Throughout most of the book, Potter neither individualizes the baby bunnies nor humanizes them in any way. They are not clothed and are not given individual names. Nor does Potter show anyone giving the bunnies any affection before they are rescued. After their rescue, Potter shows what appears to be one of them safely in its mother's arms with its father, uncle, and grandfather nearby (79). In this illustration, Potter clearly humanizes Flopsy, who is their mother, and by implication, the bunny since a real rabbit could not possibly hold a baby the way Flopsy holds her baby—but this picture occurs only after the bunnies are out of danger. Not humanizing the baby bunnies before or during their abduction helps child readers handle the kind of tension involved in the possibility of the baby bunnies' being eaten.

The Tale of Peter Rabbit and *The Tale of the Flopsy Bunnies* involve real dangers, but these early tales are not nearly as dark as *The Tale of Samuel Whiskers* and *The Tale of Mr. Tod*. In *The Tale of the Flopsy Bunnies*, the villain is a comical Mr. McGregor and his equally comical wife, and although the threats they present are very real, the two of them are nowhere near as vicious as Tommy Brock or Mr. Tod.[2] At first, it seems ironic that the fox's tale seems darker and the fox appears to be a greater villain than the rabbit-destroying humans of the earlier books since in reality, the greatest threat to wild animals, at least in Potter's England, is people and their activities. And though the McGregors and Mr. Tod as well as Tommy Brock engage in activities that at times are comical, the enmity between Tommy Brock and Mr. Tod has a vicious, human side to it. In fact, Sale quite rightly points out that the enmity between these two "is closer to human enmity than" that between fox or badger (160). This closeness to human enmity and Potter's ability to make the characters both animal and human add to the horror of the book. It is interesting that in a later book, *The Tale of Pigling Bland*, Potter creates a human villain, Mr. Peter Thomas Piperson, who rivals—perhaps even outdoes—Mr. Tod and Tommy Brock for nastiness.

In the beginning of *The Tale of Mr. Tod*, Potter immediately announces that this book involves characters different from those in most of her other books: "I have made many books about well-behaved people. Now, for a change, I am going to make a story about two disagreeable people, called Tommy Brock and Mr. Tod" (7). Actually, "disagreeable" is an understatement. Their being comic figures by the time the book ends makes them no less vicious. Incidentally, Mr. Piperson never becomes a comic figure.

In Potter's illustrations, Mr. Tod resembles the fox that tries to make a dinner of Jemima Puddle-duck and her eggs. Some readers feel it is the same fox. Others argue that the fox in *The Tale of Jemima Puddle-Duck* cannot be the same as the one in *The Tale of Mr. Tod*, since the earlier book says, after the dogs chase Mr. Fox away, "nothing more was ever seen of the foxy-whiskered gentleman" (51).[3]

In this later book, Potter writes, "Nobody could call Mr. Tod 'nice.' The rabbits could not bear him; they could smell him half a mile off. He was of a wandering habit and he had foxy whiskers; they never knew where he would be next" (7). The rabbits are not domesticated; they have none of the protections that Jemima has on the farm where she lives; she consequently loses her instinctive ability to recognize how dangerous a fox is. She would not hesitate to call the fox "nice," although she does not use that exact word. Instead, she "thought him mighty civil and handsome" (23). In *The Tale of Mr. Tod*, the adult rabbits know the fox is a villain and regard him as such. If they were simpletons, like Jemima, they could not survive in the wild.

Tommy Brock is also a villain, but, unlike Mr. Tod, Tommy Brock is villainous, it seems, only when the opportunity for vile actions presents itself to him. In *The Tale of Mr. Tod*, such an opportunity appears. Potter's description of Tommy Brock is fairly long, especially by Beatrix Potter's standards:

> Tommy Brock was a short bristly fat waddling person with a grin; he grinned all over his face. He was not nice in his habits. He ate wasp nests and frogs and worms; and he waddled about by moonlight, digging things up.
>
> His clothes were very dirty; and as he slept in the day-time, he always went to bed in his boots. And the bed which he went to bed in, was generally Mr. Tod's [10].

Note the adjective "not" before "nice" in this quotation when Potter writes about Tommy Brock's habits. Some critics argue that Potter, who is usually so accurate about details of natural history, gets things wrong when she treats the usual habits of Tommy Brock. However, this badger may be an exception to the rule.[4] Potter adds, "Now Tommy Brock did occasionally eat rabbit-pie; but it was only very young ones occasionally, when other food was really scarce" (10), hardly words that endear him to readers. The echo here of *The Tale of Peter Rabbit*—Mrs. McGregor, after all, cooked Peter's father in a pie—becomes even more disturbing when Peter and Benjamin look inside Mr. Tod's house later in the story and see preparations for rabbit pie on the table. And Tommy Brock's eating only "very young" rabbits also hardly endears him to readers: it makes him appear to be a coward who goes after only helpless prey. Still, Tommy Brock is, Potter writes, "friendly" with Old Mr. Bouncer, who is Peter's uncle and Benjamin's father and the grandfather of the bunnies that Tommy Brock steals. However, Mr. Bouncer and Tommy Brock have one thing in common: they both dislike "the wicked otters and Mr. Tod; they often talked over that painful subject" (10–11). In this book, Benjamin's father is no longer the courageous, resolute, forceful person he is in *The Tale of Benjamin Bunny*; he is "stricken in years. He sat in the spring sunshine outside the burrow, in a muffler; smoking a pipe of rabbit-tobacco" (11). He is almost a stereotypical grandfather figure, living with his son and daughter-in-law and baby-sitting with his grandchildren, who sleep inside the burrow, and he does not pay as much attention to them as he obviously should. The bunnies are clearly not the same ones in *The Tale of the Flopsy Bunnies*. They must be from a later litter. Unlike the bunnies in *The Tale of the Flopsy Bunnies*, these bunnies are completely helpless: they have just begun "to open their blue eyes and kick." When the story begins, they sleep in a burrow separate from the main burrow. Mr. Bouncer babysits for them, but on the occasion narrated in the book, "To tell the truth—old Mr. Bouncer had completely forgotten them" (12).

Tommy Brock comes across Mr. Bouncer sitting in front of the burrow. Mr. Bouncer invites him inside. They talk and smoke. Mr. Bouncer falls asleep. Flopsy and Benjamin return home, wake Mr. Bouncer, and discover the babies are gone (12–16). Mr. Bouncer clearly fails at his grandfatherly duties; consequently, "He was in disgrace; Flopsy wrung her ears, and slapped him" (16).[5]

Tracking Tommy Brock, Benjamin follows him to one of Mr. Tod's many houses, a stick house that looks very much like the one in *The Tale of Jemima Puddle-Duck*.[6] The house smells strongly of Mr. Tod, and Mr. Tod is apparently at home. Benjamin runs away and begins again to follow Tommy Brock's trail. While following, Benjamin comes across his cousin Peter and enlists his help in rescuing the bunnies. He tells Peter that Tommy Brock "bagged" his "family … in a sack" and asks, "have you seen him?" (18–22). Yet even in the middle of this horrible set of activities, Potter injects what may be some humor not only with the pun of "bagged" but also by having Peter ask Benjamin, "Tommy Brock? How many, Cousin Benjamin?" and having Benjamin answer, "Seven, Cousin Peter, and all of them twins!" (22). Since the word "twin" usually refers to two things and there are an odd number of baby bunnies, Potter may be injecting a little humor into this situation to lighten it up a little for young readers. However, it seems doubtful that many young readers would be concerned about the meaning of "twins." Adult readers probably recognize that Benjamin simply tells Peter that they all are litter mates and look alike.

Peter says that Tommy Brock carries a sack with something wiggling in it that Tommy Brock says are "*caterpillars*," but Peter thinks whatever is in the sack is "kicking rather hard, for caterpillars" (23).[7] After Benjamin tells Peter exactly what happened, Peter deduces that the bunnies are still alive and that Tommy Brock, who ate some things at Benjamin's house, will not eat the bunnies until breakfast. Peter also shows his intelligence by deducing that, since Mr. Tod is in his stick house, Tommy Brock goes to his other house. Peter and Benjamin then follow Tommy Brock to Mr. Tod's other house. On the way, they pass Peter's sister, Cotton-tail, who sits in her doorway with her bunnies playing around her. She says she saw Tommy Brock passing with a sack: "He had nodded, and pointed to the sack, and seemed doubled up with laughter" (26–27), making him even more villainous since he acts this way in front of the abducted bunnies' aunt. When Peter and Benjamin ask Cotton-tail whether her husband is at home, she does not answer but begins to talk about Tommy Brock. Then, Benjamin worries that Tommy Brock will soon be cooking his babies and urges Peter to hurry. Benjamin, however, says he knows Cotton-tail's husband is at home since he saw his ears "peeping out of the hole." Peter responds, "They live too near the rocks" where Mr. Tod's house is "to quarrel with their neighbours" (27). Nonetheless, Peter's bravery in accompanying his cousin contrasts with Cotton-tail's husband's cowardice in not helping his wife's cousin rescue his nephews and nieces.

Peter and Benjamin arrive near Mr. Tod's hill-top house, which Potter describes in frightening terms as

> something between a cave, a prison, and a tumble-down pig-stye [sic]. There was a strong door, which was locked and shut.
> The setting sun made the window panes glow like red flame; but the kitchen fire was not alight. It was neatly laid with dry sticks, as the rabbits could see, when they peeped through the window [29].

The glowing windowpanes give the house a hellish appearance. Still, when Benjamin sees that the fire is not lit, he knows the rabbit babies are not yet being cooked and sighs "with relief." However, Potter adds,

> there were preparations upon the kitchen table which made him shudder. There was an immense empty pie-dish of blue willow pattern, and a large carving knife and fork, and a chopper.
> At the other end of the table was a partly unfolded tablecloth, a plate, a tumbler, a knife and fork, salt-cellar, mustard and a chair—in short, preparations for one person's supper.
> No person was to be seen, and no young rabbits. The kitchen was empty and silent; the clock had run down [30–31].

Tommy Brock, who is now in Mr. Tod's house, clearly intends to make the bunnies into a rabbit pie. The clock has run down, and time seems to have run out for the baby bunnies. Their deaths seem imminent and inevitable.

The two adult rabbits are much smaller than Tommy Brock and Mr. Tod, who will later appear on the scene. Thus, the rabbits must rescue the bunnies by using their heads and by blind luck. The whole scene is frightening. The rabbits go to the other side of the house, which is "damp and smelly, and overgrown with thorns and briars." Benjamin says, "Oh my poor rabbit babies! What a dreadful place; I shall never see them again!" Peter and Benjamin creep to the bedroom window and see signs that Tommy Brock entered the house through the window. And he is asleep on the bed: "'He has gone to bed in his boots,' whispered Peter" (32). Wearing boots in bed—something Potter earlier in the book writes Tommy Brock habitually does—shows both

Tommy Brock's filthy habits and his contempt for Mr. Tod since he now lies in the fox's bed.

The sun sets, and the scene becomes decidedly gothic: "an owl began to hoot in the wood. There were many unpleasant things lying about, that had much better have been buried; rabbit bones and skulls, and chickens' legs and other horrors. It was a shocking place, and very dark" (34). Going back to the front of the house, the two rabbits try unsuccessfully to enter it. The moon rises, but by its light, the rabbits can see no baby bunnies though "The moonbeams twinkled on the carving-knife, and made a path of brightness across the dirty floor" (35). But the rabbits notice that when they shake the window, the door to the oven shakes "in answer," actions that let Benjamin and Peter know that the babies are alive in the oven. However, the adult rabbits cannot get into the house, and the babies "were quite incapable of letting themselves out; they were not old enough to crawl" (37–38), words that show how helpless Benjamin's babies are.

The adult rabbits spend the night digging a tunnel to the kitchen (40), but before they can finish their tunnel, Mr. Tod approaches his house. The rabbits, Potter writes, then "did the most foolish thing that they could have done. They rushed into their short new tunnel, and hid themselves at the top of it, under Mr. Tod's kitchen floor" (39–40). Mr. Tod "was in the very worst of tempers," for he "had had an unsatisfactory night" (41). As befits his title of "Mr.," Mr. Tod carries a cane and wears a waistcoat (42). As he approaches his house, he sees "unmistakable signs of badger" (43). Entering his house, he sees things set out in his kitchen for Tommy Brock's "supper (or breakfast) […]" (45). He smells "fresh earth and dirty badger," a smell that overpowers "all smell of rabbit" (45). The word "all" is important here. It lets readers know that Mr. Tod is unaware of the baby bunnies in his oven or the adult rabbits beneath the kitchen floor. Hearing snoring coming from his bedroom, he looks into it and sees Tommy Brock. He flies from his house in a rage. Potter then describes his fox-like actions of creeping into his house and then running out again, actions that last for twenty minutes (47). These actions match those of John Joiner in *The Tale of Samuel Whiskers*. They are, it seems, what Potter feels are typical canine actions.

Gradually, Mr. Tod, still going in and out of his house, approaches his bedroom, where he sees Tommy Brock in his bed. Mr. Tod brings into his house his walking stick and a coal-scuttle, two things that can serve him as weapons, but decides not to use them to attack the badger (47). Tommy Brock continues snoring, but Potter writes that Tommy Brock opens and shuts one eye even as he continues snoring (49), making it clear to readers that the badger is only pretending to be asleep.

Then, the story becomes truly comic, yet the baby bunnies are still in the oven, a fact that undercuts the humor. Still the humor gives the young readers some relief from the anxiety Potter is building. Carpenter calls *The Tale of Mr. Tod* Potter's "blackest" book as well as "the funniest," referring in particular to what happens in the book after Mr. Tod finds Tommy Brock in his bed ("Excessively Impertinent" 295). Mr. Tod rigs an elaborate booby-trap for Tommy Brock, something that would make Rube Goldberg proud. He rigs with rope a bucket of boiling water over the bed, intending to soak Tommy Brock with it when Mr. Tod pulls a rope he has fastened to the bucket. At one point while rigging his booby-trap, his foot even goes through the roof of the tunnel the rabbits dig, but he thinks the tunnel is the work of Tommy Brock (49–59). In a picture Potter places in the action describing Mr. Tod's work rigging his trap, she clearly shows Tommy Brock with one eye open looking at the bucket of boiling water that Mr. Tod hangs over Tommy Brock's head (58). Tommy Brock, of course, knowing the booby-trap is there, does not get caught in it. But Mr. Tod thinks his plan works so well that Tommy Brock is killed when the bucket falls on him. Instead, he discovers Tommy Brock sitting at his kitchen table pouring out a cup of tea which the badger then throws at Mr. Tod (64–66). The fox and the badger then have a terrible fight during which the furnishings in Mr. Tod's house get upset and during which the kettle in which Tommy Brock heats the water for tea falls on Mr. Tod's tail. The two combatants roll out of the house and down the hill while they are still fighting. Potter then writes, "There will never be any love lost between Tommy Brock and Mr. Tod" (70–73). For some reason, in spite of Potter's words, Carpenter asserts that both Mr. Tod and Tommy Brock die as a result of their battle ("Excessively Impertinent" 295). Perhaps he interprets the idea of perpetual enmity between Mr. Tod and Tommy Brock as applying only to their species rather than to them as individuals. Still, this may involve a little too much extrapolation for the young children at whom she aimed the book.[8]

    The story ends with the rescue of the baby rabbits and their return home. The ending makes clear what readers already know from their willingness to go after the babies: Benjamin and Peter are heroic. Instead of being a coward in works after *The Tale of Peter Rabbit*, Peter is anything but a coward in this work. However, unlike he is in *The Tale of Peter Rabbit*, from the moment he enters the story, Peter recognizes that he and Benjamin face an adversary (and then adversaries) stronger than themselves. Only through ratiocination and luck can they achieve their goal of rescuing the babies. They have amazing luck: Tommy Brock does not eat the bunnies as soon as he gets to Mr. Tod's house; Tommy Brock's smell masks that of the rabbits, so Mr. Tod does not know the rabbits are there; Mr. Tod thinks Tommy Brock dug the tunnel the rabbits really dug; the fox and badger's fight takes them outside of Mr. Tod's house, giving Benjamin an opportunity to go inside and grab the bunnies; it also is "perhaps" fortunate, Potter writes, that the babies are in the oven so that they do not get hurt during the fight between Tommy Brock and Mr. Tod (70).

Peter uses his head to work the actual rescue of the bunnies. He recognizes that the fox's and badger's rolling down the hill provides the ideal opportunity to enter Mr. Tod's house and grab the bunnies, telling his cousin, "Now run for it! Run in, cousin Benjamin! While I watch at the door" (74). It may seem to some readers that Peter's waiting outside to watch is less brave then running in to get the bunnies, but after all, the bunnies are Benjamin's children, and Peter's position outside the house is closer to where the fox and badger are than Benjamin's position inside the house. Benjamin, frightened, feels the fox and badger are coming back, but Peter thinks that they have probably "fallen down the stone quarry." He pushes Benjamin into the kitchen, telling him to be sure to shut the oven door "so that he won't miss them" (74), again thinking more clearly than Benjamin. Peter's use of "he" probably refers to Tommy Brock since Mr. Tod seems to have no knowledge that the bunnies are in the oven. After Benjamin gets the bunnies and takes them out of the kitchen, rejoining Peter, he leaves it up to Peter to decide whether they can get away or should hide. Peter then, "pricked his ears; distant sounds of fighting still echoed in the wood." Then, Potter writes, "Five minutes afterwards two breathless rabbits came scuttering away down Bull Banks, half carrying half dragging a sack between them, bumpetty bump over the grass. They reached home safely, and burst into the rabbit hole" (77). Thus, they have gone full circle, tracing a much more circuitous route than Peter alone does in *The Tale of Peter Rabbit*. Old Mr. Bouncer once again finds himself in the good graces of his daughter-in-law. The victorious bunnies recount the tale of their adventure, but at the end of the story, Potter writes, "they had not waited long enough to be able to tell the end of the battle between Tommy Brock and Mr. Tod" (80), again alluding to the ongoing enmity between the badger and the fox as well as the outcome of the individual fight between Tommy Brock and Mr. Tod.

One big difference between Peter in *The Tale of Mr. Tod*, when compared to *The Tale of Peter Rabbit*, is Peter's attitude. In this later book, he does not enter the dangerous area and ignore the danger that is there. He is fully aware the whole time that he is risking his life. He also goes into danger not for his own sake, not for food so he can gorge himself, but to save Benjamin's children. And he never gives himself up for lost. He has thus matured in many ways.

At the end of the story, Potter shows that order returns to the world of the rabbits. Benjamin and Peter overcome two adversaries, each of whom is much larger and much more powerful than they are. They do so through cooperation, bravery, ratiocination, and luck. In a sense, the two heroic characters are reborn when they leave the top of Bull Banks and return home with the babies. Their return also enables the babies to have a rebirth; however, Potter ends the story before readers can find out anything about the results of such a rebirth. Nonetheless, Peter and Benjamin are true heroes, overcoming two ogres, both of whom eat rabbits. They enter the lair of the adversary and return victorious, saving not just themselves, as Peter does in *The Tale of Peter Rabbit*, but also the baby rabbits who could not possibly save themselves. Their victory, then, does not save the world, but certainly saves the family.

The Tale of Pigling Bland

Peter Hollindale labels *The Tale of Pigling Bland* (1913) a "mock-romantic story" and "a celebration of ultimate confidence in life" ("These Piglets" 144). Given Potter's love of Shakespeare and her use of the structure of his plays for the structure of some of her own works, Hollindale's label seems accurate. At the end, *The Tale of Pigling Bland* certainly is a celebration of ultimate confidence in life. Pigling Bland goes on a journey that turns out to be fraught with peril. It is really unclear whether he goes to market to find a job or to become someone's dinner. In the beginning, the tale has echoes of "Hansel and Gretel" since Aunt Pettitoes and the narrator send away Bland and Alexander so "there will be more to eat without them" (15), and they may end up in someone's oven just as Hansel and Gretel might. However, Alexander returns home where, the narrator says she "disposed" of him "in the neighbourhood; and he did fairly well when he had settled down" (30).

Bland, however, never returns home. He overcomes obstacles that seem insurmountable. At several points along the way, death seems inevitable for him. However, he overcomes all those obstacles and is victorious at the end. As he and Pig-wig make their final escape, every indication is that they are well on their way to finding a new home for themselves, thus completing one variation of the generic structure of children's books. The story seems, then, not just a celebration of ultimate confidence in life but also of the possibility of rebirth leading to a happy ending, the kind of happy ending Potter herself hoped for and eventually obtained in her marriage to William Heelis.

Margaret Lane associates *The Tale of Pigling Bland* with *The Tale of Mr. Tod*, especially in connection with descriptions of kitchens in each, calling *The Tale of Pigling Bland* "another near-gruesome night piece" (*Tale of Beatrix Potter* 125). Both tales are really gruesome, although both have happy endings.

The Tale of Pigling Bland ends with a happy union in spite of many things that mitigate against its occurring: the dance at the end signifies that a kind of order is established in the world of Pigling Bland and Pig-wig. Clearly, the tale has a source in Potter's life, especially in connection with her marriage to

William Heelis that occurred in 1913, the same year as the publication of *The Tale of Pigling Bland*. The composition of the story seems to have overlapped with the courtship between Heelis and Potter, if indeed it could be called a courtship in any traditional sense of the term.[1] Potter, however, denied that the tale was based on her relationship to William Heelis. In a letter to Margaret Hough, dated 4 November 1913, Potter writes that she does use a location where she and William Heelis walked on Sunday afternoons and adds that if she puts William in one of her books, it will have to be as an animal that is tall and thin (*Beatrix Potter's Letters* 214).[2] Her disclaimer is in some ways strange. The words about making William a thin and tall animal seem themselves to be a kind of joke. At any rate, for her to think she needed to make some kind of defense of the idea that the book is not related to her and William itself indicates that she very well may have been thinking of the two of them, especially when she adds that the location is one in which she and William often walked. Her own escape into marriage, especially after the tragedy of Norman Warne's death and her parents' callousness in connection with that death, seems to be part of the motivation for the happy ending to what is otherwise a very dark tale. That she would make William a tall thin animal seems beside the point since no one would argue for a one-to-one correspondence.

The story also grows out of Potter's own direct experiences with pigs. When she was a farmer, she usually had a matter-of-fact attitude toward the animals she raised. Although she made pets of some of her animals, including a pig, she recognized that pigs are, for farmers, commodities. She even puts herself as narrator in the book: the narrator uses the pronoun "I" and encourages the pigs' mother to send Pigling Bland and his brother, Alexander, to market. After the pigs' mother, Aunt Pettitoes, tells the two pigs to "Observe sign-posts and milestones" and "do not gobble herring-bones," the narrator tells them, "remember, … if you once cross the county boundary you cannot come back" (20). This is a strange rule, but it eventually spells freedom for Pigling Bland. The narrator also gives the two brothers their "licenses … permitting two pigs to go to market in Lancashire" and adds that she has "had no end of trouble in getting these papers from the policeman" (21). This material could easily refer to Potter's own problems with her parents involving her forthcoming marriage to William Heelis as well as the objections they had to the marriage that never occurred between Beatrix Potter and Norman Warne. However, such a reading is not necessary for enjoyment of the story.

In the story, the pigs are apparently going to a market, not where they will be slaughtered, but where they will be hired. Still, the idea of being slaughtered is inescapable with their journey to market and becomes even more obvious in the case of Pigling Bland, first, when he takes shelter for the night in a chicken coop. As Bland enters the coop, a hen on a perch clucks, "Bacon and eggs, bacon and eggs"; a cockerel scolds; "Trap, trap, trap! Cockle, cackle, cackle!" a white hen sitting on eggs clucks, "To market, to market! Jiggety jig," all of which alarm Bland so much that he decides he will leave at daybreak. Then, he falls asleep (37). Peter Thomas Piperson enters the coop and puts Bland along with six chickens into a hamper and carries it into his house.[3] While being carried in the hamper, Bland manages to hide the papers for Alexander and himself, along with some peppermints Aunt Pettitoes gave him, in his clothes before Mr. Piperson gets to his house. There, Piperson lifts Bland out. Bland then sees that his kidnapper is "an offensively ugly elderly man, grinning from ear to ear" (38–40). Once in the house, Piperson feeds Bland. His actions clearly indicate that he is considering slaughtering Bland: after consulting his almanac, he realizes that it is "too late in the season for curing bacon" (44). The next morning, Mr. Piperson carries the hens out to a neighbor who is giving him and "the hens a lift," but before he goes, he tells Bland "not to meddle with nought," and that if Bland does meddle, he says, he will "come back and skin ye!" Bland thinks that if "*he* had asked for a lift, too, he might have been in time for market." However, Potter adds, Bland "distrusted Peter Thomas" (46–47).

Bland finishes his breakfast and begins to clean up. While cleaning, he sings a rhyme about Tom, Tom, the Piper's Son and hears a voice chiming in "Over the hills and a great way off" (48). He later discovers that the voice is that of Pig-Wig, a pig Piperson holds captive. She tells Pigling Bland that she will become "Bacon, hams" (55). The same fate obviously awaits Pigling Bland. This knowledge leads the two pigs to plot their escape, but most of the plotting is left to Pigling Bland. Again, Potter clearly does not hesitate to treat some of what may be considered the less pleasant, more gruesome, facts of farm life.

The tale, then, follows the general plot of so many of Potter's stories: a central character gets into a situation from which he appears unable to escape and then manages to escape. It also follows what, for so many years, Potter hoped would become the general outline of her own life and what eventually did become the outline of that life. At the time of writing the story, Potter could only hope that she would have the kind of happy outcome that Pigling Bland and Pig-Wig achieve. They are able to escape because, when Piperson comes home, he makes "lots of porridge" and forgets "to lock the meal chest." He locks "the cupboard door," but does not shut it correctly. He then goes to bed and tells Bland not to wake him before twelve (52). Bland then discovers Pig-wig, although he hears her earlier and pushes peppermints under the door where she is (48–52). She asks Bland for more porridge and eventually tells him she will try to escape after she eats. Bland says they cannot leave while it is dark, but the two pigs decide to leave together. Bland offers to use the paper that Alexander was supposed to use for Pig-wig (56–57). Bland stays awake all night. Early in the morning, the two pigs run off (63–65).

Even after the pigs escape from Piperson's house, they are in danger of being slaughtered when a grocer stops them and asks for their papers. Pigling Bland shows him the paper he has and the one that Alexander, his brother, lost. The grocer immediately questions how Pig-Wig could be named Alexander. Then, a fortunate accident occurs: the grocer asks a ploughman to help him with his horse, which has become lame. He knows "pigs are slippery," but feels Pigling Bland, who pretends to be lame, "could never run" (77). Yet the ending is very optimistic: when Pigling Bland says, "Now, Pig-wig, NOW," he and Pig-wig run: "Never did any pigs run as these pigs ran!" Shortly, "They came to the river, they came to the bridge—they crossed it hand in hand—then over the hills and far away she danced with Pigling Bland" (78–81). This ending, with its rhymed couplet, emphasizes the kind of harmony found at the end of the book. The final illustration in the book shows the two pigs dancing while three rabbits watch. One plays a drum; another plays the flute; the third lies on the grass and watches the dance. The sun rises on the horizon (81). The two pigs have left the county and can never return, but there is no question of their wanting to return. They can now achieve Pigling Bland's ambition to grow potatoes and to enjoy a happy life with Pig-wig.

The traps that Pigling Bland escapes to achieve his happy ending are numerous. As many of Potter's heroes do, Pigling Bland escapes through a combination of ratiocination and luck. Fortunately for him, Mr. Piperson desires to sleep late. Bland pretends to be lame, but the grocer's horse really is lame because of a pebble in his hoof, causing the grocer to leave the two pigs and approach the ploughman since the grocer is sure that a pig as lame as Bland pretends to be "could never run" (77). Pigling Bland concocts the plan to escape from Piperson. Strangely, Pig-wig, who knows death awaits her, makes no plans on her own to do so. And Pigling Bland realizes that they must wait until daybreak to escape and again wait until the ploughman is far enough away and preoccupied so that they can successfully escape. He is also courageous enough to keep thinking clearly in excruciating circumstances, even pretending to be lame, probably because he knows that doing so may lead the grocer to think he cannot run. Thus, Pigling Bland is a real hero who takes advantage of circumstances to achieve his happy ending.

The Tale of Johnny Town-Mouse

The Tale of Johnny Town-Mouse (1918) is a retelling of one of Aesop's fables, "The Town Mouse and the Country Mouse." Like most of Aesop's fables, "The Town Mouse and the Country Mouse" is rather short. In the 1912 translation of V.S. Vernon Jones, it is one fairly long paragraph that tells the story of a Town Mouse and a Country Mouse who "were acquaintances." The Country Mouse invites the Town Mouse to "see him at his home in the fields." When the Town Mouse gets there, they dine on "barleycorns and roots." The Town Mouse does not like the food and says, "my poor dear friend, you live here no better than the ants" and invites the Country Mouse to come stay with him and see what the Town Mouse eats. When the Town Mouse goes back to town, he brings the Country Mouse with him. When they get to town, the Town Mouse shows the Country Mouse "a larder containing flour and oatmeal and figs and honey and dates." The Country Mouse begins to eat, but soon after he begins eating, someone enters the larder. The mice run away and hide "in a narrow and exceedingly uncomfortable hole." After all gets quiet, the mice leave the hole, but someone else comes in, so once again they scuttle away. The Country Mouse then says "goodbye to his host," and adds, "You live in the lap of luxury, [...] but you are surrounded by dangers; whereas at home, I can enjoy my simple dinner of roots and corn in peace'" (112–13).[1]

Potter got the basis of her tale from Aesop's tale, but she makes the tale entirely her own. L. Lear and Zach both call *The Tale of Johnny Town-Mouse*, "the most autobiographical of Potter's little books."[2] Potter even injects herself directly into the end of the book to say that she prefers living in the country. However, she takes from Aesop's story the bare plot element of contrasting the lives of the two mice. She also follows Aesop in showing the dangers her town mouse faces and showing none of the dangers her country mouse faces. For Potter, who elsewhere treats directly the dangers animals face in the wild, that Timmy Willie, her country mouse, faces no dangers in the country seems extremely strange. She may omit from the story the very real dangers a mouse in the country faces in order to make her point: "One place suits one person, another place suits another person. For my part, I prefer to live in the country, like Timmy Willie" (57). In fact, from the start, she weights the story in favor of the country, something that is understandable coming from Potter in 1918, when this story was first published. Still, the story is much more propagandistic and much less realistic than Potter's fantasies tend to be.

Potter bought Hill Top Farm in 1905 and married William Heelis in 1913. Since her marriage, she lived in Sawrey. Linda Lear writes that this story shows Potter's "deep understanding of animal nature" (294), words that are certainly difficult to understand in connection with *The Tale of Johnny Town-Mouse* and open to doubt. In fact, by leaving out the dangers that Timmy Willie would face in the country, Potter seems very untrue to her usual depiction of the lives small animals lead both in the wild and in man-made environments. According to Leslie Linder, Timmy Willie lives in Sawrey, and Johnny lives Hawkeshead, a town about two and one-half miles from Sawrey (*History* 243); at least, the illustrations in the book are based on those locations. However, it is difficult not to associate Johnny Town-mouse's home with the house where Beatrix grew up in Bolton Square in London. Like the life of Mr. Jeremy Fisher, the life of Johnny Town-mouse seems to be a satire of (perhaps even a parody of) the life her father led in London, with abundance of material goods and a marked scarcity of the things that could make children happy.

In Potter's retelling of the tale, Timmy Willie goes to town before Johnny comes to the country. Timmy goes not by invitation but by accident. Every week, a hamper of food goes to town. One week, Timmy falls asleep in the hamper and ends up making the trip. As Potter puts it, "Johnny Town-mouse was born in a cupboard. Timmy Willie was born in a garden. Timmy Willie was a little country mouse who went to town by mistake in a big hamper" (7). Timmy Willie creeps into the hamper, eats some peas, and falls asleep. He awakens when the carrier lifts the hamper into his cart: as the cart moves, "Timmy Willie trembled amongst the jumbled up vegetables" (11). Timmy Willie ends up in "a house where the hamper was taken out, carried in, and set down" (12). The place is full of noises unfamiliar to Timmy Willie, who "was almost frightened to death" (15). When the cook starts to unpack the hamper, "the terrified Timmy Willie" springs out (15). In stereotypical fashion, the cook springs on a chair and screams, "A mouse! a mouse! Call the cat. Fetch me the poker [...]!" Timmy Willie tries to hide in a hole in the skirting board (16). In so doing, he crashes "into the middle of a mouse dinner party, breaking three glasses" (19). This introduction of Timmy Willie into town life clearly foreshadows the difficulty he will have in town.

At first, Johnny Town-mouse inquires, "Who in the world is this?" but recovering his manners, he politely introduces Timmy to "nine other mice, all with long tails and white neckties. Timmy Willie's own tale was insignificant," but Johnny and his friends are "too well bred to make personal remarks," except for one who asks Timmy whether he has "ever been in a trap" (20). In the illustrations, Potter shows Timmy Willie with a very short tale. She gives no explanation for the shortness. Still, the mouse's question to Timmy Willie clearly illustrates a danger a town mouse would be more likely to face than a country mouse; that is, the town mice would be more likely to lose parts of their tales in a mousetrap than a country mouse would. It also, of course, refers to the kind of dress a city dweller might wear at a dinner party: a coat with long tails. Living in the country, Timmy Willie seems ignorant about the proper attire for a formal party; at least, he does not expect to be in a formal party, so he has no opportunity to dress appropriately, and of course, he has no way to make his own tail longer. Actually, the discussion of the length of tails involves a joke on Potter's part.[3]

Timmy eats a sumptuous meal consisting of things he never had before. He is afraid to eat the strange dishes, but he eats them, behaving "with company manners." The constant noise upstairs makes him so nervous that he drops a plate. Johnny says of the plate, "Never mind, they don't belong to us" (23). Two young mice wait on the table. They "come tumbling in, squeaking and laughing" several times. "Timmy Willie learnt with horror that they were being chased by a cat. His appetite failed, he felt faint. 'Try some jelly?' asked Johnny Town-mouse" (24).

Discovering that Timmy prefers going to bed to eating strange food, Johnny offers him what he says is "a most comfortable sofa pillow," but it has a hole in it and smells of cat. Timmy prefers "to spend a miserable night under the fender" (27). Timmy Willie finds life in the house very disturbing and longs "to be at home in his peaceful nest in a sunny bank. The food disagreed with him; the noise prevented him from sleeping. In a few days he grew so thin that Johnny Town-mouse noticed it" and questioned him. When he hears about Timmy Willie's garden, he says, "It sounds rather a dull place? What do you do when it rains?" (31). Timmy Willie answers in terms that make his country home seem idyllic: when it rains, he sits in his "little sand burrow," shelling "corn and seeds from" his "Autumn store." He says he peeps "out at the throstles and blackbirds on the lawn, and my friend Cock Robin. And when the sun comes out again, you should see my garden and the flowers—roses and pinks and pansies—no noise except the birds and bees, and the lambs in the meadow" (32). Johnny Town-mouse expresses his disappointment with Willie, since he and his friends "have," he says, "endeavored to entertain you, Timothy William," to which Timmy replies, "Oh yes, yes, you have been most kind; but I do feel so ill" (35). Johnny recognizes how much life in town disagrees with Timmy and suggests he return to the country in the same hamper in which he came (36). Timmy gladly accepts the suggestion and returns home.

On Saturdays, when the hamper returns to Timmy's garden, Timmy sometimes looks at it since "Johnny Town-mouse had half promised a visit." But Timmy avoids getting into it (40). Winter passes, the sun comes out, and Timmy sits "by his burrow warming his little fur coat, and sniffing the smell of violets and spring grass. He had nearly forgotten his visit to town. When up the sandy path all spick and span with a brown leather bag came Johnny Town-mouse" (43). When he goes to town, Willie intrudes into a scene full of noise and chaos. Johnny enters a fairly idyllic scene. However, Johnny finds himself just as unfit for country life as Willie finds himself for town life. As soon as he arrives, Willie tells him, "You have come at the best time of the year, we will have herb pudding and sit in the sun." But Johnny immediately complains about the dampness and carries "his tail under his arm, out of the mud" (44). The picture accompanying these words shows the two mice sitting at a round table made from a stump in a kind of arbor with what looks like a glass and pitcher behind them and some kind of food—presumably an herb pudding—on a plate between them. Willie holds out a fork but looks toward the reader; Johnny stares intently at the pudding. Johnny then starts "violently" and asks, "What is that fearful noise?" Willie explains it is a cow from whom he will "beg a little milk" and adds about cows, "they are quite harmless, unless they happen to lie down upon you" (47). The picture accompanying these words shows Timmy with a pitcher moving in the direction of four cows (46). The earlier picture shows a pitcher that is red and white. The picture of Willie and the cows shows a blue and white pitcher, indicating that Willie in his country home enjoys some luxuries.

Timmy asks Johnny how "all our friends are" (47). "Johnny's account," Potter writes, "was rather middling." He then explains that he pays "his visit so early in the season" because "the family had gone to the sea-side for Easter; the cook was doing spring cleaning, on board wages, with particular instructions to clear out the mice. There were four kittens, and the cat killed the canary" (48). Again, Potter mentions the dangers of life in town without mentioning the dangers in the country, except for what is probably a joking reference to having a cow lie down on someone. The picture accompanying the words telling why Johnny visits "so early in the season" shows a mouse in the foreground wearing a blue waistcoat with a brown hat in his hand running toward a stairway with part of the kitchen in the background with a cat on a window-ledge and four kittens, with three on the floor looking up at the table and one on the table. A woman, probably the cook who was supposed to get rid of the mice, has her hands behind an open door and what look like mops and brooms in disarray on the floor in front of her (49). Johnny says, "They say we did it; but I know better" (51), probably referring to the killing of the canary but perhaps to the mess Potter shows in the picture showing the cook doing her spring cleaning (49). Potter here echoes the phrase about looking like the cat that ate the canary. However, as soon as he says, "but

I know better," Johnny asks, "Whatever is that fearful racket?" and Timmy explains that it is just a lawnmower, adding, "I will fetch some of the grass clippings presently to make your bed. I am sure you had better settle in the country, Johnny" (51). However, Johnny has no intention of moving to the country. His considering the lawnmower's noise "fearful" seems strange for someone who is familiar with town noises, especially since the picture shows a man pushing a push mower, not a power mower (50). Again, Potter seems to weight the story in favor of country life.

Johnny says he will wait to make a decision until "Tuesday week," while the hamper "is stopped while" the family is away, and Timmy responds, "I am sure you will never want to live in town again" (52). The picture accompanying these words shows the two mice again in a kind of bower made of vegetation while Johnny holds a shaft of wheat and one is beside Willie, who sits up with his legs crossed. Johnny wears a waistcoat very much like the ones the mice in town wear and like the one showing the mouse running toward the stairs, away from the chaos in the kitchen (53).

The next page begins with a simple sentence: "But he did," referring to Johnny's return to town: "He went back in the very next hamper of vegetables; he said it was too quiet!!" (54). Strangely, when he first arrives, he complains about the noise, and when he leaves, he complains about the quiet. The final picture shows Timmy Willie holding in one hand a stem with leaves and eating what looks like some kind of fruit in his other hand with a large ripe strawberry beside him and another, smaller, unripe strawberry behind it (56). This picture illustrates the end of the book where the narrator says she prefers "to live in the country, like Timmy Willie."[4]

Although *The Tale of Johnny Town-Mouse* involves a small animal's being trapped in an enclosed space and then emerging from that space, it is markedly different from Potter's other tales. One big problem in the book for adult readers familiar with Beatrix Potter's works is the way it ignores all the problems of country living. Instead, Potter depicts country life as idyllic in idyllic settings without the kinds of dangers animals face in her more realistic and more typical works. Thus, this book seems weaker than Potter's earlier works that depict without flinching the very real dangers her animals face. Instead of worrying about being caught in a trap or eaten by a cat or even a wild animal, Timmy Willie seems to have no worries and to live the kind of life found in books by writers not nearly as talented as Potter.

The Fairy Caravan: Beatrix Potter's Book for an American Audience

In the late 1920s, Beatrix Potter seemed content to live the life of a wealthy English sheep grower and spend her time buying land in the English Lake District for the National Trust. Yet in 1929, Potter published *The Fairy Caravan*. As Karen J. Lightner points out, "*The Fairy Caravan* was a direct result of the encouragement and understanding she received from her American friends" (60). Alexander McKay of David McKay Company, publishers, came from Philadelphia and persuaded her to publish a book for her American readers. On 12 December 1927, Potter wrote to one of her American friends, Mrs. Charles Hopkinson, wife of an American portraitist and landscape painter, that she wanted the book published "in America for the American market only" (*Beatrix Potter's Americans* 14). On 20 November 1942, a little over a year before her death, she wrote to her American friend Bertha Mahoney Miller, editor of the *Horn Book*, that up until *The Fairy Caravan*, she had always preferred to have one publisher publish her books. Then, she added that she decided to publish with a different publisher in America because the book contained what she called "a rather different sort" of tales that were "too personal—too autobiographical—what do you call it?" She printed them, she wrote, as the result of a kind of vanity: she wanted to see them in print without paying to have them printed (*Beatrix Potter's Americans* 192).

Vanity seems to have been involved in another way. In a letter to another American, Elizabeth Booth, on 12 June 1943 (a little over six months before Potter's death, on 22 December 1943), Potter wrote about the "pleasure [...] American unknown correspondents' letters" gave her, adding that Americans "really appreciate" her books, but in England, the books have "the popularity of a 'best seller' toy book—enormous sales, but mainly toy book; a convenient present." She added that *The Tailor of Gloucester*, her favorite book, sold better in America than in England (*Beatrix Potter's Americans* 197). George Speaight defines "toy books" as "cheap picture books" (92). Clearly, Potter, late in life, felt that English audiences did not value her books the way she wanted them valued. Larger than her books for small children, *The Fairy* Caravan, she felt, fit into a category with *The Tailor of Gloucester*—a book bought on its merits as literature rather than a mere gift. She apparently felt that Americans appreciated her books as literature, as indicated by Americans' appreciation for *The Tailor of Gloucester*.

In the 20 November 1942 letter to Miller, Potter writes that she also allowed *The Fairy Caravan* to be published in the United States "to save copyright there" and mentions the pirating of *The Tale of Peter Rabbit* as a result of its not being copyrighted in America (*Beatrix Potter's Americans* 192), thus depriving her of revenue.

When, for the sake of British copyright, Potter published *The Fairy Caravan* in England, instead of using Warne, she published a privately bound edition with George Middleton, printers and publishers in Ambleside, Westmoreland, a town about seven miles from Near Sawrey. It is strange that in her correspondence, she at times seems almost slightly ashamed of *The Fairy Caravan*, wanting it to be seen only by American, not British, readers. On 12 December 1927, as she was working on the book, she writes in a letter to Mary-Abigail Coolidge, another American friend, the one to whose son the book is dedicated (*Fairy Caravan* 3), that the stories in it "are more and more peculiar" and calls them "funny spider webs" (*Beatrix Potter's Americans* 17). Incidentally, she also gave the name of Mrs. Coolidge's son, Henry P., to one of the guinea pigs in the book (13). Yet she apparently decided that once published, the book was all right: on 30 June 1929, she wrote to McKay that the book, "ain't so bad after all" (*Beatrix Potter's Americans* 25), and on 11 October 1929, she wrote McKay, "Take out a few feeble pages—the book is none so bad" (*Beatrix Potter's Americans* 28); and on 24 February 1930, she wrote to McKay, comparing *The Fairy Caravan* to *The Tailor of Gloucester*, calling it "not everybody's book—but much favored by a few" (*Beatrix Potter's Americans* 35). Her likening it to *The Tailor of Gloucester* is, for her, high praise. Yet on 27 October 1930, in a letter to McKay, she called the book, "an indigestibly big mouthful" (*Beatrix Potter's Americans* 40). Still, in the 20 November 1942 letter to Miller, looking back on the publication of *The Fairy Caravan*, Potter admits that the *Caravan* did not sell as well as her rabbit books, but she "was quite satisfied" (*Beatrix Potter's Americans* 192).

Even though Potter was hesitant about writing and publishing *The Fairy Caravan*, Linda Lear quite rightly claims that she got "a great deal of pleasure" from it (352). In fact, on 19 September 1935, she wrote to Marian Frazer Harris Perry, another American friend who had visited Potter in the Lake District, that she wrote *The Fairy Caravan* to "amuse" herself (*Beatrix Potter's Americans* 68), and on 19 March 1942, she wrote to Miller about all her works that she "made stories to please myself because I never grew up!" (*Beatrix Potter's Americans* 177).¹ Obviously, in the last analysis, *The Fairy Caravan* did please her.

Linder quotes a long passage from Potter in which she claims to discuss the origin of the idea for a fairy caravan (*History* 293). Published in different form in *Horn Book* for May 1942, the passage became part of an essay by Potter entitled "The Lonely Hills." In "The Lonely Hills," she tells of watching what she calls "a weird dance, to the music of Piper Wind," in which four wild fell ponies went around a tree, "round and round in measured canter [...]; round and round reversed; arched necks, tossing manes, tails streaming." She writes that she "watched a while, crouching behind a boulder," and then she asks, "Who had taught them? Who had learned them to 'dance the heys' in that wilderness?" She goes on to write that when she stood, "They stopped, stared, and snorted; then galloped out of sight." She had seen, she writes, trained horses going around a circus ring, "but these half wild youngsters had never been handled by man" (154–55). In the passage that Linder quotes (but not in "The Lonely Hills"), Potter then asks, "Had they too seen Pony Billy?" a central character in *The Fairy Caravan* (*History* 293).

In "The Lonely Hills," she then recalls the even earlier time when she saw "unshod footprints, much too small for horses' footmarks, much too round for deer or sheep" and "wondered" whether they were "footmarks of a troop of fairy riders," and declares that, the "finding of those little fairy footmarks [...] first made me aware of the Fairy Caravan" ("Lonely Hills" 155). Linder, however, in his treatment of the material, immediately adds that Potter actually used the idea of a fairy caravan in 1903 in *The Tale of Tuppenny*, a tale Potter never published alone but included, in greatly revised form, as the first chapter of *The Fairy Caravan* (*History* 293).² However, the caravan that ends the version Linder publishes is very different from the one in *The Fairy Caravan*. A traveling showman runs it who has a tent, a band, five polecats and weasels, and performing fleas as well as Tuppenny and a dormouse (308). It lacks the magic of the caravan in *The Fairy Caravan*.

The Fairy Caravan is much longer than Potter's little books, even greatly exceeding books like *The Tailor of Gloucester*, *The Tale of Mr. Tod*, and *The Tale of Little Pig Robinson*, the last of which was also published first in America by McKay and intended primarily for American audiences. *The Fairy Caravan* is also in some ways more difficult to read because of its length and its heavy reliance on Northern British colloquialisms. In fact, realizing that the book needed some explanations for American audiences, Potter penciled in notes in the copy for Alexander McKay's children, explaining many of the rural North British terms used in the book (Linder 295). Obviously, Potter intended the book for a slightly older audience than the very young audience her usual books seem aimed at.

The Fairy Caravan: Potter's Book for an American Audience 155

The Fairy Caravan begins with a preface in which Potter borrows from a nursery rhyme:

> As I walk'd by myself,
> I talked to myself,
> Myself said unto me—

Then, she writes that the tales in the book "have walked and talked with me." She did not, she writes, intend to print them, but did so "on the insistence of friends beyond the sea" (5). Thus, she emphasizes in the book itself the book's personal nature and its being written primarily for Americans, those "friends beyond the sea."

Since material in *The Fairy Caravan* can be traced back to 1903, its composition, like that of *The Tale of Little Pig Robinson*, really is a work of many years.[3] *The Fairy Caravan* begins by telling about Tuppenny, a guinea pig, who lives in "a town called Marmalade" in "the Land of Green Ginger" (9). He runs away from Marmalade, eventually joining ALEXANDER AND WILLIAM'S CIRCUS, the group that travels in the caravan (11–20).

The contrast between Marmalade and the caravan forms the basic structure of the first part of the book. The rest of the book has been characterized as a "bit of a jumble" of stories thrown together (Chrystie 430) and, kindlier, as a series "of stories within stories within stories" (Hart). Actually, it is more of a tapestry of stories strung along the narrative thread the travels of the fairy caravan provides. In fact, Lear speaks of the book as a "tapestry of her [Potter's] memories" and claims that "All in all, she was pleased with" its weaving together of memories into a "fanciful, entertaining tale." Lear writes that Potter even told McKay the tales in the book are "fact—except possibly: the fairies" (354). Note the tentativeness about her last phrase here. Even the tales involving the fairies may be "fact." The term *caravan* itself is a pun in the book. It refers to the caravan in which the animals travel as well as the book itself, which is a kind of a caravan on which the individual stories ride.[4]

The contrast between life in Marmalade and life in the fairy caravan is multifaceted. It involves town versus country, with the country with its spirit of egalitarianism being more appealing than the highly classed town. Since the country is more appealing than the town, *The Fairy Caravan* makes a nice companion piece for *The Tale of Johnny Town-Mouse*.[5]

Snobbery and bigotry pervade Marmalade based on the hair-lengths of guinea pigs: long-haired Abyssinian cavies and more common short haired guinea-pigs (9–10). Yet the short haired guinea pigs are too cowardly to try on themselves the concoction a pair of rats from outside the town sell that is supposed to make hair grow longer. Instead, they try it on poor Tuppenny (13).

In the 1903 version of "Tale of Tuppenny," the barber in the town sells what he calls the Quintessence of Abyssinia that is supposed to grow hair.

Most of Tuppenny's hair was "pulled out," causing him to suffer. In parentheses, Potter explains that she does not know why his hair was pulled out, but she has "no doubt that he deserved it" (306). As a result of losing his hair, Tuppenny became "indifferent to appearances" (307).[6] Still, his friends persuade him to go to the barbershop where the barber applies the concoction. At first, nothing happens, so his friends get Tuppenny to return to the barbershop twice and have more of the Quintessence of Abyssinia applied to his hair. His hair begins to grow at a rapid rate, so he goes to the barber to have it cut. After he spends all his money having his hair shaved, his family members cut his hair and use the hair to stuff pincushions (307). The barber's shop becomes deserted, so he closes it and runs away. Rats take over the shop and drink the remaining bottles of the concoction, but it does not cause their hair to grow. And Tuppenny joins up with the traveling showman (308).

In *The Fairy Caravan*, the guinea pigs lie to Tuppenny to get him to allow them to try the hair-growing lotion on him, telling him they bought the lotion "to cure his toothache and chilblains" (15). After they apply the lotion, Tuppenny's hair will not stop growing, so his wife pulls it out, causing him much pain and causing him to run away (20). Thus, Tuppenny is an object of much more scorn and ridicule in the book than in the earlier story. When he gets to the caravan, the animals immediately accept him. Jane Ferret gives him hot balm tea and a baked apple. She thus stands in marked contrast to the guinea pigs who use him as an object of experimentation and his wife who mistreats him. The animals of the circus admire his wonderful hair. Xarifa the Dormouse immediately wants to put it up with hairpins and to comb it gently so as not to hurt Tuppenny (26). Pony Billy, one of the proprietors of ALEXANDER AND WILLIAM'S CIRCUS (he is the WILLIAM of the name), finds a place for Tuppenny in the circus, inviting him to ride in the tilt-cart. The other animals plead with him to join them, promising his "share of fun, and peppercorns, and sugar candy." Tuppenny, of course, accepts (27).

One of Potter's central themes in work after work is that of rebirth, something that is in *The Fairy Caravan* clearly associated with spring; in fact, the caravan's travels go from winter to spring, and the book contains many descriptions of new spring growth. A rebirth central to the story is associated with Tuppenny. When he leaves Marmalade, he goes on a long, frightening journey (21). His hair stops growing and his chilblains disappear, so much so that he feels, Potter writes, "like a new guinea-pig" (22), indicating that at least the semblance of a rebirth occurs. When he reaches the caravan, he remembers his name, but seems to remember little else except that "his hair had been a grievance" (26). His lack of memory reinforces the idea that his life is now beginning anew. Ikey Shepster, the starling, calls him a "new long-haired animal" (30). Tuppenny becomes a welcomed

The Fairy Caravan: Potter's Book for an American Audience 157

member of the caravan family, a family characterized by cooperation and love. Thus, a real rebirth occurs.

Potter weaves realistic descriptions of scenery and farms and realistic accounts of Herdwick sheep life, including rescues from high ledges and winter snows, with more fanciful kinds of writing. Her book is, Alice M. Jordan writes, "one of the rare tales in which fancy and reality are happily blended" (10), a comment that also holds true in connection with many of Potter's other works. In it, Potter recounts fairytales, including a version of "Rumpelstiltskin" in the tale entitled "Habbitrot" (97–104). She tells a version of "Belling the Cat" (198–200); and she tells the tale of "The Fairy of the Oak," whose tree is destroyed but she ends up living in a bridge made from the oak's wood and blesses all who pass over it (216–24). According to Leslie Linder, this last tale is "original" with Beatrix Potter (*History* 350). Potter also tells a tale that can be traced back to the Bible (Matthew 7:15) and to Aesop's *Fables* of a wolf in sheep's clothing pretending to try to rescue some lambs; in Potter's version, a shepherd saves the lambs from being devoured (82–84). In fact, Potter repeatedly extolls the virtues of the shepherds who work in the Hill Country. *The Fairy Caravan* also contains allusions to "Cinderella," "Puss in Boots," "Little Goody Two-Shoes," and numerous nursery rhymes, including some that provide the entertainment the circus puts on at Codlin Croft Farm, a farm Potter says she based on several farms in the British Hill Country ("Beatrix Potter's Explanatory," 300), the area she loved and where she lived after she finally escaped from her parents' house in London. It also has tall tales, including the story entitled "Demarara Sugar" about some hens mistaking snow for demerara sugar (123–33); the tale Sandy tells about Squire Brown's parrot and the hawk in which the parrot gets the hawk to release him by saying words he often heard the squire say, "I'm riding today, John Geddes," (133–34); and the tale of "Louisa Pussycat's mouse seminary," in which Louisa ends up eating all of her pupils (178–82).

The Fairy Caravan even contains a hero quest that Potter explicitly calls a "quest" (118), in which Pony Billy goes into the enchanted Pringle Woods to rescue Paddy Pig, who eats toadstools, thinking they're tartlets, gets sick, and thinks he is stuck forever in the hollow of a tree (136–45). In fact, Pony Billy acts heroically repeatedly in the narrative, pulling the caravan through Pringle Woods (108–11) and traveling at night to get the cat named Mary Ellen to help care for Paddy after having just rescued him (163–73). He constantly shows concern for the well being of the other animals in the circus, most of whom are much less able to take care of themselves than Billy is.

The whole of *The Fairy Caravan* is a fairy story, as the title indicates. The guinea pigs in the City of Marmalade talk to one another, the animals in the caravan talk to one another and to other animals, and the circus that travels in the caravan is invisible to "big people," that is, to grown humans, because the members of the circus carry fern seed. Also important is Potter's managing to capture the essence of the Northern English countryside that she loved so well and to communicate it to her American audience.

In all but length, including more extensive landscape descriptions, *The Fairy Caravan* is then not so different from Potter's other books. For all of her insistence that it is "too personal—too autobiographical" for English audiences, her choice of an American publisher really does seem to have involved practicality and vanity: she felt that it would find a more appreciative audience in America and make more money there, in part because Americans took her work more seriously and in part because prior American copyright would keep the book from being pirated in America.

The Tale of Little Pig Robinson

Leslie Linder writes that *The Tale of Little Pig Robinson* (1930) was Potter's last one in what he calls "the *Peter Rabbit* series" but one of her earliest stories. Linder dates the beginning of its composition to April 1883, when Potter wrote a letter to her father describing a scene she observed at Ilfracombe (*History* 256), a resort town on the North Devon coast that she was visiting. It is, however, doubtful that it really is one of the first stories she ever wrote, especially since she revised it extensively for publication, though it is undeniably one of the first stories she ever began.

In his essay on Potter's works, Graham Greene treats *The Tale of Little Pig Robinson* as the end point of Potter's work (at least up to 1933, the year Greene's essay was published). He writes that in 1930, Potter "had not returned to the great comedies" of her earlier work. She had also "gone on beyond the great near-tragedies" of works like *The Tale of Mr. Tod* and *The Tale of Pigling Bland*. *The Tale of Little Pig Robinson* Greene calls Potter's *Tempest*. He seems to find the work disappointing when he writes at the end of his essay in the *London Mercury*, "It was all very satisfying for a pig Robinson"; however, "in that rarified air no bawdy Tommy Brock could creep to burrow, no Benjamin pursue his feud between the vegetable frames, nor Puddle-Duck search in wide-eyed innocence for 'a convenient dry nesting-place'" ("Beatrix Potter: A Critical Estimate" 245).

It is in the note at the end of Greene's reprint of his essay about Potter in his *Collected Essays* that he says she wrote to him that *Little Pig Robinson* was indeed the last published of her books but was "the first written" (240), words that Linder and others who write about Potter echo.

Linda Lear, however, claims that when Alexander McKay asked for another book after publishing *The Fairy Caravan*, Potter used Edward Lear's "The Owl and The Pussycat," with additions from Defoe's *Robinson Crusoe* and various events based on her own experiences with her pet pigs to create it (354).[1] Linda Lear's claim about the writing of *The Tale of Little Pig Robinson* seems much more likely than that of Potter herself in the letter to Greene and that of Linder. In the letter Potter sent to Greene, it seems possible that she was trying to stop Greene from ever again trying to write about her, the same kind of thing she did with at least two other writers: Margaret Lane and Janet Adam Smith. Potter's picture letter from 1883 most likely contains the original of some of the material in *The Tale of Little Pig Robinson*. It describes several scenes involving the port at Ilfracombe, but says nothing about a pig (*Letters* 12).[2] Judy Taylor, in her *Letters to Children from Beatrix Potter*, reproduces a letter Potter sent to Noel Moore on 11 March 1892, and under an illustration from *The Tale of Little Pig Robinson*, Taylor notes that Potter used scenes from her own holidays in writing *The Tale of Little Pig Robinson* (21), indicating that Potter drew from several sources in creating the book. Perhaps some of those sources involved scenes she saw after she began publishing her other books.

Even Linder notes that, in later years, when Potter came upon the letter she originally wrote to her father about the port at Ilfracombe, she wrote in pencil on the envelope that it is "an early impression leading to Pig Robinson," and on a background sketch for the book, Linder notes that Potter wrote that in the book, she describes a harbor based on that at Ilfracombe (Linder 256), again indicating that the book is the work of many years extending from the first impressions of Ilfracombe rather than one of Potter's first stories. Thus, in several ways, the composition of *The Tale of Little Pig Robinson* spread over many years. At any rate, Potter embodies in Pig Robinson's tale several of the important themes found throughout her work, especially that of escape from a situation that seems to involve a certainty of death for the protagonist, in this case Little Pig Robinson himself, and the way Potter combines fairly wild fantasy with stark realism.

Ruth K. MacDonald agrees that Potter began the tale in 1893, but points out that she revised it in 1901 and 1902 and implies that in 1929, when David McKay and Warne wanted another tale, she revised it for publication (83). Alexander Grinstein traces what Potter wrote about the tale in her letters, including quoting her as having called the tale "dreadful rubbish" (251–52, 255).

On 28 March 1894, Potter sent a letter to Eric Moore from Falmouth, a port town on the River Fal in Cornwall. In it, she writes that dogs, cocks, and hens are on the ships and that she knew the story of "the owl & the pussy cat, who went to sea in a peagreen boat," quoting from Edward Lear's poem and indicating that even that early she was thinking about "The Owl and the Pussycat" but had not seen anything like that until that very day, thus combining material from Edward Lear into her letter. She then writes about a curly-tailed white pig on the deck of a ship docked there. The sailors on the ship, she writes, always take a pig on their voyages, and it seems to enjoy the trip, but when the sailors get hungry, the pig becomes their food. Then she writes that if the pig, "had any sense," it would escape from the ship in a boat and row away. She includes a sketch of the ship's captain, boatswain, and cook chasing the pig. In discussing her sketch, she tells Eric that the cook waves a knife and fork at the pig because he wants to use the pig to make sausages. She also includes a picture of the pig escaping from the ship and, another picture set ten years later, showing the pig living on Robinson Crusoe's island (*Letters to Children* 26–27).[3] The letter to Eric clearly contains an early version of a part of *The Tale of Little Pig Robinson*, but the book itself contains much more material than the brief sketch in the letter does. In fact, the material about the pig's escaping the ship takes up a fairly small part of the book, although it is easy to see that the whole book leads up to the climax in which the pig escapes.

The letter to Noel Moore containing an early version of *The Tale of Peter Rabbit* is dated 4 September 1893, more than seven months *before* the letter to Eric about the pig on the boat, and the day after writing the picture letter about the rabbit to Noel, Potter wrote a picture letter to Noel's brother Eric containing an early version of what became *The Tale of Mr. Jeremy Fisher*.[4] Potter also sold in 1894 to Ernest Nister, publisher, a series of nine drawings of a frog going fishing that Nister used in an annual for 1894 entitled *Comical Customers at the New Stores of Comical Rhymes and Stories* to illustrate words not by Potter but by Clifton Bingham. This series of drawings closely resembles several main elements of *The Tale of Mr. Jeremy Fisher*.[5] Still, in a letter dated 2 November 1943, Potter writes to Reginald Hart about finding part of her story about Pig Robinson that she dated 1893, again indicating an early origin of the story and possibly dating its origins even earlier than the origins of *The Tale of Peter Rabbit*. However, it seems fairly certain that parts of the story were composed at various points during Potter's life, so to call it the first story she ever wrote is a distortion of the facts. Any claim by Potter that *The Tale of Little Pig Robinson* was the first she wrote obviously stretches the truth—unless there is some undiscovered manuscript somewhere containing an early version of the entire story, a manuscript that predates even the picture letter to Noel Moore containing the early version of *The Tale of Peter Rabbit*. At any rate, Potter's early picture letters as well as the incomplete portion of *The Tale of Little Pig Robinson* indicate that even before Potter began writing her little books for children, the idea of escape from an untenable situation was in her mind. Considering the situation in which she lived, it is not surprising she should have thought of escape and even of a kind of rebirth, especially when Potter was in her twenties in the early 1890s and still living with her parents and dependent on them for money.

In *Beatrix Potter: Artist, Storyteller and Countrywoman*, Judy Taylor writes that after the publication of *Little Pig Robinson*, people noticed the way it parallels Hugh Lofting's *The Story of Dr. Dolittle: Being the History of His Peculiar Life at Home and Astonishing Adventures in Foreign Parts Never Before Printed*, published in 1920. Potter found this idea amusing, Taylor writes, since Potter claims that she did not know of Hugh Lofting's story until one of her American friends sent her a copy. Taylor quotes Potter as writing that she "cribbed" Pig Robinson's adventures "'per' Stevenson's *Kidnapped*," and adding the trite maxim that "There is nothing new under the sun" (171–72). That *Robinson Crusoe* is one of the sources of Potter's book is obvious not only from her title and the name of the pig[6] but also from her writing at the end of her book that readers can find the island's description in "Robinson Crusoe" and explaining that Pig Robinson's island is similar to Crusoe's (118). However, Robinson's island is also markedly different from Crusoe's.

Also, Potter uses "The Owl and the Pussycat" to tie the book together, introducing the reader to it at the beginning of Chapter 2 when she refers to it and even quotes from Lear's poem about the boat and the pig in it (32), thus introducing the idea of a pig being an important character in her book. In a sense, she implies, the whole of *The Tale of Little Pig Robinson* is an explanation of how the pig got to the island in Edward Lear's poem. Toward the end of the book, Potter writes about the island where the pig lives that she has not been there, so she relies on the Owl and the Pussy Cat, who honeymooned there after Little Pig Robinson got there (118–19), thus adapting Lear's poem to her own purposes. She also has two dogs from early in her story—Stumpy and Tipkins—visit Little Pig Robinson on the island (119), thus adding to the unity of her story as she explains how a pig arrived on the island.

Greene's comparison of *The Tale of Little Pig Robinson* to Shakespeare's *Tempest* leads in an interesting direction. *The Tempest*, usually considered Shakespeare's last play or at least the last play he wrote by himself, has often been treated as his farewell to the theater. Although numerous critics, such as Mark Van Doren, point to problems with this idea, Van Doren does write about the play, "It may well be that Shakespeare in 'The Tempest' is telling us for the last time, and consciously for the last time, about the world" (322–23). The idea that Shakespeare is giving a kind of farewell to the theater still is widely held.[7] This idea was available to Potter. In an essay published in 1905, Edward Dowden, for example, asserts, "we identify Prospero in some measure with Shakespeare himself" (140). And in his 1833 essay, Greene seems to echo this idea in relation to *The Tale of Little Pig Robinson* when he writes that in it, "Miss Potter too had reached her island, the escape from tragedy, the final surrender of the imagination to safe, serene fancy," and quotes the part of Potter's tale that deals with the shore being "covered with oysters"; acid-drops and sweets growing on trees; yams "ready cooked," and a breadfruit tree growing "iced cakes and muffins ready baked" (245). Thus, Greene sees *The Tale of Little Pig Robinson* as a kind of farewell by Potter to the kind of books for which she is best known: her little books for children. And although *The Tale of Little Pig Robinson* is fairly long, it is her last *little* book for children, although it isn't so little. As she wrote elsewhere, she was tired of writing those books. Of course, Potter objected to what Greene wrote. However, she would have, it seems, objected to anything he wrote about her, just as she objected to things others wrote about her, no matter how accurate and how well intentioned. Still, as with most of what Greene wrote about Potter, his observations on *The Tale of Little Pig Robinson* seem insightful and should be taken seriously. Whether intentioned on Potter's part or not, the book is a kind of farewell to the little books. Though its origin is early in Potter's life, its completion is late in her life. It is a kind of compendium of many of the themes that run through her little books, and it does seem to be a kind of conclusion to the series. In a sense, it brings full circle the idea of an escape, in this case not from a false Eden but to a real Eden. In her first book, *The Tale of Peter Rabbit*, Peter acts as though, when he enters Mr. McGregor's garden, he has entered an Eden with many good things to eat, but it turns out to be a fallen Eden complete with a serpent—Mr. McGregor—that eats rabbits. Little Pig Robinson escapes from being eaten on board the *Pound of Candles* into a garden that presents no threat to him of being eaten and that provides him with many good things to eat.

One of the sources Potter mentions for *The Tale of Little Pig Robinson* is Robert Louis Stevenson's *Kidnapped* (1886). Potter's Little Pig Robinson is obviously kidnapped. In Stevenson's novel, David goes onboard a ship, supposedly to tour it, and ends up being kidnapped, just as Little Pig Robinson does. However, the adventures of Robinson and David are otherwise similar in few ways. Potter may have gotten a few plot elements from Stevenson's novel, but obviously put them together with episodes from her own life, using having seen a pig on the ship at Ilfracombe as a springboard for her imagination. She combined elements from Stevenson's tale with her own observations and her reading in Edward Lear as well as other authors, including Shakespeare, to create her tale of Little Pig Robinson's abduction.

The first chapter of *The Tale of Little Pig Robinson* involves a reminiscence of the narrator (presumably Potter herself) of childhood trips she took to the seashore. Although the real town Potter visited is not mentioned in the tale, it is clearly based on what she saw at Ifracombe and at Sidmouth, another of the seaside towns, this one on the coast of the English Channel in Devon, where the Potters vacationed in April 1898. In fact, she wrote a picture letter to Noel Moore from Sidmouth on 17 April 1898.[8] The change from Sidmouth to Stymouth is, of course, very appropriate for a story about pigs, as is the name of the farm on which Robinson and his aunts live: Piggery Porcombe. Right away in her tale, Potter begins treating talking animals who wear clothes and do work of various sorts. In addition to Robinson and his family, Susan, a cat, fetches fish for Betsy (8) from Betsy's husband's boat, the *Betsy Timmins* (18). Everyone goes to meet the boats, except for a dog named Stumpy, who walks along with a parcel in his mouth (11). Names of ships moored in the harbor include *Margery Daw* (from a nursery rhyme), *Jenny Jones* (from a folk song), *Goldielocks* (81), and a brig named *Little Bo Peep*. Also, the *Pound of Candles* is moored there, a ship that will figure in the story of Pig Robinson, as will Stumpy and another little dog named Tipkins. On the *Pound of Candles* is a yellow cat, who plays a significant role in Robinson's tale, and a pig.

Although the work lacks the compression that her little books usually have, it does have a kind of unity. Early in the book, the reader hears of a yellow cat and a pig onboard the *Pound of Candles* (17), a cat that will be instrumental in Robinson's escape. Susan the cat brings herring to Betsy, and then Susan eats her dinner. Then, she sits by the fire and thinks about a cat and pig she sees on the *Pound of Candles*. Susan could not understand what a pig is doing on a ship, "But," Potter concludes her first chapter, that she, that is, the narrator, knows "all about" that pig (21). Thus, she introduces the adventures of Little Pig Robinson.

The *Pound of Candles* really is an appropriate name for a ship with a pig on board. The pig can serve for food for the crew and a source of fat that can be used to make candles. These two ideas are central to Pig Robinson's fate. In fact, when Robinson hears the ship's name, it reminds him of things one can get from a pig. Nonetheless, in his naiveté, he allows the ship's cook to lead him onto the *Pound of Candles*, captained by Barnabas Butcher (79), another very appropriate name.

Robinson's aunts send him away to sell their eggs, get them soap, and do marketing, even though both of them fear that he is too young to make the trip. When the donkey cart that usually makes the trip breaks down, Aunt Dorcas and Aunt Porcas feel they cannot make the trip themselves because they are too fat to get over the stiles near Stymouth (27), so they decide they have no choice but to send Robinson (28). There is, of course, at least one other thing that can be done: they can wait the week it will take to repair the cart. As it turns out, their worries are well founded since Robinson shows himself to be much too young to make the trip and return safely.

Like Pigling Bland, Robinson never returns home. Bland plays a major role in his own escape from danger; Pig-wig helps, but Bland does most of the planning and thinking involved in the escape, and Pig-wig benefits greatly from Bland's intelligence and resourcefulness. Robinson is fortunate enough also to have a helper in the cat on the *Pound of Candles*, who helps convince Robinson that he needs to escape, comes up with a plan so that Robinson can escape, and through use of his brain, enables Robinson successfully to carry out the plan. The cat, however, does not escape with Robinson. Robinson, then, is in some ways similar to some of Potter's other characters who are largely passive in their escapes from danger, characters such as both Peter and Benjamin in *The Tale of Benjamin Bunny*, Jemima in *The Tale of Jemima Puddle-Duck*, and Tom in *The Tale of Samuel Whiskers*. However, Jemima and Tom are for the most part wholly passive in their ultimate rescues while Robinson is very active in his.[9] Once he realizes the danger he is in, he is more than willing to follow the cat's directions that ultimately lead to his escape to the island of the bong tree. He, then, is also in some ways similar to the more active heroes, such as Peter in *The Tale of Peter Rabbit* and Pigling Bland in *The Tale of Pigling Bland*. The escape itself symbolizes his maturation from helpless child to more mature adult who participates actively in the actions. He goes from being a foolish little pig who thoughtlessly allows himself to be led onto the *Pound of Candles* and to be fattened by the cook, to becoming a more mature adult who works to achieve freedom that involves escaping from what looks like an inevitable death. He also becomes capable of taking care of himself, something he is unable to do before he leaves the *Pound of Candles*. When Stumpy and Tipkins visit him on his island, Robinson is content and healthy (119), clear indications of his maturity, of his ability to take care of himself. Thus, Potter's central character grows from a child to a self-assured and competent adult. He escapes from what looks like certain death and is reborn as an adult. He even goes through a kind of symbolic preparation for burial when, to prevent him from being sunburned, the sailors cover him with sailcloth (101). The picture accompanying these words shows two sailors putting sailcloth over the sleeping pig: they are about to cover his head (100). The picture, then, adds symbolically to the idea of Robinson's being prepared for burial. Throughout her little books, Potter thus returns to the theme of escape and rebirth, a theme that seems to have been central to her own life.

Robinson's aunts do a wholly inadequate job of preparing him for his journey. They are right in hesitating to send Robinson alone, but overcome their doubts because they are unwilling to wait a week for the carrier man to repair his donkey cart so he can deliver the aunts' goods to Stymouth and bring back the things the aunts need: soap, blue bag (a brand of starch), tea, yeast, cabbage seed, and darning wool. Obviously, all these are things they could do without for one week, even if they were people instead of pigs. Before sending Robinson away, the aunts tell him what to do and give him instructions for the eight-mile round trip. They tell him to be wary of some things that make sense—gunpowder, ships' cooks, pantechnicons, sausages, shoes, and ships—and at least one that makes little or no sense—sealing-wax (30). This list, however, cannot possibly be of much help to Robinson who has no experience by which to understand it. One of the things on the list—sausages—makes perfect sense if the word refers to the possibility that Robinson will be made into sausages but makes no sense if it just refers to sausages made from other pigs: what pig would refuse to eat a sausage? Gunpowder could present real dangers, but readers have no reason to suspect that Robinson has been exposed to guns and explosives. People could use shoes to kick Robinson, and pantechnicons (large vans for transporting furniture) could involve real danger for him when he gets to Stymouth (50). The warning to beware of ships is a good one, but Robinson wants to be nice to people and accommodate them, so when a man invites him to board the *Pound of Candles*, he is anxious to oblige him although he feels uneasy: his only fault, the narrator says, if he had one, is to be unable to say no. When a sailor offers him snuff, he accepts it, even though snuff makes him sick, thinking he can give it to his Aunt Dorcas. In return, Robinson offers the sailor some barley sugar. Robinson has no way of knowing that he has encountered the greatest danger of all the things on the list that his aunt tells him to beware: a ship's cook. The cook eats a large quantity of the barley sugar Robinson offers him, pulls Robinson's ear, compliments Robinson, and comments about Robinson's five chins, another obvious foreshadowing of what the cook intends to do. But poor Robinson has no past knowledge that would enable him to recognize the danger he is courting (77–79).

The cook lures him onto the *Pound of Candles*, supposedly just to show Robinson around. A merchant who has dealt with Robinson's family, Mr. Mumby, calls out to Robinson to prevent him from going with the cook, but the street is too noisy for Robinson to hear. Mr. Mumby is then distracted by a customer entering his shop (80). Some of the animals who know Robinson are too busy or distracted to stop Robinson (83). Old Sim Ram, for example, knows Robinson but is involved in counting bales as they are lifted onto the ship; Sim Ram's sheepdog, Timothy, also knows Robinson, but watches a dog fight, so he pays no attention to the pig.

As Robinson boards the ship, he sees Captain Barnabas Butcher, who directs the loading of the ship and speaks of things that are being loaded, including food, but when he begins to count "a joint of …," he stops abruptly on seeing the cook with Robinson (83–87). Robinson misses the reference to the kind of food they hope Robinson will become. The cat on board the *Pound of Candles*, when he sees Robinson, winks and in other ways tries to indicate to Robinson that something bad is happening. Even though Robinson never saw a cat act like this before, Robinson shows his naiveté by inquiring of the cook whether the cat is sick, so the cook throws a boot at the cat (perhaps one of the shoes of which Robinson is supposed to beware). The cook then takes Robinson in the cabin and gives him muffins that the pig eats until he falls asleep. When he wakes up, the ship is under weigh (87–88).

To make sure the child reader knows what Robinson does not know, namely, that Robinson is in grave danger, before Potter tells of Robinson's getting on the ship, Potter writes that once Robinson is missed, the police conduct an investigation about what happened to Robinson, but then it is too late (80); thus, the child reader knows that some kind of serious inquiry is being made about Robinson's disappearance. The cook fattens Robinson during the voyage, intending to butcher and cook Robinson as a feast for Captain

Butcher's birthday. But Robinson has no way to guard himself against ship's cooks and cannot possibly recognize that the man who approaches him in Stymouth is a ship's cook who poses great danger to the pig.

Once the ship leaves port, Robinson wakes and quickly becomes desperate, but he soon learns that his desperation has no impact on the ship's crew except to serve as a source of amusement and then anger: he runs around the deck singing over and over a song about "Poor Pig Robinson Crusoe!" But the sailors at first just laugh at him, and, when he upsets some of them by running between their legs, they get angry. The ship's cook then threatens to make Robinson into pork chops (90–91), thus foreshadowing for the reader and even for Robinson the fate the cook has in store for Robinson. As a result, Robinson faints (91). Clearly, he has no idea up to this time of the danger he is in.

But Robinson's feeling of desperation is short-lived. The members of the crew treat Robinson very well, especially when it comes to feeding him, and Robinson seems to have no idea why they are feeding him so well. The cook feeds Robinson as much as he wants, and Robinson eats a lot of food (93), thus unwittingly cooperating with the cook's plan to fatten him up for the slaughter.

The cat ultimately figures prominently in Robinson's escape; he is instrumental in saving Robinson from becoming the center of a feast celebrating the captain's birthday. The cat keeps trying to give Robinson hints about the danger the pig is in, even warning the pig about problems of over-eating, but Robinson pays no attention (94). In a very fanciful line drawing that accompanies the words about Robinson's eating so much, Potter shows the pig eating from a bowl with plates, mugs, and eating and cooking utensils piled near him (95).

In an aside that is apparently designed to get the child reader to not be overwhelmed by Robinson's danger, Potter explains some of the cat's actions by referring to the poem about "The Owl and the Pussycat," explaining that the cat's outlook results in part from the cat's separation from the owl. In Potter's version of Edward Lear's poem, the owl is a snowy-owl that sails off on a whaler heading for Greenland while the *Pound of Candles* with the cat on it heads for the tropics (94). As a result, the cat neglects its work, which consist of blacking boots and serving as a valet to the captain, and instead spends all his time in the rigging and at night serenades the moon (97). Thus, Potter also helps explain the kind of motive the cat has in ultimately opposing the captain and the crew in their desire to enjoy Robinson as the main part of the feast for the captain's birthday.

One day, when the ship is becalmed and the crew can go fishing in the jolly boat, Robinson, who is sleeping on the deck, overhears a conversation between the mate and the cook who have remained on the boat. This conversation makes him realize that the cat is telling the truth. The mate says that Robinson should not be allowed to sleep in the sun. The cook asks why, and the sailor responds that sunstroke causes the crackling to be ruined. "Crackling" is a reference to the skin of roast pork. Then, Robinson gets covered with sailcloth. The cook wonders whether the pig heard what the mate said, and the mate replies that the pig cannot get off the ship anyway, but the cook still worries that hearing what the mate said might upset Robinson's appetite (101–02). Another ominous sign occurs when the captain reports that the ship is within an archipelago and orders that the cat come to black his shoes and learns the cat is in the boat fishing. He loses his temper and orders that the cat be fetched. The captain leaves, and the mate says to the cook that if the captain does not quickly cheer up, he will not be able to enjoy the roast pork that will be served for his birthday (102–03).

Since the ship is becalmed, the crew leaves the boat in the water and plays cards (104), two things that prove very fortunate for Robinson since the crew pays no attention to what is happening on deck and their leaving the boat in the water enables Robinson to use it to escape. The cat is sent up on the mast to watch for land, and when the cat comes down, he lies: he reports that no land is in sight, so no one keeps watch during the night (104). Thus, the cat has a chance to put into action a plan to save Robinson, who by this time lies under the sailcloth shivering and crying (104). The cat first admonishes Robinson for not paying attention to the cat's earlier hints, tells him to stop crying, and says he has a plan the will easily save the pig. The plan involves Robinson getting into the jolly boat and rowing to land. In an aside, Potter writes that Robinson has been out fishing and can row; he's even caught some crabs, another of Potter's jokes embedded in the text since catching crabs is a term in rowing that means catching the oar's blade in the water and thus interfering with the rowing. The cat says Robinson does not have far to go since the cat can, when he is in the mast, see a bong tree's top. The bong tree is something else Potter borrows from Edward Lear's poem. The *Pound of Candles* cannot, the cat says, get through the islands because the water among them is too shallow for the ship. And the cat says he will "scuttle" the boats left on deck (106). The cat and Robinson put the plan into action, and thus, the cat is to a large extent responsible for Robinson's escape. Potter explains that the cat assists Robinson because of he likes Robinson and does not like the cook and captain (106).

The cat helps Robinson collect supplies for life on the island and puts holes in the three boats that remain on deck. But as the cat acts, some of the crew members who have bad hands in cards start making noises indicating they might stop playing and come on deck. The cat bids farewell to Robinson and helps him over the ship's side so he can slide down the rope and get into the boat. Then, two hands come on deck and notice on the water what one of them says is a huge "cockroach." The other says it is a "dolphinium" (109). The crew members argue loudly, so the captain, who also receives a bad hand, comes on deck and orders that his telescope be brought to him so he can see what the thing in the water is. He then discovers that his telescope disappeared along with other things Robinson has on the boat with him. He then orders the jolly boat to go see what the thing on the water is, but the jolly boat is also gone. Suspecting the thing on the water is the pig and the cat, he orders the crew to take the three boats that are on deck. When he hears the cat is asleep in the ship's rigging, he orders the crew to forget about the cat and get the pig, only to discover the boats leak too badly to chase the pig (109–11). So Robinson manages to escape. He eventually gets to the island on which the bong tree grows. It is a paradise for a pig on which food is plentiful (116–18). Potter ends the story, writing that Robinson has no desire to return to Stymouth and, as far as she knows, may be on the island still, where he grows "fatter and fatter and more fatterer [...]" (119).

Thus, Robinson reenacts the adventures of creature after creature in Potter's little books: he finds himself in a situation in which he faces what seems to be inevitable death and manages to escape from that situation. He establishes a new home for himself on an island that has everything he needs to live a happy life. The end of his adventures is straight out of numerous fairytales and myths: he lives happily ever after in what is for him a new Eden.

Sister Anne

Potter's love of fairytales led her to incorporate motifs from fairytales into her little books for children, using, for instance, material from "Jack and the Beanstalk" and other tales of ogres in works like *The Tale of Peter Rabbit* and *The Tale of Mr. Jeremy Fisher* and using "Little Red Riding-Hood" in *The Tale of Jemima Puddle-Duck* to help shape her own little books, which many people consider to be fairytales. She also made up fairytales that actually involve fairies. "The Fairy in the Oak," which she originally wrote for two girls in New Zealand, involves an oak fairy, and "Llewellyn's Well"[1] was another of her original tales involving actual fairies. She revised "The Fairy in the Oak," and it became part of *The Fairy Caravan*. She never finished "Llewellyn's Well." She also wrote her own versions of several traditional fairytales. Linder gives the texts of some of these, including "Little Red Riding Hood" (*History* 360–63) and "Cinderella" (*History* 364–74). Some of her other fairytales include "The Tale of the Faithful Dove" and "Wag-by-Wall." Linder includes the texts of manuscripts of both works, one of the second manuscript version of *The Tale of the Faithful Dove* (340–45) that Linder dates 14 February 1907 (338), and two unfinished versions of *Wag-by-Wall*, one from 25 November 1909, entitled, "The Little Black Kettle" (330–31), and the other from 1943, entitled "Wag-by-Wa'" (332–35). Both works were published posthumously in book form, *Wag-by-Wall* in 1944 and *The Tale of the Faithful Dove* in 1955. A very long (for her) retelling of a fairytale, *Sister Anne*, she intended to include in *The Fairy Caravan*, but ended up publishing it separately with illustrations by Katharine Sturges. Alexander McKay published it in 1932. Potter said her eyes were too weak for her to illustrate it herself, but she approved of the Sturges illustrations.[2]

Originally intended for *The Fairy Caravan* in a sequel in which the animals tell tales to one another, *Sister Anne* has a framing device in which one mouse tells the tale to two others.[3] In a letter to one of Potter's American friends, Mrs. J. Templeton Coolidge, dated 29 April 1932, Potter writes that she is hesitant to have *Sister Anne* published, especially without the references to the mice in *The Fairy Caravan*, since, she feels, doing so will make the tale "deadly serious" (*Letters* 346). In the published version, she retains the idea of mice telling the tale to one another. Even so, Potter writes that she feels "a blood curdling picture" should be on the tale's cover "to warn off the babes!" (*Letters* 346). In the letter to Mrs. Coolidge, Potter writes that she originally suggested to Alexander McKay throwing out the version of Bluebeard in the sequel to *The Fairy Caravan*; *Sister Anne* is the version of Bluebeard to which Potter refers. But McKay suggested printing it separately as *Sister Anne* and not using the mice as a framing device. However, she objected to eliminating the mice. She continues that she is trying to improve the book, but she is not sure "whether it is a romance or a joke," and adds that it is not "for babes." The mice, she recognizes, provide "comic relief." Still, she says that she is not sure whether McKay is right, but she left up to him the decision whether to publish it (*Letters* 346). In the published version of *Sister Anne*, Potter includes a preface in which she writes that three mice, who were cousins, sat down to spin. The first mouse said to the second, "Tell us a story, to pass the time while we spin." The second mouse asks, "What about?" and the first mouse answers, "cats." The third mouse says, "a cupboard." The first mouse says, "Very well" (5). Then the story about Sister Anne begins.

The use of the mice clearly associates this tale with the fairytale convention of talking animals. However, in the body of the tale, no animals talk, no magic occurs, no fantastic creatures appear. The mice also connect it with Potter's other works that use talking animals. In particular, the mice connect it to *The Tailor of Gloucester*, in which mice talk, write a note that humans can read, and sit in a window and spin. The first mouse's mention of cats also connects *Sister Anne* to *The Tailor of Gloucester* in which Simpkin plays such an important role. The mice also connect the tale to the nursery rhyme, "Three Little Mice Sat Down to Spin," that Potter illustrated in 1892.[4] Cats figure in the story: many wild cats roam Bluebeard's castle. The tale ends with the castle burning, and the town near the castle flourishing. The ruins of the castle remain, and "a white owl haunts the ruins." Some people claim the owl is a ghost, perhaps of one of Bluebeard's wives, perhaps even Fatima, who is the wife in the tale. However, the narrator says, if Fatima were haunting a place, it would be Lackland Hall where she lived happily after the adventures narrated in *Sister Anne* (153–54).

Sister Anne is Potter's version of the Blue Beard tales, stories about a ruthless Baron who murdered his wives. Perrault's version of the tale tells of the successful efforts of Blue Beard's final wife to avoid being murdered. Potter's main source for her tale is the Perrault version, although her tale is much longer than Perrault's. In Perrault's version, terrible as he is, Blue Beard is at first much kinder to his wife than Bluebeard is in Potter's tale. When he goes away, he allows his wife to entertain her friends and show them all the riches of his castle. He gives her the keys to the castle and tells her she can go anywhere except in one room that a particular key unlocks. This key is a magic key, and when the wife opens the room, the key becomes stained so that she cannot clean it. The wife in Perrault's tale is much more assertive than Fatima, the wife in Potter's tale. After Perrault's Blue Beard's wife discovers that the forbidden room has the remains of Blue Beard's former wives, she is terrified of him. When he tells her that because she has entered the room, she must join his former wives in it and die for having entered the room, she begins bargaining for time and manages to stall him until her brothers arrive and kill him. The main role of Anne in Perrault's story is to watch from the top of the tower to see whether the brothers are coming. Anne finally reports to the wife that two horsemen are coming. The brothers come alone and kill Blue Beard just as he is about to kill his wife.

Potter enlarges the story, giving many details setting the story in a particular time and place, one that Lovell-Smith identifies as in the north of England around 1400 (10). Lovell-Smith also uses Potter's choice of words to locate Potter's characters historically around 1400. Lovell-Smith locates the geography of the story even more specifically to places fairly close to where Potter lived in the Lake District (11), thus indicating an important way in which Potter's version of the tale would have fit into the narrative of *The Fairy Caravan*. Potter especially enlarges the role of Anne so that she becomes the real hero of the tale. Potter's Fatima is an extremely weak character who depends on Anne to save her. Anne is the forceful one who arranges for the sisters to have a plan of escape, manages to summon the brothers, one of whom comes alone to the castle while the other gathers an army to assist in the attack on the baron. Strangely, after the baron gets killed, Potter tells of Fatima's remarrying and living happily thereafter, but Potter tells nothing more of Sister Anne.[5]

In her little books for children, Potter does not hesitate to treat the dangers for her animal creatures, both those posed by other animals and those posed by people. In *Sister Anne*, she treats the vicious actions of people toward other people. Like so many folk fairytales, *Sister Anne* is full of blood and gore, so much so that, in the 29 April 1932 letter to Mrs. Coolidge, Potter herself calls the version that was to be included in *The Fairy Caravan*, "grisly" (*Letters* 346).

Potter's version of this tale is much more complicated than Perrault's version and much more complicated than Potter's other tales. From the beginning, Potter creates a sinister atmosphere, describing Bluebeard's castle and men in ominous terms. Bluebeard has gotten no heir from his seven wives, and he wants an heir. He takes as his eighth wife Fatima. At first, Bluebeard proposes that Fatima's mother marry him, but she refuses the marriage proposal, instead offering the baron her daughter's hand.

Fatima has a sister named Anne and two brothers. Fatima has pretty shallow reasons for wanting to accept Bluebeard's proposal: she likes the looks of Bluebeard's beard and looks forward to living in a castle. As soon as they are married, Bluebeard takes her to his castle. She takes with her two pigeons, two cocks that can carry messages back to her home. After only five days, Fatima sends back a message saying she is lonely and would like Anne to visit her and asks Fatima to bring another pigeon with her, the hen dove. Anne suspects something more is involved than loneliness and warns her brothers that their help may be needed. She takes with her the cock pigeon rather than the hen in case she has to get a message back to her brothers, and she warns her brothers. Thus ends section one of the tale with Anne implying that she suspects trouble and wants to be prepared for it. She also warns her brothers to read any message the pigeons bring, and if the third pigeon comes, they should saddle and hurry to Bluebeard's castle (20).

Accompanied by the family's servant, John Danson, Anne rides toward the baron's castle. Before John leaves her, she tells him to tell her brothers to watch for the pigeons and to tell Lancelot Lackland, son of Sir Anthony, that they might need his forces (24), indicating again that she thinks things may not be well with her sister. At the castle gate, Wolfram, a one-eyed porter, greets Anne and asks whether she is alone. She orders him to take her to Fatima (33).

Fatima tells Anne that Bluebeard is away a lot of the time but is good to her, giving her many gifts. But she is afraid of Bluebeard's men, so she does not go into the courtyard below. Her only companion is an old hound named Rollo. Desiring to explore the castle, Anne sees that it is "solitary and lifeless except jackdaws and cats" (41), and full of rubbish, including a broken cradle and worm-eaten gowns. There is also "a sickly smell" (43).

As the women go through the castle, they hear Wolfram singing a song that he sings repeatedly with variations:

> What did he do with her breast bone?
> Down, down, hey down,
> He made him a viol to play theron;
> Down, down, hey down! [45].

This song is not original with Potter; it is a version of an English ballad, "The Twa Sisters," about an older sister who kills her younger sister because her lover starts to turn his affections to the younger one.[6] Potter omits from Wolfram's singing of the ballad the idea of one sister killing another until late in her story when Wolfram sings one line about the murder (106). Potter locates the singer of the song in Bluebeard's castle and makes the song especially appropriate to the things occurring in the castle. Neither Fatima nor Anne early in the narrative realizes that Wolfram's song involves, as Wolfram sings it, Bluebeard's having killed his earlier wives. As Lovell-Smith points out, one big change Potter makes in her book that contrasts with the narrative in the song is that the sisters in Potters' tale love each other and that Anne does all she can to save her sister (14).

Frightened, Fatima returns to her chambers, but Anne goes below in the castle and comes across a woman named Elspeth roasting half a sheep who warns Anne that she should go away from the castle if she wishes to stay alive (51) and tells her about her niece, Marion, who was killed while trying to get out of the castle. She also implies that Bluebeard killed his seven previous wives. When Anne asks Elspeth how they can get out, Elspeth tells her of a door out of the castle. Elspeth says she can steal the key but needs outside help if they are to escape. Anne says she will signal for help (53–54).

The baron returns and leaves many times. One time he returns in a terrible temper. He kicks the dogs, hits Fatima, and swears at Anne. He is interested in marrying again, this time to a wealthy spinster, and he arranges to marry the spinster by bribing her steward who does not know Bluebeard is already married (70–72). One morning, when he is more amiable than usual, he tells his wife he is riding out again and gives her his keys so she can get his flagons and tankards out of the cupboard and polish them. He warns her, "Unlock nothing else, dost hear? No prying, no peeping!" (75). Anne picks up the keys.

Bluebeard leaves again, giving Fatima his keys, telling her to get out his tankards, but repeats, "Unlock nothing else" (77). Anne again takes the keys. The sisters clean the chamber where they stay, making much noise. Wolfram comes up demanding to know what is happening. Anne tells him to leave. He says they will talk first and advances on her. Fatima screams, and Rollo attacks. When Wolfram leaves, the women pile furniture against the door. The baron returns, and the women learn he will ride away again the next day and be gone for three days (91).

During the days the baron is gone, the sisters clean their clothes. When Anne comes back from a trip to get water, she discovers Fatima is gone. She gets Rollo to lead her to her sister. As they search, they hear Wolfram singing. They wander through the castle until Anne discovers "her sister lying like one dead" as result of the "nameless horror" she has seen. Anne takes the keys from Fatima and drags Fatima back to their room and locks the door (109).

At this point, Potter interrupts the story. Immediately after she writes of Anne dragging Fatima back to their room, Potter puts into parentheses some more information about the cousin mice: the two mice listening to the tale, "with nerves and fur on end," bite the mouse that tells the tale (110), indicating that they find the tale disturbing. This interruption may alleviate the tension for Potter's readers, especially the younger ones. Potter then returns to telling about the sisters.

When the story continues, Wolfram's attention is drawn by a banging at the gate, giving Anne an opportunity to take her sister back to their bower. Fatima regains consciousness but lies moaning in her bed and wakes during the night screaming. Anne sends a pigeon to her brothers, asking to be rescued, but the pigeon gets attacked and does not reach the brothers. In the meantime, Anne prepares "for a siege" (111–12). She goes to Elspeth and asks how she can signal to Elspeth that help has arrived. Elspeth tells her to burn a bag of feathers on the battlements. Since Wolfram hates smoke because he lost his eye in a fire, he will yell, so even if Elspeth does not see the smoke, she'll hear about it (113).

The baron returns. He confronts the sisters, and Anne tells him that Fatima is ill. He demands his keys and, looking closely at them, discovers the two sisters have been going through the castle. He drags his wife to her feet. Anne throws a flagon out the window, and Wolfram brings it up to the baron. He announces that it fell on Roger Darkness from Bowland, who waits below for the baron (114–22). Bluebeard sends the women up to their rooms and goes down to discuss with Roger Darkness the baron's marriage to the wealthy spinster. Anne gets food and takes her sister to their bower. She tells Fatima to open the door for no one but Anne or their brothers. She starts carrying water up to the bower. Roger Darkness sees her as she makes her trips. He wonders whether he has come too far into the castle. Refusing food or lodging, he leaves (124–26).

The baron and his men leave, and Anne sends up another pigeon, but a falcon gets it (132). Three days pass. Anne brings up more food. Wolfram kills Rollo. Anne releases her final pigeon (136). This one reaches Anne's brothers, who come to the castle. Elspeth starts to lead them to the women, but she hears Wolfram and returns below. John, who is Anne and Fatima's brother, reaches the castle and explores it. John kills Wolfram and the castle dogs. He takes Wolfram's keys and goes to the bower where the sisters are. John and Anne carry Fatima to the hearth and give "her warm mulled ale—and hope, and life" (140–49).

In the meantime, Henry, the other brother, goes to get help. He brings to the castle Lancelot Lackland and his men. They go into the castle and await the return of the baron. When the baron returns, he is killed "by an arrow at his own gate" (149–53). The townsmen arise to help kill the baron's men. Then, the town prospers. Fatima marries Roger Lackland and becomes "a happy wife and mother" (154).

Sister Anne is difficult to fit into the broad sweep of Potter's works. In terms of length, it resembles *The Fairy Caravan*. However, *The Fairy Caravan* fits extremely well into the sweep of her other works since it involves animals living their own lives parallel to those of people; in many ways, those lives are unknown to people, and aspects of those lives are always unknown. There are, of course, a few exceptions. Potter's narrator, who is presumably at least a guise of Potter herself, becomes a character in some of her works. In *The Tale of Samuel Whiskers*, for example, she observes Samuel Whiskers and Anna Maria moving into Farmer Potatoes' barn and makes it clear that she is indignant because Anna Maria uses Potter's wheelbarrow, writing, "I am sure *I* never gave her leave to borrow my wheelbarrow!" (66). She also includes a colored illustration that shows in the distance a figure that is probably her watching the rats running down the street (67). In *The Tale of Pigling Bland*, her role is much more problematic than it is in *The Tale of Samuel Whiskers*. She finds two of the pigs in the garden, whips them herself, and leads them from the garden by their ears; one of the pigs even tries to bite her (12). She complains to Aunt Pettitoes about her children (15). She gives advice to Alexander and Bland before they leave to go market (perhaps to be hired out, perhaps to be slaughtered). When they are ready to leave, she gives the two pigs their licenses that permit them to go to market, telling them, "I have had no end of trouble in getting these papers from the policeman" (21). Here too, she includes what is clearly a picture of herself, this time in a black and white ink sketch, handing one of the pigs—probably Bland, since the pig she is handing them to is serious—the papers the pigs need (22).[7] In these two works, then, at least one person is clearly aware of the lives the animals lead. In other works, Potter also comments directly on what is happening, as she does in *The Tale of Mr. Jeremy Fisher* (57).

Except for its happy ending, "Sister Anne," then, hardly resembles Potter's other tales. It is full of the kinds of blood and gore that her other works lack. No wonder she wanted to warn readers that it is not a book for young children. Yet like so many of her other works, it involves characters for whom all seems lost and death seems inevitable. Nonetheless, they are finally victorious over the forces that threaten them, and at least one of them achieves a large measure of happiness. Actually, Anne and her brothers achieve a victory over the forces of evil in Potter's tale. Fatima is thoroughly passive. Yet she is the one who gets rewarded in the end, but she achieves her happiness not as a result of her own exertions but as a result of the heroism of her sister and, to a lesser extent, of her brothers. Thus, the tale strangely resembles *The Tale of Jemima Puddle-Duck* and *The Tale of Samuel Whiskers*, since Fatima is, like Jemima and Tom, hardly instrumental in saving herself.

Three Posthumous Works: *Wag-by-Wall*, *The Tale of the Faithful Dove*, and *The Tale of Kitty-in-Boots*

Potter completed *Wag-by-Wall* shortly before her death on 22 December 1943. Bertha Mahony Miller arranged to have it published in the twentieth anniversary issue of *Horn Book*, but Potter died before it appeared. Linder traces its history back to November 1909 when Potter entitled it "The Little Black Kettle." In his *History of the Writings of Beatrix Potter*, Linder reproduces the text of the unfinished version of 1909, that he dates 15 November. He also gives the text of the 1943 version that Potter entitled "Wag-by-Wa'"; however, Linder also writes that on 28 August 1943, Potter used the title "Wag-by-the-Wall" (328–35). The Horn Book edition came out in 1944 with what Bertha Mahoney Miller, in "The Story of This Story," her introduction to *Wag-by-Wall*, calls "Decorations" provided by J.J. Lankes since Potter provided no illustrations herself.[1] According to Linder, in 1929, intending to incorporate the story into *The Fairy Caravan*, Potter revised the story but ultimately decided not to include it in that book (Linder, *History* 328).

The first version of the story Potter sent to *Horn Book* includes material that would place it in *The Fairy Caravan*, involving Jenny Ferret's telling the tale to Xarifa and Tuppenny while the other members of the caravan sleep. According to Miller, in the final version, Potter removed all references to *The Fairy Caravan* ("The Story of This Story").

In the tale, Sally Benson, a widow, lives alone in a small cottage. She has a cow, a clock called Wag-by-Wall, that belonged to her grandfather, and an old kettle that Sally had mended many times. The clock says, "Tic: toc: gold toes: tic: toc: gold: toes," over and over. The kettle, Sally insists, can sing. Some white owls live in Sally's shed; the female lays four eggs every summer. Sally has a daughter who "ran away" and married "a wastrel." The daughter has a daughter. When Sally's daughter writes to Sally asking for money, Sally sends it whenever she can, but after she can no longer send money, her daughter stops writing. One Christmas Eve, Sally receives a letter saying her daughter and her daughter's husband are dead and a neighbor has the child. But the neighbor cannot afford to keep the child. He asks Sally to send money so the child can come to her grandmother. Sally, however, has been facing hard times, so she has no money and is ready to go into the poorhouse. As Sally sits crying by the fire, she hears a noise up the chimney. Several large stones fall down the chimney, and one of the white owls lands on top of them. Sally picks up the owl, cleans him, and gives him milk. Then she starts to clean up the mess the things falling out of the chimney caused. Among the things, she finds a stocking tied up with string. Inside it are gold pieces that Sally's grandfather put there. When Sally finds the money, the clock strikes fourteen and from then on says, "Tick-er-tocks: Goldie-locks," referring to the child's golden hair. Sally uses the money to send for her granddaughter and to live "a cheerful contented old age." The granddaughter eventually marries a farmer. "They lived happily ever after [...] kept the singing kettle and Wag-by-Wall, the clock."

This tale follows the same pattern of many of Potter's tales, even though it does not involve talking animals and has some interesting twists. For example, the owl, not Sally, gets trapped in an enclosed space and breaks out of it using his own power. The owl's exertions in breaking out lead to the story's happy ending. Sally cleans the owl and nurses him back to health. Sally does not face certain death but an inevitable life of misery, a kind of life in death, a misery compounded by the fact that she knows she can do nothing to help her grandchild. Yet something occurs that changes her future markedly. Through no fault of her own, she gets access to her grandfather's fortune which is hidden in the stocking the owl, in his struggles, knocks out of the chimney. Sally shows she has great virtue by cleaning and ministering to the owl, but the reward's coming to her occurs not because of her virtue but because the owl happens to fall into her chimney, struggles, and as a result, dislodges the stocking containing the money. Thus, she is like Tom Kitten and Jemima Puddle-duck, both of whom survive through the intervention of others. Still, she cleans the owl before she learns that the stocking contains money. She is, then, ultimately unlike either Tom or Jemima since she shows that she is virtuous by caring for the owl, and she uses her good fortune to allow not just herself but also her granddaughter to live happy lives. The owl's escape, then, becomes the means of Sally's escape.

On 23 February 1914, Potter wrote Harold Warne about a book she was planning involving a cat that wore boots, she says, "like puss in boots." The cat is "well-behaved" during the day, but goes out poaching at night, using a pop-gun. She gets caught in a trap that Mr. Tod sets and loses a boot and a claw, so she stops poaching (*Letters* 216). Potter published one or two books a year for about twelve years, but in 1914, no book was published, probably, Linder theorizes, because of her marriage and her farming. She actually finished the text for the 1914 book, and she received galley proofs that she corrected by hand, but she never finished the illustrations (*History* 218–19). On 20 March 1914, she wrote to Harold Warne, saying she had begun some drawings for the book and telling him it was all she had to offer to the firm. She adds that she could finish the illustrations if she had the proofs, so she could place the illustrations in the text (*Letters* 217). However, she finished only one illustration. Linder reproduces the one finished illustration along with a page of the galley proofs that shows some of Potter's corrections.[2] Linder gives the text of the story, named "Kitty-in-Boots," in his *History of the Writings of Beatrix Potter* (219–24). In 2016, Warne published *The Tale of Kitty-in-Boots* as a separate book, with Quentin Blake's illustrations for the story, illustrations radically different from any Potter did for any of her books.

The story in the manuscript that Potter prepared for publication and that was set in type follows the same plot line as that in the letter of 23 February 2014, except that Kitty loses a toe instead of just a claw. That Kitty is in danger of losing her life becomes clear when Mr. Tod finds her in his trap and wonders aloud whether Kitty will complete a "catskin muff." Mr. Tod pulls from the bag he carries the tail of a black cat and moves toward Kitty (Linder 222–23).[3] Thus, he makes clear that he intends to kill and skin Kitty. But Kitty points her gun at him, so he backs off, saying he was only going to release her. He then makes a move toward her, saying, "Allow me to push forward the catch of the," words Kitty interrupts by shooting her gun at Mr. Tod; the shot goes through the sleeve of his coat (223). The shot upsets Mr. Tod, but he spends the rest of the day arguing with Kitty. Kitty, however, is smart enough to know that although she has only five bullets remaining, Mr. Tod does not know that fact, so he stays away. When night comes, he says to her that she might change her mind and leaves (223). But fortunately for Kitty, she has her wits about her the whole time, for she knows that if she lets Mr. Tod approach her or if she puts down her gun, she will end up being the other half of a catskin muff.

Kitty opens Mr. Tod's bag and finds within it Mrs. Tiggy-Winkle. After the hedgehog makes sure that Kitty will not eat her, she helps release Kitty. Kitty then vows she will never again poach. She goes home and attacks another cat, Winkiepeeps, whom she blames for all that has happened. Kitty limps for the rest of her life and confines her activities to catching rats and mice in the yard and attending tea parties "with respectable" cats, like Ribby and Tabitha Twitchit, names of cats who are also in *The Tale of Tom Kitten*, *The Tale of the Pie and the Patty-Pan*, and *The Tale of Samuel Whiskers*. So Miss Kitty survives but loses something in the process, something more than just a toe: she becomes a part of society with its ridiculous manners that Potter lampoons so nicely in her other books in which she treats cats' tea parties. Kitty goes from being an interesting, adventurous cat to being a member of society who as a result of her adventures has "an elegant limp" (224). Thus, as a result of her adventures, she becomes a respectable member of respectable society; however, in light of Potter's earlier works and of her own life, many readers cannot help but wonder whether becoming a member of respectable society is a good thing.

The Tale of the Faithful Dove also involves a creature who gets trapped, this time in a chimney, the same kind of thing that happens to the owl in *Wag-by-Wall*. According to Linder, the story exists in two manuscript versions, both from February 1907. Linder also points out that on one of the manuscripts Potter much later wrote that the story is based on fact and on another says she wrote the story for the Warne children. Potter apparently sent the manuscript to Harold Warne in 1908. However, nothing happened to it until 1918 when Fruing Warne sent it back to Potter, calling it "a brilliant little MS." But at that time, Potter felt her eyesight was failing, so she felt she could not illustrate it properly. She also worried that the story's illustrations would involve only pigeons, and birds, she felt, do not look good in clothes. She suggested that another artist could do the illustrations and even named the artist—Archibald Thorburn—but Fruing Warne rejected the idea since he felt that Thorburn's "public" was very different from Potter's and that the styles of the two artists would clash (Linder, *History* 338–39). Linder published the second manuscript version with a chart showing some of the changes between the two manuscript versions (*History* 340–45). Warne published the story in 1956 with a second edition in 1970 with color illustrations by Marie Angel.

The Tale of the Faithful Dove follows a familiar pattern: a creature, this time a pigeon, gets trapped, in this case in a chimney, just as happens to the owl in *Wag-by-Wall*, but the pigeon ends up staying in the chimney for a while. The pigeon lays and hatches an egg while in the chimney. A young boy gets the pigeons out. The mother gets free, but the escape from the chimney may lead to a worse calamity for the baby since the man to whom the boy is apprenticed wants to make the baby pigeon into pigeon pie, but the apprentice wants to keep it in a dove box. The father pigeon, who fed the mother and later the baby while they were stuck in the chimney, manages to get the baby away from the apprentice and teaches it quickly to fly. The story ends happily with the three pigeons united as a family.

Thus, all three of these tales, different as they are, involve the familiar pattern of a kind of entrapment that very well may cause death. An escape, representing a kind of rebirth, follows the entrapment. In *Wag-by-Wall*, however, the owl's literal entrapment is not as important as Sally's metaphoric entrapment, although the owl's entrapment leads to the owl's escape which in turn leads to Sally's escape: she is trapped by poverty with nothing ahead of her but misery and death. Through the actions of the owl, she escapes what seems to be her inevitable fate and achieves the fairytale ending of living happily ever after with her granddaughter and her granddaughter's husband. *The Tale of Kitty-in-Boots* and *The Tale of the Faithful Dove* involve talking animals. *Wag-by-Wall* does not; instead, Sally thinks the clock and the teakettle talk to her. And by the end of the story, what the clock says makes sense to Sally and the readers.

A Very Personal Conclusion

What critics call the *intentional fallacy* is indeed a fallacy: blithely relating the meaning of a literary work to the author's stated intentions can be misleading. Like most human beings, some authors often do not even know their true intentions. Some authors even deliberately mislead readers about their intentions. Correlating an author's biography with the author's works can also be misleading. Among other things, doing so often underestimates authors' ability to create works apart from their own experiences, to treat in their works of art things they have never directly experienced. However, elements of an author's life—and even an author's intentions—may become relevant when they are approached with caution. To do so in a way that makes sense involves finding within the work of art itself convincing evidence of a correlation. My attempts to show that in a way many of Potter's works parallel her own desire to free herself from her parents and achieve a measure of independence from them must be considered objectively. I doubt very much that Potter was consciously or deliberately trying to put elements from her own life into book after book. It seems important to me to recognize that many of my readings depend on hindsight: on the ability to see what Potter could not possibly have seen, for instance, when she was writing works like *The Tale of Peter Rabbit* and even *The Tale of Jemima Puddle-Duck*. Yet in retrospect, her own life does enact many elements of these books. Many of them are about growing up. It may seem strange to say that an author writing books when she was in her thirties and forties was writing books about growing up and adding that growing up is something she had not really experienced by that time. Yet in Potter's case, it seems correct. She had not yet achieved the kind of independence that we often associate with growing up. It really is no stranger to say that she had not experienced achieving independence when she was in her thirties and beyond than it is to say the same thing about many people. I am in my late seventies, yet I know that I still have a lot of growing up to do.

I do not mean to imply that Potter foresaw in her books the problems she would have freeing herself from the yoke her parents placed upon her. Nor do I believe that she ever completely freed herself. But her not freeing herself shows that she was human with many of the frailties and contradictions that most of us share. That she was able to create such magnificent works of art that deal with the events of growing up that gave her so much trouble indicates just how magnificent her achievements were, at least on a personal level. I believe that her own attempts to grow up, her attempts to become an adult rather than just her parents' child, find voice in book after book that she created.

Early in life, she said point blank that she thought a happy marriage is what a woman should strive for. In saying things of this sort, she showed she was very much a creature of her time. Although many of her works have been seen as subversive and really are subversive, the amount of subversion in them has been, I am convinced, exaggerated. In many ways, she was profoundly conservative, especially in connection with the kinds of privileges that she felt she, as a very rich person, was entitled to.

Potter never achieved the kind of independence that she embodied in some of her books like *The Tale of Pigling Bland* and *The Tale of Little Pig Robinson*. But readers who read any of her tales as moral fables about things like the need always to obey one's mother are just plain wrong. When reading *The Tale of Peter Rabbit*, those who see Peter's being put to bed and receiving chamomile tea as a just punishment for his disobedience are just plain wrong. Potter is not out to teach any such lesson in that tale. Instead, she says that the thing we call mother's love should be unconditional, although in her own life, a mother's love seems not to have been unconditional and possibly not present at all. In the tale, the child who rebels is treated with a degree of love Potter, apparently, never received. And Peter's mother's giving him the tea and putting him to bed are signs of her unconditional love for her child. They are things that will help him overcome problems immediately associated with his adventures: exhaustion, stomach problems, and perhaps an impending cold. In fact, in the *Tale of Benjamin Bunny*, readers discover that, at least in Potter's conception of the world in which Peter exists, Peter may have come down with a cold. I think it is important for us to recognize the kinds of courage it took for a person who thought she was born to discredit her parents to write books even as subversive as *The Tale of Peter Rabbit*, which does have at least one clear message: parents should be loving and compassionate toward their children in all circumstances. It also has another clear message that many readers strangely miss: growing up involves a certain amount of disobedience. To call these sorts of messages the morals of some of Potter's books is, however, a gross distortion of the books. In her first, *The Tale of Peter Rabbit*, the bulk of the book treats Peter's adventures in the forbidden garden, a place where he experiences a great deal of pleasure as well as pain. Still, Potter is, in effect, holding up—possibly without being consciously aware she is doing so—in front of parents an ideal standard that her own parents, at least as they appear in many parts of Potter's journal and of her letters, did not even strive to achieve.

As for her double vision and what I call her realism, I am ultimately unable to explain her ability to create realistic animals doing things those animals, if they were real, could not possibly do and still to make those animals believable within the confines of the small worlds she creates. I think critics are wrong when they read Potter as a moralist who tells us, among other things, to always listen to our mothers. Her little books are much too complex for those kinds of readings. Those readings involve, it seems, a kind of dismissal of all the realistic elements of animal and human life outside of her stories and within her stories. Human life is not so simple, nor are the lives of the creatures within her stories.

On the other hand, I think she is ultimately not as subversive as some scholars feel she is. As her diaries show early in her life and her letters show later in her life, she certainly did not reject all notions of the class system into which she was born and grew up. Although she may ridicule some elements of middle-class prosperity, as *The Tale of Mr. Jeremy Fisher* and *The Tale of the Pie and the Patty-Pan* show, she accepts many of those notions, especially the one that involves marriage as being the proper goal for a woman. Strangely, her parents' objections to her two engagements and her brother's happy marriage did not stop her from hoping her own husband, if she died, would remarry, just so his marriage did not involve "marrying, or not marrying, a servant," as her letter to Daisy Hammond and Cicely Mills of 30 March 1939 shows. This letter even seems to acknowledge the possibility that her husband might make what she seems to consider would compound his transgression: living in what she would consider sin with a woman who was not his wife. In *The Tale of the Pie and the Patty-Pan*, she does make fun of the customs of the English middle class as they involve tea parties and undermines some of the assumptions of the class system about duchesses, but at the same time, she shows that she feels that one should stay within one's own class since she views Ribby as being foolish for inviting a dog to tea rather than sticking within her own class, that is, inviting only cats to tea. A tale that also involves a tea party—"The Sly Old Cat"—also treats the very formal elements of a tea party and exposes some of the real horrors that lie beneath those elements, but in it, the cat and rat at least have, through most of the story, the surface appearance of gentility, while neither cat nor rat is ultimately as genteel as they both try to appear.

Nature within Potter's books, with few exceptions, is a beautiful place full of potential horrors. Its very placidity is a thin veneer over the dangers lurking within, such dangers as badgers ready to eat unsuspecting animals, large fish ready to eat a dandyish frog, and foxes ready to eat foolish ducks. It is also a world in which human predators pose all kinds of problems for her animal characters trying to lead their own lives. And sometimes the animal predators are simultaneously human predators. One of her strongest books, *The Tale of Samuel Whiskers*, clearly works this way. In it, she manages to create two characters—Samuel Whiskers and his wife, Anna Maria—who are wholly rat and wholly human. Their incredible diction aligns them with the most sophisticated of human beings. Their discussion of the proper way to fix a roly-poly pudding and their concern about the digestibility of the knots in the string holding it together aligns them with the most discerning gourmets. Potter puts this vocabulary and discussion into the mouths of rats who are about to eat a helpless little kitten who hears and presumably understands every word the rats say; thus, she makes them consummate human villains who have a kind of understanding of the consequences of their actions that no real rats could ever have. Yet, they are indeed rats through and through. How Potter manages to achieve this kind of synthesis is a mystery to me. Yet she does achieve it magnificently. She adds at least one more important thing to this mix: the story somehow is humorous at the same time that it is horrifying. In their squabbling, Samuel and Anna Maria become humorous caricatures of married couples who interact mainly through arguing; they are clearly based in part on such couples, many of whom are very real. Yet somehow, the humor itself makes the story all the more horrifying.

In work after work, from *The Tale of Peter Rabbit* to *The Tale of Pigling Bland*, Potter embodies the kind of love she did not have in her own life until her marriage to William Heelis. The kind of consideration Peter's mother shows for him when he returns from his adventures in Mr. McGregor's garden contrasts markedly with that which Potter's parents showed toward Potter. Although biographers view her relationship with her father as being closer than her relationship with her mother, her father reacts with anything but unconditional love in the way Potter describes him in the incident involving Potter's losing her hat at the International Inventions Exhibition her father takes her to on 29 May 1885. Even *The Fairy Caravan*, a work published after her marriage, involves the idea of coming from an unloving family relationship into a loving one: the caravan itself constitutes a new kind of family for Tuppenny, one that gives him unconditional love of a sort that he did not have in Marmalade and that Potter certainly did not have from her parents.

One of the central themes of work after work, from *The Tale of Peter Rabbit* through *The Fairy Caravan* and even the later works, is rebirth, often involving some kind of escape from a situation in which death seems inevitable but from which it is ultimately escaped. The idea of rebirth and escape becomes for her a shaping motif in many of her works. These repeated escapes, incidentally, seem to be one place where Potter sets her unrelenting realism aside and becomes sentimental.

Potter explores variations of this theme of rebirth: sometimes, the rebirth involves growth on the part of the one who is reborn; sometimes, it involves deterioration; sometimes, it involves no tangible change at all. That she desired an escape from her parents' fairly suffocating control of her is obvious. That she never wholly achieved such an escape, even after her parents' death, is also, I feel, obvious. To find oneself desiring an escape from one's parents' control and ultimately internalizing that control seems profoundly human. I am sure that Potter recognized these facts; however, I do not think she sat down and said to herself, "I want to escape my parents' control; I want to escape from the confines of being Beatrix Potter and be reborn as someone else; and I'm going to make that escape central to many of my works." Still, I do not see how she could not have been acutely aware of the centrality of that idea to her own life and her works. When she finally achieved at least as much of an escape as was possible for her in her happy marriage to William Heelis, she attained what really seems to be about as much true happiness as is humanly possible. She may have, as her cousin-by-marriage Ulla Hyde Parker felt, regretted that she had no children, but she certainly did have offspring in the form of her books. And her not wanting to be addressed as *miss* shows how complete not necessarily her own rebirth was but how complete her desire for rebirth was. But like most real people, she was full of contradictions, as is shown by her unhappiness about the pirating of her books and the loss of control over the rights to all the spin-offs from her books. She clearly wanted control over the income from her books and from the spin-offs she and others created, such as her dolls and coloring-books. Late in life, she did have a higher purpose in mind concerning the money she lost from that pirating and the loss of income from the spin-offs: she devoted her immense fortune to the buying of land for the National Trust. But even there she showed a kind of selfishness, not wanting to relinquish complete control over the land that she bought. She did not seem to care how she dressed and how she appeared to others, but she did seem to care very much about not giving up her own control over many things, including over her "offspring," that is, over her little books. And she did seem to care deeply that people show her the respect which she felt was her due.

It is rather easy to show that Potter embodied her own desires for escape and rebirth in book after book. Yet that really gets us no closer to understanding how she was able to create her books out of those desires. Many people have similar desires, although perhaps not as marked as Potter's were. Yet few of us who do share them have managed to create such wonderful works from those desires. Potter's creative process, in the last analysis, defies attempts to explain it, even though we can explain what it produced. Thus, her genius remains a mystery. Thankfully, even though we cannot understand how she managed to create her wonderful books, we are able to enjoy them anyway. When we begin to understand a little better the kinds of things she put into her books, we can, I hope, enjoy them a little more. We can understand why her books appeal to very young children and adults simultaneously. We can appreciate a story even as simple as *The Story of Miss Moppet* more when we begin to see the complex threads that Potter wove into it to produce a unified whole.

Potter left two enduring monuments behind her: the land she gave to the National Trust and the books she gave to the world. My interest in writing this book has clearly been to the latter of these monuments. I have never visited the former of them. But I have often visited the latter, alone, with my own children, and with many students. I have always found these visits enjoyable and enlightening. Potter said she wrote to please herself. On the most profound level, I read and reread her works to please myself, to nurture the child within me, the child I hope I continue to nourish until my death.

Notes

Introduction

1. The [sic] is in the published edition of the letter.

2. Margaret Lane mentions that after Beatrix Potter received money as a result of her father's gift to her of North Pacific Railway bonds, which she sold, she had some money of her own that she could use as she wished (*Tale of Beatrix Potter* 86). I really do not know the legal aspects of her situation.

3. See Lear 98.

4. This statement is in a letter dated 13 July 1903, with the annotation that the date should have been July 14 (*Letters* 78).

5. There is some disagreement about where Potter was when Norman's letter came. Linda Lear (2002) and Judy Taylor ("Introduction" 200) make a convincing case for placing her in London.

6. Perhaps a marriage to "a saint" might not have been such a good thing after all.

7. In the text as Taylor publishes it, "very" is underlined, not italicized.

8. Potter's biographers use this term frequently in their treatment of Potter, not just in connection with her childhood but also in connection with her much later life, even after her marriage in 1913.

9. As I argue later in this study, there are even indications she had a mean streak.

10. I discuss this letter at more length later in this chapter.

11. Robert Leeson's excellent essay, "Beatrix Potter: One of Nature's Conservatives," carefully traces her conservative ideas from her early journal entries to late in her life. To see her as consistently subversive of the society in which she lived seems incorrect both in terms of her life and of her writing.

12. See McDowell 312. Her grandfather Edmund Potter bought Camfield Place in 1866. Beatrix enjoyed spending time there with her grandmother. See Potter's "Memories of Camfield Place" (*Journal*, complete ed. 444–50).

13. It seems important to mention here that I am not a medical doctor, so any diagnosis I make is subject to doubt. Still, I have had direct experience of depression, and I do know that its causes are complex. I have also learned enough about it to know that one's biochemistry plays some role in cases of clinical depression. Potter certainly seems at times to suffer from clinical depression.

14. One of my doctors told me that the best thing I could do when suffering from depression was keep busy, something difficult but not impossible for me to achieve.

15. I do not find her possibly not labeling her own depression strange. When I first suffered from depression and for many years afterward, I had no idea what my problem was.

16. There are three entries in the index of the first edition of her journal pointing to Shakespeare (*Journal* 446). Strangely, I can find no such entries in the index of the complete edition although it has items in it that deal with Shakespeare.

17. This entry appears only in the first edition of the journal (445).

18. In part for these reasons, many readers find large portions of the journal exceedingly dull.

19. The mouse is actually carrying food, as Potter writes, "to her family in the wood"

(*The Tale of Peter Rabbit* 51). This fact, however, in no way negates Sendak's point.

20. As recently as January 2016, this debate still raged, as can be seen in Libby Joy's having to defend the idea that Potter liked children in an article in *The Beatrix Potter Society Journal,* entitled "Beatrix Potter and Children." Joy writes that even in old age, Potter's "understanding and enjoyment of children had never gone away..." (13).

21. Leslie Linder gives the text of this tale in *History* 247.

22. Greene would have been on more solid ground had he begun the inclusive dates with 1905, since Norman Warne died in that year, but Greene had no way of knowing about the relationship between Norman Warne and Beatrix Potter.

23. The part of the essay where Greene treats *The Tale of Mr. Tod* certainly does not seem very Freudian. Instead, it tries to read biography from a work of fiction, something that to me always seems a dangerous undertaking unless backed by something tangible from the author's life *and* work. In a headnote to Greene's essay in *"So I shall tell you a story,"* J. Taylor gives Greene's age as 28 at the time of the exchange with Potter (24).

24. The essay in Lane's *Purely for Pleasure* entitled "The Ghost of Beatrix Potter" recounts Lane's interactions with Potter, including Potter's reaction to Lane's request to see Potter and show her what Lane was writing. It also recounts her interactions with William Heelis after Potter's death, including the way Lane finally got William Heelis to cooperate with Lane's desire to write a book about Potter. An earlier, shorter version of the essay appeared in *Punch* for 14 Nov. 1962, as part of a series of essays on children's literature, entitled "Children's Classics Revisited: Margaret Lane Recalls her Brush with the Memory of Beatrix Potter." Lane also included the material, very slightly revised, in her "Epilogue" in *The Magic Years,* also entitled "The Ghost of Beatrix Potter" (199–210).

25. Smith gives the texts of the letters she received from Potter on 36 and 37–38.

26. Potter arranged for Middleton's grandfather to print some copies of *The Fairy Caravan,* so Potter could get a British copyright for the book.

27. I am indebted to the kindness of Judy Taylor, who made it possible for me to get a copy of Middleton's fascinating book. She even was kind enough to pay for it for me since I had trouble getting pounds to send to Brian Mace, the person who edited, designed, and sold the book, and he would not accept a credit card or a check in dollars.

Potter's Realism

1. The phrase here comes from Alfred Lord Tennyson's *In Memoriam.*

2. The material Lane quotes is also on 435 of Potter's *Journal,* complete ed.

3. The picture is on 10 of the 2002 edition.

4. I am one of those readers. Just as nature as Potter depicts it is at once tranquil and vicious, with each being present within the other, so her animals are true to the animal nature at the same time that they are being most human. Hollindale delivered to the Beatrix Potter Society "Aesop in the Shadows" as the seventeenth Linder memorial lecture. It then appeared in *Signal* for May 1999. Then, in 2000, the Beatrix Potter Society published it. Hollindale also argues that when Potter gets the natural history wrong—as she does in *The Tale of Mr. Tod*—she has good reason for what she does (*Aesop* 17–18).

5. Linder treats the making of the pamphlet and points out that the published work is entitled, "The Shortage of Horses" (*History* 399–400).

6. Grinstein quotes from the letter to Choyce on 305 in connection with a discussion of *The Story of Little Pig Robinson.* Many of Potter's letters remain unpublished. This particular letter, Grinstein writes, is in the collection of Nigel Jee. My only knowledge of the letter comes from Grinstein's book.

7. According to Linder, the edition of Mrs. Blackburn's book she was given is that of 1868.

8. The essays originally appeared in 1965 and 1966. Sendak delivered what he later called "Beatrix Potter/2" before that American Association of School Librarians—National Education Association Book and Author Luncheon in 1965. Sendak published both lectures in *Caldecott & Co.,* where the 1966 one appears as "Beatrix Potter/1" and the 1965 one as "Beatrix Potter/2." "Beatrix Potter/2" appears entitled "The Aliveness of

Peter Rabbit" in *"So I shall tell you a story..."* 92–96.

9. The quotation is from Victoria and Albert Museum. "Beatrix Potter: The Art of Illustration." See also the part of the Victoria and Albert Museum's Website simply entitled "The Big Green Book: Maurice Sendak's Tribute to Beatrix Potter."

10. Examples are much too numerous to list: works by Linder, Denyer, Lear, McDowell, and Taylor contain numerous examples.

Fairies, Fairytales and Beatrix Potter

1. Three exceptions are *The Tale of Mrs. Tiggy-Winkle*, *The Tale of Samuel Whiskers*, and *The Tale of Little Pig Robinson* in which Potter, as narrator, claims to have first-hand knowledge of the material she treats.

2. In "On Fairy Stories," Tolkien seems to use "fairy-story" and "fairy-tale" interchangeably, but he clearly prefers the term "fairy-story."

3. The Potter family rented Dalguise House for summers beginning in 1871. The family spent eleven summers there (Taylor, *Beatrix Potter* 28).

4. Esthwaite Water is one of the small lakes in the English Lake District where Potter later lived; as an adult, she considered Esthwaite Water extremely beautiful. Potter later bought the land on which Oatmeal Crag is situated and used the area as part of her setting for *The Tale of Mr. Tod*.

5. Thus, Tolkien insists that Lewis Carroll's Alice books are not true fairy-stories, since the stories are ultimately treated as dreams. Many other critics obviously do not share Tolkien's classification here since most treat the Alice books as literary fairytales.

6. Linder gives texts of "The Folly of Vanity," based on Aesop's "The Fox and the Crow"; "The Fox and the Stork," which Linder reproduces as it was set in type with Potter's own illustrations; and "Grasshopper Belle and Susan Emmet," based on Aesop's "The Ant and the Grasshopper" (247–50). The version of "The Fox and the Stork" appears in the illustrations inserted between pages 250 and 251.

7. See Judy Taylor, *Beatrix Potter* 150, where Taylor writes that Potter did not even start them.

Potter's Vocabulary and Readership Awareness

1. The black and white line illustration on 63 shows the tools in his bag and on the floor; the text on 65 says he put his tools back in his bag.

2. Label names in fairytales in English are very common, such as Little Red Riding-Hood, Snow White, and Puss in Boots.

3. Potter wrote to Harold Warne on 20 November 1911 explaining the meanings of one of the meanings of *Tod* (fox) and *Brock* (badger) (*Letters* 189).

4. In Taylor's edition of Potter's letters, "would consent to its production" is set in italics (283).

5. Linder reproduces the full text of the play (*History* 279–85).

6. I often suggested that my students who have no children borrow a child from a neighbor, relative, or friend to share the works we cover.

The Tale of Peter Rabbit

1. Frederick Warne and Co then became Potter's publisher. She continued to publish with the company until her death, except for some books she had published in the United States. At least one of them, *The Fairy Caravan* (1929), was a book she did not want published in England.

2. In her journal for 6 November 1895 (*Journal*, complete ed. 408), is a chart in which she lists the following plays and possibly rates herself on how well she was able to recite some of them, apparently from memory. Included in the list are *Richard III*, *Henry VI* part 2, *Midsummer Night's Dream*, *Richard II*, *King John*, *The Tempest*; *Henry VIII*, *Henry VI* part 3, *Henry IV* part III, *Henry IV* part 1, and *The Merchant of Venice*. Above *Henry* VI, part 3, Potter has the number 2, and above Henry IV part I, she has the number 3, and above *The Merchant of Venice*, she has the number 1; I have no idea what these number indicate. Following *The Merchant of Venice*, she has ½, perhaps indicating that she memorized only half the play.

3. Landes gives a careful introduction, especially to teachers, to the tale itself.

4. The picture of the cat is on 53 of *The Tale of Peter Rabbit*.

5. I think the cat looks beautiful and realistic. Ruth MacDonald says the cat looks "at its own reflection in the water" (28). Potter's illustration clearly shows fishes in the water, but I see no reflection.

6. Lindner reproduces the picture in *A History of the Writings of Beatrix Potter* opposite 110. The picture was removed from the Warne edition after the fourth printing. It was put back on page 10 when the Warne edition "with reoriginated illustrations and type" was published to mark the centenary of Warne's first publication of the book.

7. The illustration is on 22. Critics often seemingly ignore the text and say that Peter eats carrots, perhaps because readers stereotypically associate rabbits with carrots. The roots of the radishes in the illustration look like some kinds of carrots, but they also look like kinds of radishes and really are radishes, as the leaves make clear. Roger Sale argues that in her works Potter creates a small world using "small, enclosed spaces" that she carefully controls (144). Yet he apparently thinks she makes a mistake in calling what Peter eats radishes and writes of his eating carrots (see 140). Potter makes no mention of carrots in her text. In *The Tale of Pigling Bland*, Potter does mention carrots and shows one in an illustration (13) but not in a context in which rabbits eat them.

8. See 13 in [Emerson].

9. See 15 and 48 in [Emerson].

10. When my children were young, I took them to see an original production by two members of the faculty of the university in which I then taught. In it, people kept bringing in eggs from a room full of eggs supposedly off-stage. When the show was over, my children wanted to know where the university got that room full of eggs. The room's never appearing onstage and not even existing did not make it any less real for them.

11. See for example Moore 289–90.

12. See, for example, Mackay 6, 8.

13. See [Emerson] 17.

14. I have problems calling the pet Peter the real Peter, words that imply that somehow the Peter Rabbit of the tales is not real. In a very real sense, the Peter of the tales seems more real than the pet Peter, especially to modern children.

15. As I have indicated, I feel that he grows during the course of his adventures in Potter's first book.

16. I rely here primarily on two parts of *The Hero with a Thousand Faces*: the very brief outline of the phases of the monomyth on 30 and the much more extensive summary of the myth, including a diagram of it, on 245–46.

The Tailor of Gloucester

1. On several occasions, Potter called it her favorite work: see Linder, *History* 121, for example, where he quotes her on two separate occasions calling it her favorite.

2. See for example the first in a series of three tales entitled "The Elves" in *Household Stories from the Collection of the Bros: Grimm*, 170–71.

3. Linder treats *The Tailor of Gloucester* in *History of the Writings* 111–34. On 111–12, he treats the information about Prichard. On 124–34, he gives the text of the first edition, the one that Potter printed at her own expense.

4. The complete letter is available in several places. Leslie Linder includes it on page 7 in his introduction to *The Tailor of Gloucester*, a book that includes a version of the original manuscript that was sent to Freda. The Warne edition uses part of the original letter as a preface to the tale (5), but not the part in which Potter writes about herself. A facsimile copy of the letter and the version of the tale sent to Freda is available: See *The Tailor of Gloucester: A Facsimile*. A printed version of the letter is also available: see *The Tailor of Gloucester From the Original Manuscript*.

5. Linder traces the evolution of the story from the tale Potter heard to the version sent to Freda to the version Warne published (*History* 113–21). On 122–23, he gives a chart of the watercolors in the manuscript and the privately printed version. He gives the text of the privately printed version on 124–34.

The Tale of Squirrel Nutkin

1. The version I used of *The Thousand and One Days* is on Kindle. This tale has obvious similarities to "Rumpelstiltskin."

2. These are some of the most famous

of Kipling's stories in *Just So Stories*. All four were published before the book, *Just So Stories*, appeared. The 1907 American edition, on the page behind the title page, indicates that "How the Whale Got His Throat" (originally titled "How the Whale Got His Tiny Throat") was originally published in 1897; "How the Camel Got His Hump" in 1897; "The Elephant's Child" in 1900; and "How the Leopard Got His Spots" in 1901. The 1895 school edition of *The Second Jungle Book*, on the page behind the title page, indicates that "How Fear Came" was first published in 1894. "How Fear Came" involves a tale of creation and the Fall, after which "Fear, the Hairless One" appears along with death (16–24).

3. The entire letter appears, among other places, in Potter, *Letters to Children* 71–76. The illustration and the text that include Potter appear on 71 of *Letters to Children*.

4. See for example Lindner, *History* 135.

5. We used to have a pear tree in our yard. Our dogs would sit under it and watch squirrels in it eating the pears. One of their joys was chasing squirrels. Those particular dogs never caught a squirrel. At times, the squirrels would make a variety of noises that sound like those Nutkin makes and throw partially eaten pears at the one dog that was most persistent in her watching the squirrels in the tree and her desire to catch a squirrel.

The Tale of Benjamin Bunny

1. In pictures on 38 and 53, Potter shows what looks like the same robin she shows in *The Tale of Peter Rabbit*. As in the earlier tale, in *The Tale of Benjamin Bunny*, the robin looks down at the bunnies but never says a word and never appears in the text of either tale.

2. Potter does not identify the rabbit helping Peter fold. There are two bunnies in Mrs. Rabbit's lap; the one helping with the folding is probably one of Peter's sisters.

The Tale of Two Bad Mice and *The Tale of Mrs. Tiggy-Winkle*

1. See Linder, *History* 156.

2. Throughout this chapter, I use what appears to be Potter's preferred spelling of "doll's-house" as opposed to the usual American spelling of "dollhouse." Elsewhere in my book, I use the preferred American spelling. I also follow Potter's use of the singular possessive for doll's-house, even though two dolls occupy the house. But as Potter indicates, "It belonged to two Dolls called Jane and Lucinda; at least, it belonged to Lucinda," and "Jane was the cook" (8).

3. Some readers may take pleasure in recognizing that the crooked sixpence echoes the nursery rhyme about the crooked man, just as they may recognize that Tom Thumb and Huncamunca are characters from the play, *The Tragedy of Tragedies; or, The Life and Death of Tom Thumb the Great* by Henry Fielding, first performed in 1731. Tom Thumb is a character from English folklore. *The History of Tom Thumb* (1621) was supposedly the first fairytale published in English. The story is set in the time of King Arthur. Merlin comes across a man and a woman who have many things but seem unhappy. He discovers that their unhappiness results from their not having a child. The woman says that even if the child were no bigger than her thumb, she would be happy. Merlin is amused by what the woman says, so he sees to it that the woman gets a child no bigger than her thumb: thus, he is named Tom Thumb. The complete text of the tale is available in several places on the Web. One is http://www.sacred-texts.com/neu/eng/eft/eft26.htm.

4. Susan Rahn in "Tailpiece," feels that in this exchange of miniature letters, the mice are not entirely subservient, indicated by Lucinda's telling Hunca Munca to come no later than 5:45 one morning and Hunca Munca's writing back that she will come at 7:00 AM (84). Rahn's article also places the tale in terms of Potter's political opinions in addition to her relation to her parents. However, these series of episodes do not involve any obvious danger to the lives of the tales' protagonists, unless one decides that the mouse trap might present a danger to the adult mice, who seem fully aware of the danger it presents: in one picture, Tom Thumb appears to be warning his children about the danger while Hunca Munca looks on (52).

5. The lines in question in the published book are:

Lilly White and clean, oh!
With little frills between, oh!

Smooth and hot—red rusty spot
Never here be seen, oh! (*Tale of Mrs. Tiggy-Winkle* 16)

6. Numerous sources show that the character and occupation of Mrs. Tiggy-winkle are based to a large extent on Potter's interactions with Kitty MacDonald, a washerwoman at Dalguise House in Dunkeld, Scotland, where Potter spent eleven summers, beginning in 1871. Potter became extremely attached to Dalguise House and regretted when she could no longer stay there.

The Tale of the Pie and the Patty-Pan

1. See for example Grinstein 130. He sees these two stories as representing Potter's taking another step toward independence from her parents.

2. This work was not published during Potter's life. Linder points out that the story is dated "March 21st. 06" (*History* 183); Linder provides a facsimile of the manuscript of the tale beginning opposite 182 in *History*.

3. For the permutations of the title, see Linder, *History* 168–72. On *History* 173–74, Linder gives the text of what he calls "First Version of the Story of Duchess and Ribby." He subtitles it, "Something very NICE." It does involve the same two main characters as the published tale, but the interaction between them is very different.

4. I admit that I had to look up the definition of patty pan. Until I started studying the book, I had no idea what one was. But I was, nonetheless, able to enjoy the story.

5. See also the illustration on 23.

6. American children may not recognize that Dr. Maggoty here unwittingly refers to what may be one of the ingredients of the pie Duchess has just devoured: gammon.

The Tale of Mr. Jeremy Fisher

1. The only thing I can think is Greene may object to her entering the story at the end by commenting about "roasted grasshopper with ladybird sauce; which frogs consider a beautiful treat; but *I* think it must have been nasty!" (57).

2. Throughout this chapter, I copy Potter's spelling—*macintosh*—in quotations. Otherwise, I use the spelling *mackintosh*.

3. Lane gives the date as 1894 (475). Linder reproduces the drawings and text (*History* 179–82). Clifton Bingham (1859–1913) wrote verses for children's books such as *A Snow Baby: Merry Rhymes for Pleasant Times* as well as lyrics of sentimental songs, including "Love's Old Sweet Song."

4. The letter is reproduced on 119–21 of the Cotsen collection. The first picture visible on 119 is the last picture in the story; the rest of the story follows.

5. Potter uses the spelling "goloshes" throughout the story. In Potter's illustrations, Mr. Jeremy's "goloshes" appear to fit tightly over his feet, just as his slippers do when he walks around his house and greets his guests (see 6, 14, and 53).

6. Linder includes in the complete edition of Potter's journal a reproduction of a photograph Rupert Potter took of people in a boat, taken in September 1882. According to Linder, Beatrix Potter holds the oars. The bow of the boat is still on land. The photograph shows the kind of clothing the Potters apparently considered appropriate for boating. The clothing the people wear does not match that of Mr. Jeremy Fisher, but the picture shows that they were wearing anything but the kind of clothing most people would wear for a boating party in the early decades of the twenty-first century. See *Journal*, complete ed. opposite 228.

7. Mr. Jeremy's being saved by part of his ridiculous outfit contrasts nicely with Peter's being trapped by the jacket his mother so carefully buttons on him. Thus, readers can see that it is not always easy to make generalizations about the meanings to be found in Potter's works.

The Story of a Fierce Bad Rabbit, The Story of Miss Moppet, and "The Sly Old Cat"

1. The capital M appears consistently.

2. The lowercase m here is possibly to distinguish between any mouse and the Mouse.

3. Throughout the story, Potter seems to haphazardly capitalize the first letter of *Cat* and *Rat*. In this chapter, I follow her capitalization when quoting the story. In Linder's *History*, "The Sly Old Cat" has no page numbers. It follows material on 182.

The Tale of Tom Kitten

1. Lear calls the ducks in this tale "surly and slightly malevolent" (218). Malevolent seems to be an exaggeration. Foolish and self-centered seems more appropriate, especially in light of the way Potter handles Jemima in the tale bearing her name. Perhaps Lear and other critics react this way because the ducks goose step along the road, but I feel the use of the term *goose step* rather than waddling is just another of Potter's jokes.

2. The dedication is on unnumbered page 5. Lear discusses the meaning of "pickle," saying that for Potter it refers to "free-thinking exuberant people," like Potter's cousin Caroline, as well as small children and kittens that could not "contain their enthusiasms" as they "romped in her flowerbeds or apple orchard" (218). From what we know of the way some small children in Sawrey reacted to Potter, it seems that she was less tolerant of them than Tabitha is of the three kittens.

3. Mr. Drake Puddle-duck does not seem nearly as dangerous as Mr. McGregor or Samuel Whiskers.

The Tale of Jemima Puddle-Duck

1. Other critics disagree. Lear, for example, feels that *The Tale of Johnny Town-Mouse* is the most autobiographic of Potter's small books (294), an idea I shall discuss when I get to the chapter on that book. Still, Lear does write that Jemima is "imbued with certain autobiographical characteristics" (222).

The Tale of Samuel Whiskers or The Roly-Poly Pudding

1. I am not so sure that Greene's essay involves any kind of mockery, although, from what Greene writes about what Potter wrote to him (*Collected Essays* 240), Potter may have thought it did. (240).

2. I am one adult reader who has a great deal of trouble taking Potter seriously about how warm and loving a rat can be. I had a pet rat once. He was cute but not at all warm and loving. In fact, the older he got, the more he bit. I also find Samuel Whiskers and his wife, Anna Maria, thoroughly despicable rather than sympathetic figures. They may be admirable, but I cannot sympathize with them.

The Tale of Ginger and Pickles

1. Peter, his sisters, Jeremy, and Samuel do not get mentioned in the text; the illustration shows them.

2. Grinstein connects these ideas to Potter's own troubles involving some of the dolls and other items she wanted to market in connection with her stories and problems she was having getting money from Harold Warne. He even writes that *The Tale of Ginger and Pickles* may have involved Potter's "caricaturing the partnership of Harold and Fruing Warne and their business practices" (164–67). I doubt that this idea about the Warnes adds to our understanding of the book, but it may add to our enjoyment of it.

3. We used to raise wirehaired-fox terriers. Several of them were extremely good hunters of rodents. Also, compare John Joiner in *The Tale of Samuel Whiskers*.

The Tale of Mrs. Tittlemouse

1. Many of Potter's readers will be familiar with Mrs. Tittlemouse from *The Tale of the Flopsy Bunnies*.

The Tale of Timmy Tiptoes

1. Perhaps her cousin had a stuffed chipmunk. Lear comments that the illustrations in *The Tale of Timmy Tiptoes* look like stuffed animals (237).

2. I am no natural historian, but from what I gather, Potter is inaccurate here: gray squirrels do not hibernate, relying not on sleep but on stored fat and food to get through the winter. Nonetheless, it is fairly obvious that Potter was less concerned with scientific accuracy in this work than in most others, as is illustrated by her having Chippy Hackee, when he first appears in the story, carrying a night light (see the illustration on

The Tale of Mr. Tod

1. I think both works are "masterpieces," but I also consider works like *The Tale of Peter Rabbit*, *The Tale of Jemima Puddle-Duck,* and *The Tale of Mr. Jeremy Fisher* to be masterpieces, even though Greene considers the last of these works to be a failure. One of the wonderful things about Potter is her ability to produce masterpiece after masterpiece. I cannot choose a single "masterpiece."

2. Sale writes that the "later books, especially *Mr. Tod*, are harsher, more disagreeable by far than" *The Tale of Peter Rabbit* or *The Tailor of Gloucester* (157). Whether *The Tale of Mr. Tod* is "harsher" than *The Tale of Samuel Whiskers* is a matter of debate.

3. For a discussion of the relationship—or lack of relationship—between Mr. Tod and Jemima Puddle-Duck's fox, see Lane, *Magic Years* 186–87.

4. See, for example, Lane, *Magic Years* 189.

5. I have some problems with this passage: Flopsy's slapping her father-in-law certainly looks like elder abuse. Potter, however, seems to feel the actions are justified.

6. Compare *The Tale of Jemima Puddle-Duck* (26) to *The Tale of Mr. Tod* (19).

7. The italics are Potter's.

8. From everything in the book and from the book's length, it does seem probably that Potter had in mind a slightly older audience than she had in mind for her other books that involve Peter Rabbit.

The Tale of Pigling Bland

1. Lear writes that Potter fell in love with Heelis "slowly and companionably," just as Potter did with Norman Warne (249).

2. She refers to the illustration of the pigs looking at the sunrise on 67.

3. The name, *Piperson,* alludes to some nursery rhymes. "Tom Tom the Piper's Son" is a figure in nursery rhymes that Potter alludes to repeatedly in the book. In one, "Tom stole a pig" and Piperson steals pigs. In another, Tom is a Piper's son who can play only one song: "over the hills and far away," a line to which Potter also alludes in *The Tale of Pigling Bland.* There are, of course, many variants of these songs.

The Tale of Johnny Town-Mouse

1. The Jones translation of Aesop treats Town Mouse and Country Mouse as proper nouns, capitalizing the first letter of each. The 2002 edition of Potter's tale, with text based on the first edition of 1918, treats neither of these terms as proper nouns. This version consistently capitalizes the J in *Johnny* and the T in town when they are used as part of Johnny's name, but does not capitalize the m in *mouse*. I try to follow what seems to be Potter's usage when discussing her tale directly and, of course, when quoting her, as well as Jones' usage when discussing or quoting his translation.

2. Lear does on 294; Zack does on 219.

3. I doubt that Potter did much measuring of the lengths of the tails of mice. If she did, she probably discovered that their tails' lengths differ, among other things, according to species and to the ages of the mice. However, as Hollindale points out, Timmy Willy is a vole (*Aesop* 11), and voles, which are related to mice, do have much shorter tails than mice do. One of the common names for *vole* is *meadow mouse*.

4. Leeson carefully traces and documents Potter's preference for the country from her childhood through her later years (see especially 35–36). Her dislike of London no doubt lay behind a large part of this preference. She also seems to have distinguished between small, decidedly rural towns like Near Sawrey, where Potter herself chose to live, and Hawkshead, the basis for the town where Johnny lives. However, some of Potter's dislike of London may be involved in her treatment of the town where Johnny lives in this story.

The Fairy Caravan: Beatrix Potter's Book for an American Audience

1. In a very real sense, she never did grow up since she never had a chance to be a child.

2. Linder publishes *The Tale of Tuppeny* in *History* 306–08.

3. In a note to his essay, "Beatrix Potter: A Critical Estimate," that appears at the end of his essay as it is published in *Collected Essays* (1969), Graham Greene writes that in a letter he received from Potter, she writes him that *The Tale of Little Pig Robinson*, "Although the last published of her books, was in fact, the first written" (240 n). The exact date of Potter's letter to Greene is unknown as is the exact text. Calling *The Tale of Little Pig Robinson*, her "first written" tale, is, of course a distortion. See the discussion of this matter in the chapter of this book treating *The Tale of Little Pig Robinson*.

4. My personal feeling is that the structure of *The Fairy Caravan* is like that of some of Thoreau's books, such as *A Week on the Concord and Merrimack Rivers* and *Cape Cod*, in which the so-called digressions are really parts of the overall fabric of the book.

5. It is difficult not to see the differences between life in Marmalade and life on the caravan as a reflection of differences Potter felt in her own life in London and her life in the Lake District. Even further, Tuppenny's change from ill health to sound health mirrors Potter's change from her sickly childhood to her robust adult life in the Lake District.

6. Potter's having her own hair cut off when she was a child suffering from illness may have been in the back of her mind when she wrote this version of "The Tale of Tuppenny." The words, "no doubt he deserved it," may reflect Potter's own feelings of guilt and inadequacy.

The Tale of Little Pig Robinson

1. Edward Lear's poem spells Pussycat as one word. Many modern editions spell it Pussy-cat or Pussy-Cat. Potter's preference seems to be "Pussy Cat." Thus, the spelling in this chapter is not consistent since when quoting Potter, I use her spelling. Edward Lear's *Book of Nonsense* was first published in 1846; however, "The Owl and the Pussy-cat" first appeared in 1871 in Edward Lear's *Nonsense Songs, Stories, Botany, and Alphabets*, so Potter probably received her copy of it soon after the book's publication. Linda Lear says Potter received her copy at age four

and one-half (34). Defoe's book was first published in 1719 as *The Life and Strange Surprizing Adventures of Robinson Crusoe, of York, Mariner: Who Lived Eight and Twenty Years, All Alone in an Un-inhabited Island on the Coast of America, Near the Mouth of the Great River of Oroonoque; Having Been Cast on Shore by Shipwreck, Wherein All the Men Perished but Himself. With an Account how he was at last as Strangely Deliver'd by Pyrates. Written by Himself.*

2. This letter, however, may not be the one Linder had in mind. He had access to many more letters than I do.

3. The printed text of the letter is reproduced entirely on 26. The reproduction of the original letter is on 26–27.

4. Linder discusses the dating of the letters to Noel and Eric (*History* 175).

5. For the date of publication, Lear gives 1894 (n. 71, 475). Linder writes that Potter's drawings appeared in one of the Nister firm's children's annuals for the mid-1890s and the reproduces the drawings with the captions from the annual (*History* 179–82).

6. On 90, the pig even refers to himself as Pig Robinson Crusoe.

7. See for example an essay available on the Internet entitled "*The Tempest*: Shakespeare's Farewell to his Art," written in 1993 and revised in 2009, where Robert Zaslavksy shows that he believes that *The Tempest* is a kind of farewell to Shakespeare's art and contains "his ultimate view of existence."

8. Taylor reproduces this letter in *Letters to Children* 52–54. She even mentions a dog named Stumpy who seems to be one of the sources for Stumpy in *The Tale of Little Pig Robinson*.

9. It could be argued that Jemima is unwittingly active in her escape since she tells Kep why she is getting onions. She, of course, has no idea what the onions are for. Kep figures out very quickly what they are for.

Sister Anne

1. In his *History of the Writings of Beatrix Potter*, Linder gives the texts of both of these tales (*History* 351–59).

2. See Potter's letter to Alexander McKay, 18 December 1932 (*Letters* 352).

3. In a letter to Mrs. J. Templeton Coolidge

written 29 April 1932, Potter explains that she intended a sequel to *The Fairy Caravan* consisting largely of tales the animals tell to one another rather than narrating things that happened to them (*Letters* 346).

4. See Lear 130.

5. I rely here on the Charles Welsh 1901 translation of Perrault's tales, published by D. C. Heath in the United States and available in Project Gutenberg. Potter probably read the tales in the original French. Lovell-Smith traces additional sources Potter may have used for the Bluebeard story (9–11). I also use Welsh's spelling—*Blue Beard*—when writing of Perrault's tale and Potter's spelling—*Bluebeard*—when writing of Potter's tale.

6. Francis James Child in his collection of *English and Scottish Popular Ballads* lists many variants of this ballad. The version online at http://www.sacred-texts.com/neu/eng/child/ch010.htm, based on the Little, Brown edition of 1860, gives 25 of them, but cautions that the etext may lack some of the variations of some of the popular ballads.

7. It is interesting that in this illustration, the pig that is not receiving the papers is dancing—something Bland does in the illustration at the end of the book (81).

Three Posthumous Works: *Wag-by-Wall*, *The Tale of the Faithful Dove*, and *The Tale of Kitty-in-Boots*

1. The Horn Book edition of *Wag-by-Wall* has no page numbers. "The Story of This Story" is signed, Bertha E. Mahony, using Miller's maiden name.

2. Following 218 in *History*.

3. Page numbers here refer to the version Linder published in *History*.

Works Cited

A note on the texts: in the 2002 Warne edition of Potter's works, only the illustrations have new copyrights. The text is covered only by the original copyrights. An exception is The Tailor of Gloucester: *since many of the illustrations "are either lost or faded beyond use," Warne decided to use a first edition of the book to produce some of the pictures. (See the copyright page on* The Tailor of Gloucester, *unnumbered page 4 in the text.)*

Aesop's Fables. Trans. V. S. Vernon Jones. Introd. G. K. Chesterton. Illus. Arthur Rackham. 1912. Facsimile ed. New York: Avenel Books, [1975]. Print.

Amazon.co.uk. *COMICAL CUSTOMERS At the New Stores of Comical Rhymes and Stories.* https://www.amazon.co.uk/COMICAL-CUSTOMERS-Stores-Comical-Stories/dp/ .

Anthony, E. James. "Foreword." *The Remarkable Beatrix Potter,* by Alexander Grinstein. Madison, CT: International Universities Press, 1995. xv-xvii. Print.

Avery, Gillian. "Beatrix Potter and Social Comedy." *Bulletin of the John Rylands University Library of Manchester* 76.3 (1994): 185-200. Print.

Beeton, Isabella. *The Book of Household Management Comprising information for the Mistress, Housekeeper, Cook, Kitchen-Maid, Butler, Footman, Coachman, Valet, Upper and Under House-Maids, Lady's-Maid, Maid-of-all-Work, Laundry-Maid, Nurse and Nurse-Maid, Monthly Wet and Sick Nurses, etc., etc.—also Sanitary, Medical, & Legal Memoranda: with a History of the Origin, Properties, and Uses of all Things Connected with Home Life and Comfort.* 1861. Adelaide, Australia: eBooks@Adelaide 2006. http://www.mrsbeeton.com/.

Campbell, Joseph. *The Hero with a Thousand Faces.* Bollingen series 17. Princeton: Princeton UP, 1972. Print.

———. *The Masks of God: Primitive Mythology.* New York: Viking, 1959. Print.

Carpenter, Humphrey. "Excessively Impertinent Bunnies: The Subversive Element in Beatrix Potter." *Children and Their Books: A Celebration of the Work of Iona and Peter Opie.* Ed. Gillian Avery and Julia Briggs. Oxford, England: Clarendon Press, 1989. 271-98. Print.

———. *Secret Gardens: A Study of the Golden Age of Children's Literature.* Boston: Houghton Mifflin, 1985. Print.

Child, Francis James, ed. *English and Scottish Popular Ballads.* Boston: Little, Brown and Co., 1860. http://www.sacred-texts.com/neu/eng/child/ch010.htm.

Chrystie, Helen. "Two Hemispheres." *Saturday Review of Literature* 16 Nov. 1929: 418, 430. Print.

Cotsen, Margit Sperling. *The Beatrix Potter Collection of Lloyd Cotsen.* Ed. Judy Taylor, Anne Stevenson Hobbs, and Ivy Trent. Los Angeles: Cotsen Occasional Press, 2004.

Defoe, Daniel. *The Life and Strange Surprizing Adventures of Robinson Crusoe, of York, Mariner: Who Lived Eight and Twenty Years, All Alone in an Un-inhabited Island on the Coast of America, Near the Mouth of the Great River of Oroonoque; Having Been Cast on Shore by Shipwreck, Wherein All the Men Perished but Himself. With an Account how he was at last as Strangely Deliver'd by Pyrates. Written by Himself.* London: W. Taylor, 1719. http://www.pierre-marteau.com/editions/1719-robinson-crusoe.html.

Dennison, Matthew. "*Over the Hills and Far Away*": *The Life of Beatrix Potter*. London, England: Head of Zeus, 2016. Print.

Denyer, Susan. *At Home with Beatrix Potter: The Creator of Peter Rabbit*. New York: Harry N. Abrams, Inc., 2004. Print.

Dowden, Edward. "Shakespeare's Last Plays." *Shakespeare: A Critical Study of his Mind and Art*. 3rd ed. New York: Harper & Brothers, 1905. 369–82. Rpt. "Shakespeare's Last Plays." *The Tempest: Critical Essays*. Ed. Patrick M. Murphy. New York: Routledge, 2001. 140–49. Print.

Eliade, Mircea. *The Sacred and the Profane: The Nature of Religion*. Trans. Willard R. Trask. New York: Harcourt, Brace & World, 1959. Print.

[Emerson, Ann, ed.] *The History of* The Tale of Peter Rabbit. London: Warne, 1976. Print.

Evans, Heather A. "Kittens and Kitchens: Food, Gender, and *The Tale of Samuel Whiskers*." *Victorian Literature and Culture* 36.2 (2008): 603–23. Print.

Fielding, Henry. *The Tragedy of Tragedies; or, The Life and Death of Tom Thumb the Great*. Full text of "The tragedy of tragedies; or, The life and death of Tom Thumb the Great. With the annotations of H. Scriblerus Secundus. Edited by James T. Hillhouse." New Haven: Yale UP, 1918. https://archive.org/stream/tragedyoftragedi00fieluoft/tragedyoftragedi00fieluoft_djvu.txt.

Fletcher, John. "On Some Complexities of Beatrix Potter." *International Fiction Review* 4 (1977): 71–72. Print.

Foote, Timothy. "A Tale of Some Tails, and the Story of their Shy Creator." *Smithsonian* (Jan. 1989): 80–91. Print.

Goldberg, Christine. *Turandot's Sisters: A Study of the Folktale AT 851*. New York: Garland Publishing, 1993. Print.

Greene, Graham. "Beatrix Potter: A Critical Estimate." *London Mercury* (January 1933): 241–53. Print.

———. "Beatrix Potter." *Collected Essays*. New York: Viking, 1969. 232–40. Print.

[Grimm, Jacob, and Wilhelm Grimm]. "The Elves." *Household Stories, from the Collection of the Bros. Grimm*. Trans. Lucy Crane. Illus. Walter Crane. 1886. New York: Dover Publications, 1963. 171–74. Print.

———. "Little Red-Cap." *Household Stories, from the Collection of the Bros. Grimm*. Trans. Lucy Crane. Illus. Walter Crane. 1886. New York: Dover Publications, 1963. 132–35. Print.

Grinstein, Alexander. *The Remarkable Beatrix Potter*. Madison, CT: International Universities Press, 1995. Print.

Gristwood, Sarah. *The Story of Beatrix Potter*. London, England: National Trust, 2016. Print.

Hart, Laura. "A Book Review of Beatrix Potter's '*The Fairy Caravan*.'" *Fell Pony Journal* (Summer 2004). www.parrett.net/~hart/fairy_caravan_book_review.htm.

Heelis, John. *The Tale of Mrs. William Heelis: Beatrix Potter*. Rev. ed. Stroud, England: Sutton Publishing, 1999. Print.

The History of Tom Thumb. 1621. ISTA Flash Drive 9.0. *The World's Wisdom in the Palm of Your Hand*. http://www.sacred-texts.com/neu/eng/eft/eft26.htm.

Hobbs, Anne Stevenson, introd. and ed. *Beatrix Potter's Art: Paintings and Drawings*. London: Warne, 1989. Print.

Holland, Evangeline. "The Dandy." *Edwardian Promenade: Your #1 Source for Edwardian History*. 10 Apr. 2008. http://www.edwardianpromenade.com/fashion/the-dandy/.

Hollindale, Peter. "Aesop in the Shadows." *Signal* 89 (May 1999): 115–32. Print.

———. *Aesop in the Shadows*. London: Beatrix Potter Society, 1997. 17th Linder memorial lecture. Print.

———. "These Piglets Fled Away." *Signal* 74 (May 1994): 141–48. Print.

Hyde Parker, Ulla. *Cousin Beatie: A Memory of Beatrix Potter*. London: Warne, 1981. Print.

Jordan, Alice M. "'The Fairy Caravan' by Beatrix Potter." *Horn Book* (Nov. 1929): 9–11. Print.

Joy, Libby. "'Beatrix Potter and Children.'" *Beatrix Potter Society Journal and Newsletter* 119 (Jan. 2016): 12–13. Print.

Kipling, Rudyard. "How Fear Came." *The Second Jungle Book*. School ed. Garden City, NY: Doubleday, Doran & Company, 1895. 1–28. Print.

———. *Just So Stories*. Garden City, NY: Doubleday, Doran & Company, 1907. Print.

Kutzer, M. Daphne. "A Wildness Inside: Domestic Space in the Work of Beatrix Potter." *Lion and the Unicorn* 21.2 (1997): 204–14. Print.

Landes, Sonia. *Curriculum Guide to The Tale of Peter Rabbit*. Cambridge, MA: Book Wise, 1987. Print.

Lane, Margaret. "Beatrix Potter: The Missing Years." *Purely for Pleasure*, New York: Knopf, 1967. 291–99. Print.

―――. "Children's Classics Revisited: Margaret Lane Recalls her Brush with the Memory of Beatrix Potter." *Punch* 14 Nov. 1962. 712–15. Print.

―――. "The Ghost of Beatrix Potter." *Purely for Pleasure*, New York: Knopf, 1967. 279–89. Print.

―――. *The Magic Years of Beatrix Potter*. London: Warne, 1978. Print.

―――. "The Secret World of Beatrix Potter." *Beatrix Potter: Thirty Years of Discovery and Appreciation: A Selection from Talks Given to the Beatrix Potter Society, 1980–2010*. Ed Libby Joy and Judy Taylor. [London]: Beatrix Potter Society, 2010. 18–31. Print.

―――. *The Tale of Beatrix Potter: A Biography*. 2nd rev. ed. London: Warne, 1985. Print.

Lanzendorfer, Joy. "How Beatrix Potter Invented Character Merchandising: Faced with Rejection, the Author Found her Own Path to Fame and Fortune." *Smithsonian.com*. http://www.smithsonianmag.com/arts-culture/how-beatrix-potter-invented-character-merchandising-180961979/.

Lear, Edward. *Nonsense Songs, Stories, Botany, and Alphabets*. London: Robert John Bush, 1871. https://ufdc.ufl.edu/UF00026002/00001/5j.

Lear, Linda, *Beatrix Potter: A Life in Nature*. New York: St. Martin's, 2007. Print.

Leeson, Robert. "Beatrix Potter: One of Nature's Conservatives." *Beatrix Potter's Attitudes and Enthusiasms: Papers Presented at the Beatrix Potter Society Conference, Ambleside, England, July 1994*. Ed. Enid Bassom, Rowena Knox, and Irene Whalley. [London]: Beatrix Potter Society, 1995. Beatrix Potter studies 6. 23–38. Print.

Lightner, Karen J. "The Fairy Caravan 'Explained.'" *Beatrix Potter Studies* 7 (1997): 60–74. Print.

Linder, Leslie. *A History of the Writings of Beatrix Potter Including Unpublished Work*. 2nd ed. London: Warne, 1971. Print.

―――. Introduction. *The Tailor of Gloucester from the Original Manuscript*. New York: Warne, 1968. 5–9. Print.

Lofting, Hugh. *The Story of Doctor Dolittle: Being the History of his Peculiar Life at Home and Astonishing Adventures in Foreign Parts. Never Before Printed*. New York: Frederick A. Stokes, 1920. Print.

Lovell-Smith, Rose. "Of Mice and Women: Beatrix Potter's Bluebeard Story, Sister Anne." *Children's Literature Association Quarterly* 38.1 (Spring 2013): 4–25. Print. [Also available online in Project Muse.]

MacDonald, Ruth K. *Beatrix Potter*. Boston: Twayne Publishers, 1986. Twayne's English authors series 422. Print.

Mackey, Margaret. *The Case of Peter Rabbit: Changing Conditions of Literature for Children*. New York: Garland, 1998. Print.

Mahoney, Bertha E. "The Story of this Story." *Wag by Wall*. Boston: Horn Book, 1944. Print.

McDowell, Marta. *Beatrix Potter's Gardening Life: The Plants and Places That Inspired the Classic Children's Tales*. Portland, OR: Timber Press, 2013. Print.

Middleton, George. *Echoes of Ambleside and Beyond: Reminiscences and Recollections of an Ambleside Octogenarian*. Kendal, England: MTP Media Ltd., 2015. Print [Middleton copyrighted the material in 2012].

Mitchell, W. R. *Beatrix Potter: Her Lakeland Years*. Ilkley, England: Great Northern Books, 2010. Print.

Moore, John H. "A Captive of the Shawnees, 1779–1784." *West Virginia History* 23.4 (July 1962): 287–96. Print.

Morse, Jane Crowell. "Introduction." *Beatrix Potter's Americans: Selected Letters*. Ed. Jane Crowell Morse. Boston: Horn Book, 1982. ix-xii. Print.

Nodelman, Perry. *The Pleasures of Children's Literature*. 3rd ed. Boston: Allyn and Bacon, 1992. Print.

Norman, Andrew. *Beatrix Potter: Her Inner World*. South Yorkshire, England: Pen & Sword History, 2014. Print.

Pardoe, [Julia]. *The Project Gutenberg ebook of The Thousand and One Days: A Companion to the "Arabian Nights."* London: William Lay, 1857. http://www.gutenberg.org/ebooks/36301.

Perrault, Charles. *The Project Gutenberg e-Book of The Tales of Mother Goose As First Collected by Charles Perrault In

1696. Trans. Charles Welsh. Introd. M. V. O'Shea. Illus. D. J. Munro. Boston: D. C. Heath & Co., 1901. http://www.gutenberg.org/files/17208/17208.txt.

Potter, Beatrix. *Beatrix Potter: A Holiday Diary with a Short History of the Warne Family*. Ed. Judy Taylor. London: Beatrix Potter Society, 1996. Print.

———. *Beatrix Potter's Americans: Selected Letters*. Ed. Jane Crowell Morse. Boston: Horn Book, 1982. Print.

———. "Beatrix Potter's Explanatory Notes About the Text." *A History of the Writings of Beatrix Potter Including Unpublished Works*, by Leslie Linder. London: Warne, 1971. 299–302. Print.

———. *Beatrix Potter's Letters*. Selected and introd. Judy Taylor. London: Warne, 1989. Print.

———. *The Fairy Caravan*. Philadelphia: David McKay, 1929. Print.

———. *The Journal of Beatrix Potter from 1881–1897*. Complete, rev. ed. Transcribed from her code writings by Leslie Linder. London: Warne, 1989. Print.

———. *The Journal of Beatrix Potter from 1881–1897*. Transcribed from her code writing by Leslie Linder. London: Warne., 1966. Print.

———. "Kitty-in-Boots." *A History of the Writings of Beatrix Potter Including Unpublished Work* by Leslie Linder. 2nd ed. London: Warne, 1971. 219–24. Print.

———. *Letters to Children from Beatrix Potter*. Ed. Judy Taylor. London, England: Warne, 1992. Print.

———. "The Lonely Hills." *Horn Book* (May-June 1942), 153–56. Print.

———. "'Roots' of the Peter Rabbit Tales." *Horn Book* (May 1929): 69–72. Print.

———. *Sister Anne*. Philadelphia: David McKay Co., 1932. Print.

———. "The Sly Old Cat." Reproduction in Facsimile. *A History of the Writings of Beatrix Potter Including Unpublished Work* by Leslie Linder. 2nd ed. London: Warne, 1971. Opposite 182. Print.

———. *The Tailor of Gloucester From the Original Manuscript*. New York: Warne, 1968. Print.

———. *The Tailor of Gloucester: A Facsimile of the Original Manuscript and Illustration*. New York: Warne, 1968. Print.

———. *The Tailor of Gloucester*. 1903. London: Warne, 2002. Print.

———. *The Tale of Benjamin Bunny*. 1904. London: Warne, 2002. Print.

———. *The Tale of Jemima Puddle-Duck*. 1908. London: Warne, 2002. Print.

———. *The Tale of Johnny Town-Mouse*. 1918. London: Warne, 2002. Print.

———. *The Tale of Kitty-in-Boots*. Illus, Quentin Blake. New York: Warne, 2016. Print.

———. *The Tale of Little Pig Robinson*. 1930. London: Warne, 2002. Print.

———. *The Tale of Mr. Jeremy Fisher*. 1906. London: Warne, 2002. Print.

———. *The Tale of Mr. Tod*. 1912. London: Warne, 2002. Print.

———. *The Tale of Mrs. Tiggy-Winkle*. 1905. London: Warne, 2002. Print.

———. *The Tale of Mrs. Tittlemouse*. 1910. London: Warne, 2002. Print.

———. *The Tale of Peter Rabbit*. 1902. London: Warne, 2002. Print.

———. *The Tale of Peter Rabbit*. 1902. New York: Warne, 1987. Print.

———. *The Tale of Pigling Bland*. 1913. London: Warne, 2002. Print.

———. *The Tale of Samuel Whiskers or The Roly-Poly Pudding*. 1908. London: Warne, 2002. Print.

———. *The Tale of Squirrel Nutkin*. 1903. London: Warne, 2002. Print.

———. *The Tale of the Faithful Dove*. Illus. Marie Angel. Middlesex, England: Warne, 1971.

———. *The Tale of the Flopsy Bunnies*. 1909. London: Warne, 2002. Print.

———. *The Tale of the Pie and the Patty-Pan*. 1905. London: Warne, 2002.

———. *The Tale of Tom Kitten*. 1907. London: Warne, 2002. Print.

———. "The Tale of Tuppenny." *A History of the Writings of Beatrix Potter Including Unpublished Work* by Leslie Linder. 2nd ed. London: Warne, 1971. 306–08. Print.

———. *The Tale of Two Bad Mice*. 1904. London: Warne, 2002. Print.

———. *Wag-by-Wall*. Illus. J. J. Lankes. Boston: Horn Book, 1944.

Rahn, Susan. "Tailpiece: *The Tale of Two Bad Mice*." *Children's Literature* 12 (1984): 78–91. Print.

Reed, Clifford M. "Beatrix Potter's Unitarian Context." *Beatrix Potter: Thirty Years of Discovery and Appreciation: A Selection from Talks Given to the Beatrix Potter Society, 1980–2010*. Ed. Libby Joy and Judy

Works Cited

Taylor. [London]: Beatrix Potter Society, 2010. 143–66. Print.
Sendak, Maurice. "Beatrix Potter/1." *Caldecott & Co.* New York: Michael di Capua Books: Farrar, Straus and Giroux, 1988. 61–70. Print.
———. "Beatrix Potter/2." *Caldecott & Co.* New York: Michael di Capua Books: Farrar, Straus and Giroux, 1988. 71–76. Print.
Sipe, Lawrence R. "Contemporary Urban Children Respond to *Peter Rabbit.*" *Beatrix Potter's Peter Rabbit: A Children's Classic at 100.* Ed. Margaret Mackey. Lanham, MD: Children's Literature Association and Scarecrow, 2002. 3–18. Print.
Smith, Janet Adam. "The World of Beatrix Potter." *"So I shall tell you a story": Encounters with Beatrix Potter.* Ed. Judy Taylor. London: Warne, 1993. 33–39. Print.
Speaight, George, with Brian Alderson. "From Chapbooks to Pantomime." *Popular Children's Literature in Britain.* Ed. Julia Briggs, Dennis Butts, and M. O. Grenby. Aldershot, England: Ashgate, 2008. Print.
Taylor, Judy. *Beatrix Potter: Artist, Storyteller and Countrywoman.* 1986. Rev. ed. Middlesex, England: Warne, 1996. Print.
———. "Introduction to the Diary." *Beatrix Potter: A Holiday Diary with a Short History of the Warne Family.* Ed. Judy Taylor. London: Beatrix Potter Society, 1996. 9–14. Print.
———. "Introduction." *Letters to Children from Beatrix Potter.* Ed. Judy Taylor. London: Warne, 1992. 6–11. Print.
———. "Notes from the Hill." *Beatrix Potter Society Journal and Newsletter* 140 (April 2016): 14–15. Print.
———. "Postscript." *Beatrix Potter: A Holiday Diary with a Short History of the Warne Family.* Ed. Judy Taylor. London: Beatrix Potter Society, 1996. Print.
———, ed. *"So I shall tell you a story": Encounters with Beatrix Potter.* London: Warne, 1993. Print.

Taylor, Willow. *Through the Pages of My Life: And My Encounters with Beatrix Potter.* London, England: Beatrix Potter Society, 2000. Print.
Thompson, Stith. *The Folktale.* New York: Dryden Press, 1946. Print.
Tolkien, J. R. R. "On Fairy-Stories." *Tree and Leaf.* 1988. London, England: HarperCollins, 2001. 3–81. Print.
Van Doren, Mark. *Shakespeare.* New York: Henry Holt, 1939. Print.
Victoria and Albert Museum. "Beatrix Potter: The Art of Illustration." *V&A: Victoria and Albert Museum: The World's Greatest Museum of Art and Design.* 2015. http://www.vam.ac.uk/content/articles/b/-beatrix-potter-the-art-of-illustrating/.
———. "The Big Green Book: Maurice Sendak's Tribute to Beatrix Potter." *V&A: Victoria and Albert Museum: The World's Greatest Museum of Art and Design.* 2012. http://www.vam.ac.uk/users/node/3920.
Weideger, Paula. "Tales of the Real Beatrix Potter: How Could Mrs Heelis, the Curmudgeonly Sheep-Farmer, also be the Fey Storyteller who Created Peter Rabbit 100 Years Ago?" *The Independent.* 6 Oct. 1993. http://www.independent.co.uk/life-style/tales-of-the-real-beatrix-potter-how-could-mrs-heelis-the-curmudgeonly-sheepfarmer-also-be-the-fey-storyteller-who-created-peter-rabbit-100-years-ago-paula-weideger-went-to-cumbria-to-investigate-the-mystery-1508937.html.
Zach, Emil. *The Art of Beatrix Potter.* Foreword Steven Heller. Introd. Linda Lear. Afterword Eleanor Taylor. San Francisco: Chronicle Books, 2016. Print.
Zaslavsky, Robert. "*The Tempest*: Shakespeare's Farewell to his Art." Doczonline.com. http://www.doczonline.com/wp-content/uploads/2009/03/tempest-rz.pdf.
Zipes, Jack. *Fairy Tales and the Art of Subversion: The Classical Genre for Children and the Process of Civilization.* New York: Wildman, 1983. Print.

Index

Aesop 46-47, 147, 191*Fairies*n6, 196*Johnny*n1
Aiken, Charles 8
Anthony, E. James 83
Arnold, Matthew 8
Avery, Gillian 62, 118

Baum, L. Frank 51
"Belling the Cat" 157
Bible 52, 157
Bingham, Clifton 95, 194*Jeremy*n3
Bird's Place 16-17; *see also* Camfield Place
Blackburn, Mrs. Hugh (Jemima Wedderburn Blackburn) 38, 190n7
Blake, Quentin 179
"Blue Beard" 171-72
Booth, Elizabeth 152
British National Trust 2, 13, 28-29, 31, 152, 186, 187

Camfield Place 189n12; *see also* Bird's Place
Campbell, Joseph 64-65, 192n16
Carpenter, Humphrey 15, 40-41, 50, 55, 112-13, 114, 115, 120
Carroll, Lewis 51, 191*Fairies*n5
Child, Francis James 198*Sister*n6
Choyce, Louisa (Louie) 37, 190n6
"Cinderella" 103, 157, 170
Clark, Carolyn 13, 14-15
Coolidge, Henry P. 153
Coolidge, Mary-Abigail Parsons (Mrs. J. Templeton) 153, 170-71, 172, 198*Sister*n3
Cotsen, Lloyd 94, 194*Jeremy*n4
Crompton, Abraham 13

Dalguise House 19-20, 44, 191*Fairies*n3, 194*Mrs*n6
Defoe, Daniel 159, 197*Little*n1, 197*Little*n6
Denyer, Susan 2, 191n10
Dennison, Matthew 62
depression 13, 16-22, 30, 55, 189n12, 189n13, 189n15, 197*Fairy*n6

Eliade, Mircea 31
"The Elves and the Shoemaker" 66, 192*Tailor*n2

Evans, Heather A. 109, 116, 118, 121
Evens, Edmund 36-37

fairies 33, 36, 43-47
The Fairy Caravan 5, 13, 17, 45, 46, 47, 52, 152-58, 170-71, 172, 175, 177, 185, 190n26
"The Fairy in the Oak" 47, 170, 191*Peter*n1, 197*Fairy*n5, 198*Sister*n3
fairytales 22, 33, 34, 43-47, 51, 52, 65, 66, 68, 74, 84, 152-58, 169, 170, 172, 191*Vocabulary*n2
Fielding, Henry 193*nTwo*3
Fletcher, John 118, 120
Flower, Sir William 9
The Folly of Vanity 24, 191*Fairies*n6
Frederick Warne and Company 1, 8, 11, 55, 160, 191*Peter*n1, 192n6

Gaddum, Molly 95
Gladstone, W.E. 19
Goldberg, Christine 71
Goldielocks 164
Grahame, Kenneth 38
Graves, Robert 39
Greene, Graham 25-26, 55, 94, 113, 114, 134, 159-60, 162-63, 190n22, 190n23, 194*Jeremy*n1, 195*Samuel*n1, 197*Fairy*n3
Grimm, the brothers 43, 66, 110, 120, 190, 192*Tailor*n2, 200,
Grinstein, Alexander 9, 17, 37, 105, 126, 160, 190n6, 194*Pie*n1, 195*Ginger*n2
Gristwood, Sarah 113

Hamer, Samuel 13
Hammond, Daisy 30, 184
"Hansel and Gretel" 43, 143
Hart, Alison 24
Heelis, Sylvester May 33
Heelis, William 2, 5, 10-11, 12, 14, 16, 22, 23, 30, 35, 143-44, 148, 185, 190n24
Herdwick Sheep 16, 36, 39
Hill Top Cottage 2
Hill Top Farm 2, 9, 148
Hobbs, Anne Stevenson 22

Index

Hollindale, Peter 36, 50, 51, 142, 190n4, 196*Johnnyn*3
Hopkinson, Mrs. Charles 152
Horn Book 8, 44, 51, 152, 154, 177, 198*Threen*1
Hutton, Caroline 38
Hyde Parker, Ulla 11, 12, 17, 23-24, 34, 186

International Inventions Exposition 20-21

"Jack and the Beanstalk" 47, 57, 170
Jordon, Alice M. 157
Joy, Libby 190n20

Kipling, Rudyard 73, 192-93n*Squirrel*1
Kutzer, Daphne 114

Lake District 2, 9, 16, 28, 30, 86, 152, 172, 191*Fairiesn*4
Landes, Sonia 56, 191*Petern*3
Lane, Margaret 10-11, 12, 15, 17, 18, 26-27, 35-36, 44, 95, 11, 143, 160, 190n24, 190n2, 194*Jeremyn*3, 196*Todn*3
Lankes, J.J. 177
Lear, Edward 64, 159, 162, 167, 197*Littlen*1
Lear, Linda 8, 9, 10, 13, 14, 18, 19, 21, 34-35, 40, 86, 147, 148, 153, 159-60, 191n10, 195*Tomn*2, 195*Jemiman*1, 196*Piglingl*, 197*Littlen*5
Leeson, Robert 189n11, 196*Johnnyn*4
Lennel 13
Letters to Children from Beatrix Potter 23, 25, 34, 63, 70, 84, 94, 95, 130, 160-61, 193*Squirreln*3, 197n8
Linder, Leslie 18, 35, 44, 46, 49, 66, 67, 94, 95, 101, 130, 154, 157, 159, 160, 170, 177-79, 180, 190n5, 190n6, 190n7, 190n21, 191n10, 191*Fairiesn*6, 191*Vocabularyn*5, 192*Tailorn*3, 192*Tailorn*4, 192*Tailorn*5, 193n*Squirrel*4, 193n*Two*1, 193n*Two*2, 194*Pien*2, 194*Pien*3, 194*Pien*6, 194*Jeremyn*3, 194*Jeremyn*6, 195*Slyn*3, 197*Fairyn*2, 197*Littlen*2, 197*Littlen*4, 197*Littlen*5, 198*Sistern*1, 198*Threen*2, 198*Threen*3
"Little Goody Two-Shoes" 157
"Little Red Riding-Hood" 43, 47, 110-13, 120, 170, 191*Vocabularyn*2
"Llewellyn's Well" 170
London Zoo 130
"The Lonely Hills" 45, 154
Lovell-Smith, Rose 172, 173-74, 197*Sistern*5

MacDonald, Kitty 194*Kittyn*6
MacDonald, Ruth K. 95-96, 160, 191*Petern*5
Mace, Brian 190n27
Mackinlay, Jean Sterling 52
Marjorie Daw 164
Matheson, D.M. 28-29
McDowell, Marta 191n9
McKay, Alexander 5, 13, 14, 52, 152, 153, 154, 155, 159, 180, 170, 171, 198*Sistern*2

Middleton, George 29-30, 153, 190n26
Millais, John 19, 34
Miller, Bertha Mahony 8, 51-52, 152, 177, 198*Threen*1
Mills, Cecily 30, 184
Mitchell, W.R. 30, 41
Monk Coniston 13, 28, 29
Moore, Annie Carter 8, 18
Moore, Eric 94, 95, 160-161, 197*Littlen*4
Moore, Freda 67, 192*Tailorn*4, 192*Tailorn*5
Moore, Hilda 63
Moore, Noel 4, 56, 63, 67, 70, 94, 160-61, 197*Littlen*4
Moore, Nora 70
Morley Memorial Collage for Working Men and Women 9
Morse, Jane Crowell 12
Mrs. Beeton's Book of Household Management 57, 111, 117

Near Sawrey 2, 9, 70, 126, 130, 148, 153, 195*Tomn*2, 196*Johnnyn*4
Newton, Isaac 97
Nister, Ernest 95, 161, 197*Littlen*5
Nodelman, Perry 63-64,
Norman, Andrew 12, 1, 17, 23
nursery rhymes 145, 146, 155, 157, 164, 196*Piglingn*3

Oedipus 71
Old Testament 8, 23

Paget, John 9
Pardoe, Julia 71
Perrault, Charles 110, 120, 171-72, 198*Sistern*5
Perry, Marian Frazer Harris 10
Potter, Bertram 7, 15, 18, 30, 36
Potter, Helen Leech 7, 9, 10, 13, 14, 15, 16, 18, 19, 92-93
Potter, Kate 21
Potter, Rupert 7, 10, 13, 15, 16, 19, 20-21, 96, 100, 189n2, 194*Jeremyn*6
Pourquoi tales 73, 74
Prichard, John 66-67, 192*Tailorn*3
Ptolemy 97
"Puss in Boots" 157, 178-79

Rahn, Susan 193*Twon*4
realism 33-42, 53, 80, 184
riddles 71-73
"'Roots of the Peter Rabbit Tales" 44
Rowson, Neville and Eileen 130
"Rumpelstiltskin" 157, 192*Squirreln*1

Sale, Roger 113, 135, 192n7, 195*Todn*2
Scott, Mary Welsh 30
Sendak, Maurice 22, 37, 39-40, 56, 189n19, 190-91n8

Index

Shakespeare 52, 55, 85, 143, 162, 189n16, 191Petern2, 197n7
"The Shortage of Horses" 37, 190n5
Sister Anne 36, 52, 170-76
"The Sly Old Cat" 88, 101-104, 184
Smith, Janet Adam 25, 27-28, 160, 190n25
Speaight, George 152-53
Stevenson, R.L. 118, 162, 167
The Story of a Fierce Bad Rabbit 101-104
The Story of Dr. Dolittle 161
The Story of Miss Moppet 7, 44, 101-104, 187
"The Story of This Story" 177, 198Threen1
Sturges, Katharine 170

The Tailor of Gloucester 1, 36, 40, 42, 46, 52, 66-68, 152-53, 154, 171, 192Tailorn1, 192Tailorn4, 196Todn2
The Tale of Benjamin Bunny 38, 62, 64, 75, 76-81, 82, 136, 164, 183, 193Benjaminn1, 193nBenjamin2
The Tale of Ginger and Pickles 33, 50, 126-27, 195Gingern1, 195Gingern2, 195Gingern3
The Tale of Jemima Puddle-Duck 7, 31, 33-34, 49, 53, 55, 56, 64, 109-13, 114, 117, 118, 120, 135, 137, 164-65, 170, 176, 178, 182, 195Todn1, 196Todn3, 196Todn6, 197n9
The Tale of Johnny Town-Mouse 46-47, 147-51, 155, 195Jemiman1, 196Johnnyn1, 196Johnnyn4
The Tale of Kitty-in-Boots 178-81
The Tale of Little Pig Robinson 5, 38, 39, 51, 52, 64, 154, 155, 159-69, 183, 190n6, 191Fairiesn1, 197Fairyn3
The Tale of Mr. Jeremy Fisher 7, 31, 38, 40, 41, 42, 49, 64, 81, 88, 94-100, 126, 135, 148, 161, 170, 176, 184, 194Jeremyn5, 194Jeremyn7, 196Todn1
The Tale of Mr. Tod 25, 26, 31, 33, 38, 49-50, 62-63, 64, 75, 78, 81, 134-42, 154, 159, 179, 190n23, 190n4, 191Fairiesn4, 196Todn1, 196Todn8
The Tale of Mrs. Tiggy-Winkle 35, 46, 82-87, 105, 128, 129, 179, 191Fairiesn1, 193-4, 194Mrsn6
The Tale of Mrs. Tittlemouse 128-29, 195Tittlemousen1
The Tale of Peter Rabbit 1, 3, 7, 8, 18, 22, 23, 27, 31, 33, 38, 39, 40, 41, 44, 46-47, 49, 50, 51, 52, 53, 55-65, 67, 69, 70, 74, 76, 77, 78, 79, 80, 81, 82, 94, 100, 101, 105, 107, 120, 122-23, 126, 132, 135, 136, 140, 141, 142, 153, 161, 163, 165, 170, 182, 183, 185, 189-90n19, 190-91n8, 192Petern4, 192Petern5, 192n6, 192n7, 192n14, 192n15, 193Benjaminn1, 194Jeremyn7, 195Tomn3, 195T6odn1, 196Todn2
The Tale of Pigling Bland 7, 31, 38, 39, 40, 45-46, 50-51, 64, 135, 143-46, 159, 164, 165, 176, 183, 185, 192n7, 196Piglingn2, 198Sistern7

The Tale of Samuel Whiskers. Or the Roly-Poly Pudding 7, 31, 33, 40, 42, 45, 47, 50, 55, 56, 64, 74, 81, 106, 108, 114-21, 122, 126, 134, 135, 139, 164-65, 176, 178, 179, 185, 191Fairiesn1, 195Tomn3, 195Samueln2, 195Gingern3, 196Todn2
The Tale of Squirrel Nutkin 1, 3, 7, 47, 67, 69-75, 81, 193Squirrelnl5
"The Tale of the Birds and Mr. Tod" 46
The Tale of the Faithful Dove 24, 170, 180-81
The Tale of the Flopsy Bunnies 7, 49, 74, 81, 122-25, 134, 135, 137, 195Tittlemousen1
The Tale of the Pie and the Patty-Pan 41, 88-93, 104, 119, 179-80, 184
The Tale of Timmy Tiptoes 3, 50, 130-33, 195Timmyn1, 195-96Timmyn2
The Tale of Tom Kitten 41, 49, 53, 102, 105-108, 114, 179, 195Tomn1
The Tale of Tuppenny 154-56, 197Fairyn2
The Tale of Two Bad Mice 15, 40, 42, 82-87, 103, 126, 128
Taylor, Judy 11, 15, 22, 23, 24, 25, 28, 29, 34, 37, 94, 160, 161-62, 189n5, 190n23, 190n27, 191n10, 191Fairiesn7, 191Vocabularyn 4
Taylor, Willow 23-24
Tennyson, Alfred Lord 190n1
Thompson, Bruce Logan 28-29
Thompson, Stith 43-44, 71
Thorburn, Archibald 180
Thoreau, Henry David 197Fairyn4
Tolkien, J.R.R. 43, 44-47, 71, 191Fairiesn2, Fairiesn5
"The Twa Sisters" 173-74
2 Bolton Gardens 8, 22, 44, 83-84, 97, 148

Van Doren, Mark 162
Victoria and Albert Museum (South Kensington Museum) 39, 41, 42, 191n9
violence 33-34, 40, 184-85

Wag-by-Wall 170, 177-78, 180-81
Warne, Amelia (Milly) 10, 11, 37
Warne, Freda 67, 192Tailorn5
Warne, Fruing 14, 22, 24, 52, 180, 195Gingern2, Warne, Harold 9, 101, 128, 178-179, 180, 191Vocabularyn3, 195Gingern2
Warne, Louie 101
Warne, Mary 51
Warne, Norman 8, 10, 11, 15, 17, 30, 49, 85, 144, 189n5, 190n22, 196Piglingl
White, E.B. 51
Wordsworth, William 8
World War I 1, 37
World War II 1
Wright, Mrs. M.E. 38

Zach, Emily 84, 130, 133, 147

www.ingramcontent.com/pod-product-compliance
Lightning Source LLC
Chambersburg PA
CBHW020836020526
44114CB00040B/1224